A NEWER WORLD

KIT CARSON,
JOHN C. FRÉMONT,
AND THE CLAIMING
OF THE AMERICAN WEST

DAVID ROBERTS

SIMON & SCHUSTER

SIMON & SCHUSTER
Rockefeller Center
1230 Avenue of the Americas
New York, NY 10020

Designed by Karolina Harris
Maps by Jeff Ward
Manufactured in the United States of America
1 3 5 7 9 10 8 6 4 2
Library of Congress Cataloging-in-Publication Data
is available.
ISBN 0-684-83482-0

For Sharon—
With memories of the West where we grew up
And of the West we explored together—my enduring love

CONTENTS

PREFACE: THEY LED THE WAY 17

ONE: SAVAGE SUBLIMITY

ONE: A DISORDER OF ENORMOUS MASSES 23
TWO: ONE-CENT REWARD 50
THREE: INDIAN KILLER 79

TWO: THE CONQUEST OF CALIFORNIA

FOUR: CHILDE HAROLD'S PILGRIMAGE 107
FIVE: THE HOWITZER IN THE SNOW 123
SIX: PERFECT BUTCHERY 141
SEVEN: NEMESIS 163

THREE: HORROR DESOLATION DESPAIR

EIGHT: HARDSCRABBLE 183
NINE: CAMP DISMAL 200
TEN: WOLF BONES 216
ELEVEN: THE STRONG AND THE WEAK 234

FOUR: THE LONG WALK

TWELVE: ROUNDUP 247
THIRTEEN: THE SIEGE OF TSÉLAA' 259
FOURTEEN: HWÉÉLDI 270

CONTENTS

Epilogue 287
Note on Sources 297
Acknowledgments 303
Index 305
Photo Credits 320

A NEWER WORLD

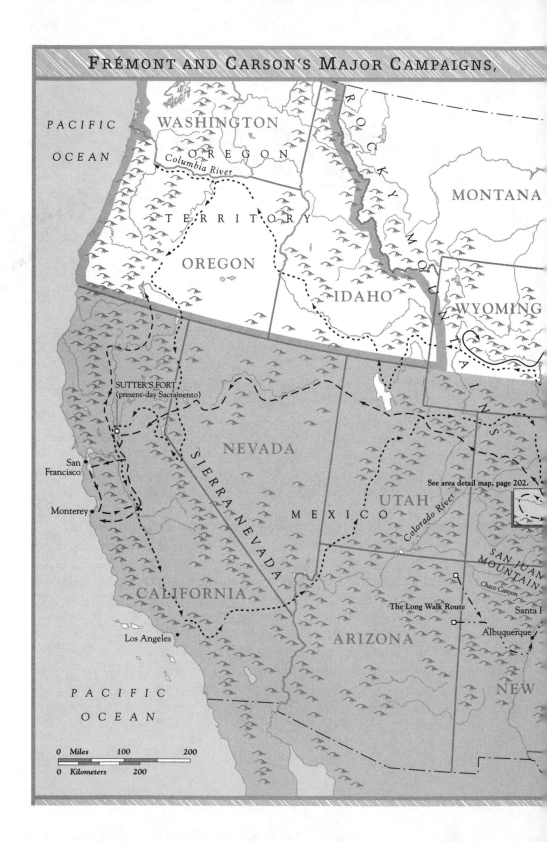

PACIFIC

OCEAN

WASHINGTON

OREGON

Columbia River

MONTANA

T E R R I T O R Y

OREGON

IDAHO

WYOMING

R O C K Y   M O U N T A I N S

SUTTER'S FORT
(present-day Sacramento)

San
Francisco

Monterey

NEVADA

S I E R R A   N E V A D A

See area detail map, page 202.

UTAH

M E X I C O

Colorado River

SAN JUAN
MOUNTAINS

Chaco Canyon

The Long Walk Route

Santa F

CALIFORNIA

Los Angeles

ARIZONA

Albuquerque

NEW

PACIFIC

OCEAN

| 0 | Miles | 100 | | 200 |
| 0 | Kilometers | | 200 | |

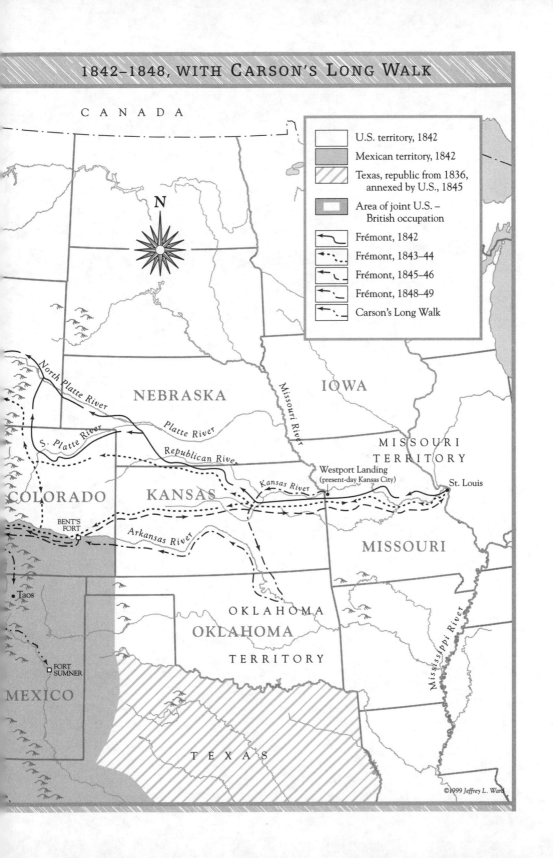

1842–1848, WITH CARSON'S LONG WALK

CANADA

N

	U.S. territory, 1842
	Mexican territory, 1842
	Texas, republic from 1836, annexed by U.S., 1845
	Area of joint U.S. – British occupation
	Frémont, 1842
	Frémont, 1843–44
	Frémont, 1845–46
	Frémont, 1848–49
	Carson's Long Walk

North Platte River

NEBRASKA

Missouri River

IOWA

Platte River

S. Platte River

Republican River

MISSOURI
TERRITORY

Kansas River

Westport Landing
(present-day Kansas City)

St. Louis

COLORADO

KANSAS

BENT'S
FORT

Arkansas River

MISSOURI

Taos

OKLAHOMA

OKLAHOMA

TERRITORY

Mississippi River

FORT
SUMNER

MEXICO

TEXAS

©1999 Jeffrey L. Ward

Come, my friends,
'Tis not too late to seek a newer world.
—"Ulysses," ALFRED, LORD TENNYSON

PREFACE:
THEY LED THE WAY

HAD anyone taken a poll in the late 1850s or early 1860s, John C. Frémont would probably have been chosen as America's greatest explorer, living or dead. During the same period, Kit Carson, still very much alive, had become a dime-novel hero so storied that citizens and journalists knocked each other aside to catch a passing glimpse of him in a hotel or on the street.

On five expeditions between 1842 and 1854, Frémont covered more ground west of the Mississippi than had any other explorer. At the same time, Carson had risen from an unknown trapper to become the country's most famous mountain man, scout, and Indian fighter.

Today, Frémont's star has so far faded that the majority of Americans under the age of fifty have never heard of him. Kit Carson's fame persists, but as a kind of silhouette on the screen of the West, a two-dimensional cardboard paragon in the mold of Daniel Boone, Davy Crockett, or Buffalo Bill: exactly what he accomplished, most moderns would be hard put to say. Even fewer moderns remember that Carson and Frémont rode their separate paths to glory by twining their fates inextricably together.

The two men met by chance on a steamboat on the Missouri River in 1842. Out of work and broke, Carson was hired by Frémont to guide his first expedition. During the following years, Frémont made Carson famous as the hero of his government reports, which were bestsellers in their day. And Carson time and again not only saved Frémont's expeditions from disaster: he several times saved Frémont's life.

During the last century and a half, many biographies of both men have been written. Yet no previous book has focused on the vital interconnection between these two American heroes, so utterly different in character and ambition. Though their paths would ultimately diverge, each man remained fiercely loyal to the other through the rest of his life.

A *Newer World* is not intended to be a dual biography. Instead, I have chosen to dwell at length on four campaigns that epitomize the two explorers' triumphs and failures, believing that each campaign contains the kernel of a stirring, seldom-told adventure tale. Those campaigns are Frémont's first expedition in 1842, with Carson as guide, which penetrated the Wind River Range in Wyoming and made the first ascent of Fremont Peak, then the finest mountaineering feat yet performed in North America; the so-called Conquest of California in 1845–46, by which Americans wrested the future Golden State from a weak Mexican government in a pseudowar whose details remain murky today; Frémont's disastrous fourth expedition in 1848–49, during which, scouting an impossible railroad route along the 38th parallel in midwinter, he lost 10 of his 33 men in the San Juan Range and saw them resort to cannibalism; and Carson's 1863–64 roundup of the Mescalero Apaches and the Navajos, leading to the Long Walk and a five-year incarceration of more than 9,000 natives at a concentration camp called Bosque Redondo.

As these episodes, mingling courage and despair, wisdom and folly, unfold, the diametrical natures of Carson and Frémont seem to glance off each other, the one playing the foil to the other. If Carson comes off as considerably more sympathetic than his commander, it is in part because his style of heroism—taciturn, plainspoken, oblivious to his own renown—matches the aesthetic of our modern age better than the more Victorian style of Frémont's derring-do—flamboyant, oratorical, and always conscious of the judgment of posterity.

To deepen my understanding of these four campaigns, I traveled virtually every step of their itineraries, by car and on foot. Some of the settings where Frémont and Carson's deeds took place have been turned into touristic monuments, such as the reconstructed Bent's and Sutter's Forts, complete with rangers and interpretive displays. Others lie almost as lost in the wilderness as they were in the 1840s. Retracing Frémont's route up the Wind River peak later named for him, trying to match the terrain with his dramatic account; visiting the forlorn, empty hollows where the mountain-man rendezvous of the 1830s turned riotous and violent; trying to find the northern California riverbank where Frémont's troops perpetrated an Indian massacre that has all but slipped through the cracks of history; fondling the lichen-furred splinters of tree stumps high in Colorado's La Garita Mountains that Frémont's desperate men had chopped 148 years before; or winding among slickrock domes and slot canyons north of Navajo Mountain, where the great chief Hoskininni successfully evaded Carson's roundup—on such sojourns into obscure landscapes in the still untamed West, I felt a kinetic connection with the men I was writing about that no amount of poring over books and manuscripts could have supplied.

Too few historians of the exploration of the West have made any real effort to comprehend that pageant from the Indian point of view. In recounting the deeds of Carson, Frémont, and their brethren, American chroniclers have all too often lapsed into an easy celebration of the inevitable course of manifest destiny. Even such skeptics as Bernard De Voto and Wallace Stegner have seldom tried to conceive the whole business from the point of view of, say, the Blackfeet or the Navajos.

Yet there is no escaping the fact that the Americanizing of the West was at the same time an unprecedented cultural tragedy. After ransacking the anthropological literature and consulting with Native Americans, I felt it obligatory to pause in my story now and again to try to imagine it from the point of view of its inevitable victims—the Indians who were so often attacked, infected with fatal diseases, resettled on reservations far from their homelands, and deliberately massacred. If this effort has succeeded, I hope it adds complexity to the reader's understanding not only of Carson and Frémont, but of the mythic West.

Yet in the end, my aim is not to debunk such pioneers as Carson and Frémont. Once loosed, manifest destiny was an irreversible flood. For all his flaws, I see Frémont finally as something of a hero—an abolitionist ahead of his time, a brave and stoic leader who won unquestioning loyalty from good men. And there is no question in my mind that Carson, so hard to plumb on the personal level, deserves to be regarded as a hero. One of the overarching themes of his life is the man's evolution from the blithe and thoughtless killer and scalper of Indians in 1829 to arguably their most effective champion and advocate in the West in the 1860s.

On the Kit Carson monument in Santa Fe, a brown sandstone obelisk three blocks north of the plaza, an inscription on the north side reads

Pioneer
Pathfinder
Soldier

But the inscription on the west side is more succinct:

He Led the Way

From that phrase, so full of the period chauvinism of its day, I take my half-ironic motto. In their absence, other men might have spearheaded the tide of conquest and emigration that Americanized the West. But Carson and Frémont led the way.

SAVAGE SUBLIMITY

1

A DISORDER OF
ENORMOUS MASSES

THEY set out, fifteen men on fifteen mules, shortly after dawn on August 12, 1842, carrying two days' worth of food—dried buffalo meat, macaroni, and coffee. In the lead, as usual, rode Kit Carson, threading a trail through tangles of downed limber pine, across tilted slabs of granite where the mules' hoofs skated and slipped, beneath waterfalls and around cobalt lakes. And as usual, calling the shots from the middle of the pack, John C. Frémont straddled his mule as the alien landscape enfolded him, his quicksilver spirit veering between exultation and despair. Directly ahead of the party loomed its goal, the peak Frémont had judged loftiest in all the Rocky Mountains, snowfields gleaming in the sun, rock towers spiking the sky.

As yet, these two were nobodies, Kit Carson and John Frémont, their deeds discussed, if at all, only within the arcane circles of their peers and cronies. But this summer's jaunt would make them famous, launching a joint passage into the realms of myth that would place them, before the century's end, among America's eternal heroes. From the 1842 expedition onward, their destinies and renown would be intertwined; yet in all the West, no pair of adventurers more different in character than Carson and Frémont could be found.

Ten weeks before, the two men had first met, aboard a steamboat crawling the Missouri River upstream from St. Louis. Twenty-nine years old, a southerner born in Savannah and raised in Tennessee, Virginia, and South Carolina, Frémont had escaped a life of incipient dandyism to become an ambitious lieutenant in the Corps of Topographical Engineers, a branch of the U.S. Army. He had served adequately on several surveying trips in the South and Midwest, but the present journey was Frémont's first thrust into the Great West, as well as his break in life. For the first time, he was in charge of an expedition. The explicit mandate given Frémont was to survey the first half of the Oregon Trail; his implicit charge was to keep an eye out for the best places to build forts along the way to safeguard emigrants from the "redskins" who (in the phrase of the day) "infested" the territory.

Frémont needed a guide who knew the West. Three years his elder, out of Kentucky via a hardscrabble homestead on the Missouri frontier, Carson had run away from home at the age of sixteen. For thirteen years he had trapped beaver and fought Indians from California down to Chihuahua, from New Mexico up to Idaho, without amassing the most modest fortune or dulling one whit his wanderlust. Now, with the collapse of the beaver trade, he was simply another down-on-his-luck mountain man looking for work. Aboard the steamboat, in response to Frémont's earnest questions, Carson (as he recalled many years later) "told him that I had been some time in the mountains and thought I could guide him to any point he wished to go."

By mid-August, the expedition had traversed a thousand miles of prairie, ascending a series of rivers: the Missouri, both the North and South Platte, and the Sweetwater. On August 7, the team had traversed South Pass—the ill-defined saddle, some 7,500 feet above sea level, that affords the easiest crossing of the Continental Divide between Mexico and Canada—and turned the south end of the majestic Wind River Range. Now, for the ascent of what would come to be known as Fremont Peak, the lieutenant divided his party, leaving twelve men beside a lake on the western fringe of the range to stand guard against the Blackfeet Indians, who Frémont feared would seize the first opportunity to ambush his team.

For all his western experience, Carson had never before penetrated the Wind Rivers. Both he and Frémont seriously underestimated the range's defenses. What from a distance looked like a straightforward slope leading to the mountain (which days before, from the plains, Frémont had singled out as clearly the apex of the chain) proved to hide a wildly convoluted terrain. Unguessed chasms thwarted their progress, the forest grew in places too dense to ride through, and chaoses of sharp-edged talus made for treacherous footing. By nightfall, the team had found a grassy bottom among the pines where the mules were turned out to graze and the men set up their bivouac.

For all the difficulties thrown across his path, Frémont pushed into the heart of the range in a state of rapture. "It seemed as if," he later wrote, "from the vast expanse of uninteresting prairie we had passed over, nature had collected all her beauties together in one chosen place." An avid if uncritical self-taught botanist, Frémont gathered samples wherever he went: here, he waxed ecstatic over "a rich undergrowth of plants, and numerous gay-colored flowers in brilliant bloom." (Looking over Frémont's pressed specimens four months later, anticipating the lieutenant's second western expedition, the great Harvard botanist Asa Gray wrote to his equally luminary Princeton colleague John Torrey, "I wish we had a collector to go with Fremont. . . . If none are to be had, Lieut. F. must be *indoctrinated*, & taught to collect both dried spec. & seeds. Tell him he shall be *immortalized* by having the 999th Senecio called *S. Fremontii*. . . .")

Yet Frémont's rapture was darkened with a sense of awe that bordered on dread. In the primeval wild into which he had trespassed, the young lieutenant discerned "a savage sublimity of naked rock." As crag and ridge and abyss forestalled his blithe plans, he felt all but trapped within "a gigantic disorder of enormous masses."

In the morning, still optimistic, Frémont moved three miles deeper into the range, through "a confusion of defiles," until his party came to a clearing with a magnificent view of their objective. Here the leader set up an advanced base, leaving the mules with several men and all their camping equipment. After an early dinner, the would-be alpinists set out on foot, carrying neither coats nor food: "The peak appeared so near, that there was no doubt of our returning before night. . . ."

Once again, Frémont misjudged the Wind River Mountains. "We

were soon involved in the most ragged precipices . . . , [which] constantly obstructed our path, forcing us to make long *détours*; frequently obliged to retrace our steps, and frequently falling among the rocks." One man averted death as he pitched toward a cliff's edge only by "throwing himself flat on the ground." By late afternoon, the men were close to exhaustion, and Frémont himself had succumbed to a violent headache and vomiting.

Stretching 110 miles across western Wyoming, with its countless lakes, its meadows fringed with evergreens, its cirques teeming with solid walls of granite and gneiss, the Wind River Range has become today a favorite playground for backpackers, fishermen, and mountaineers. From Elkhart Park, at 9,100 feet on a mountain shoulder above Fremont Lake, a well-traveled trail winds fifteen miles north and east toward Titcomb Lakes.

The path winds up a shallow vale, then angles across a plateau thick with limber pines and Engelmann spruce, making a gratuitous jog north to treat pilgrims to a splendid panorama at Photographers Point, where they gain their first view of distant Fremont Peak. Forest Service crews have chainsawed downed tree trunks out of the way, but in the trackless woods on either side, fallen, mossy logs form a maze of obstacles that would still make for tortuous going on muleback.

The best guess of modern historians as to where Frémont entered the Wind Rivers is at Boulder Lake, some dozen miles south of Elkhart Park. Approaching the mountains from South Pass, Frémont might easily have believed he was taking the shortest route to his objective; but the delusions of mountain foreshortening that bedeviled all early climbers in the West thus added those dozen miles to the party's ordeal. It is possible that the path Carson found through tangles and ravines during the party's first two days veers close to the Titcomb trail, but equally likely that the 1842 explorers wandered several miles farther east.

By mid-August, the summer's riot of wildflowers has peaked and waned, leaving only the hardier survivors: not only the profusions of purple asters over which Frémont raved, but swaths of Indian paintbrush, elephantela (with its tiny pink trunklike blossoms), buttercups, blue lupine, and magenta fireweed blooming down the stalk. Squirrels skitter among the pine needles, and Canada jays, emboldened by the crumbs a summer's troop of hikers have dropped along the trail, perch on nearby branches.

Ten miles in, the trail skirts Seneca Lake. The odds are good that Frémont's party passed by here, for it lies on the direct route to Titcomb Basin, southeast of Fremont Peak. For all the vexations of trail finding in the forest, for all the scrapes and scares of negotiating granite slabs and cliffs, in the Wind Rivers, Frémont's spirit soared with joy. As he emerged upon an unexpected lake (possibly Seneca), "a view of the utmost magnificence and grandeur burst upon our eyes. With nothing between us and their feet to lessen the effect of the whole height, a grand bed of snow-capped mountains rose before us, pile upon pile, glowing in the bright light of an August day."

The evening of August 13, on the north side of a sizable lake with a rocky island in the middle of it, the team prepared for a second bivouac. Island Lake, as Frémont named the site of their nocturnal vigil, is the first point on the party's mountain itinerary where the modern traveler can be sure of walking in their 1842 footprints. The lake lies close to timberline, at 10,346 feet—3,400 feet of altitude and three miles as the hawk soars beneath the summit of Fremont Peak.

On a broad flat rock, the men stretched their weary bones in hopes of sleep. They had nothing to eat, and not even their coats to cover themselves. Before dusk, the best hunters had set off hoping to shoot a bighorn sheep or two, but had come back empty-handed. The men built a bonfire of downed pine, but a gale out of the north robbed the bivouackers of its heat. Most of the worn-out party endured the ten hours of darkness without a wink of sleep.

Frémont, however, had already proved himself the most stubborn of explorers. Despite vomiting late into the night, he rose on August 14 still determined to conquer the mountain. As he later jauntily wrote, "[W]e were glad to see the face of the sun in the morning. Not being delayed by any preparation for breakfast, we set out immediately."

By the end of his voyaging, twelve years hence, Frémont could lay fair claim to having explored more terrain west of the Mississippi than any other American. The historian Allan Nevins would subtitle his 1928 biography of the man *The West's Greatest Adventurer.* Frémont would enter the pantheon of his country's heroes tagged with the resounding sobriquet the Pathfinder.

Yet compared to the monumental government expeditions to the West that had preceded his, Frémont's 1842 voyage does not easily lend itself to pioneering superlatives. Lewis and Clark's journey of 1804–6 fulfilled Thomas Jefferson's empyrean expectations: to explore the Louisiana Purchase and beyond, all the way to the Pacific; to search for a northwest passage by river across the continent (Lewis and Clark proved there was none); and to gauge the potential of that vast wilderness for American commerce and settlement. The next two western expeditions—Zebulon Pike's in 1806–7, and Stephen Long's in 1819–20—furthered the reconnaissance of the Great Plains and the Rocky Mountains, as well as probing the Spanish stronghold in the Southwest.

But Frémont's 1842 mission was a comparatively modest one—essentially, to make an accurate map of the first half of what was already being called the Oregon Trail. The journey's covert purpose, Frémont comprehended well: for his push west might help serve the intrigues of politicians who dreamed of seeing the American flag wave not only over Oregon, but Texas and California as well. Only three years after Frémont set out from St. Louis, the editor of the *New York Morning News*, John L. O'Sullivan, would publish a manifesto whose key words became the catch phrase that rallied tide after tide of American expansionism. It was, O'Sullivan wrote, the "manifest destiny of this nation to overspread the continent allotted by Providence for the free development of our yearly multiplying millions."

It required, however, a linked chain of fortuitous events to place Frémont in charge of the expedition that would launch his lasting fame. As the survey took shape in the minds of its government sponsors, it was assumed that Joseph Nicollet would lead the party, as he had the 1838–39 jaunt into the Midwest; once again, Frémont would serve as a useful but decidedly subordinate second-in-command. An astronomer, cartographer, and member of the French Legion of Honor, Nicollet had fled his native land in 1830 for political reasons; within a decade, he had landed a cherished job as explorer for the War Department. A brilliant innovator, Nicollet was the first to use the barometer to measure altitudes; one historian calls him "the first systematic modern cartographer." It was Nicollet, on the 1838–39 expedition, who taught Frémont everything the young lieutenant knew about mapping and surveying.

By 1842, however, Nicollet was gravely ill with cancer. It was almost more than he could do to write up the report of his previous journey, let alone lead another one.

The great American champion of westward expansion was Thomas Hart Benton of Missouri, who had served in the Senate since 1821. A close confidant of Thomas Jefferson, Benton had tirelessly lobbied for expeditions to take up the challenge laid down by Lewis and Clark; in the last meeting he ever had with an ailing Jefferson, in 1824, their talk had been of the need for further exploration of the unknown West.

By 1840, as Nicollet's mapmaker, Frémont had won the attention and approval of the stormy senator from Missouri. But it was far from a foregone conclusion that, in default of Nicollet, a twenty-nine-year-old lieutenant in the Topographical Corps would be entrusted to lead the survey up the Missouri and the Platte.

And Frémont came very close to ruining not only his chance at command, but his whole career—by falling in love with Benton's daughter. Jessie was fifteen when she met the twenty-six-year-old Frémont. They courted discreetly, then were secretly married by a Catholic priest on October 19, 1841. When Jessie presented her father with this startling *fait accompli,* the senator flew into one of his legendary rages, then banished his son-in-law from the house. Still only seventeen, Jessie stood firm, declaring her fealty to the man she loved, and Benton was so moved that he performed an about-face. By early 1842, the rash lieutenant had become Benton's protégé.

To finance the expedition, Benton pushed a $30,000 appropriations bill through Congress. Within the senator's heart burned a clandestine passion to flood the West with Americans, and so drive out the British, who were gaining more than a foothold in Oregon. Clandestine, because relations with Great Britain would be seriously compromised by any overt avowal of such an American goal.

Thus the official orders for Frémont's expedition make no hint of paving the way for emigrants or of claiming land for the United

States. The only document that has ever come to light, a laconic five-sentence directive from the chief of the Bureau of Topographical Engineers, demands only that Frémont "make a Survey of the Platte or Nebraska river, up to the head of the Sweetwater." The party's whole foray into the Wind River Range was thus technically—and characteristically—a case of Frémont's deliberately overstepping his mandate.

By his late twenties, the explorer was a man driven by restless curiosity. His love of nature ran deep, and his enthusiasm for botany and geology far exceeded that of a dilettante. Yet in view of his ultimate glory as "the West's greatest adventurer," it is striking that at the age of twenty-eight, Frémont had no particular interest in the West. He was the prototype of that classic nineteenth-century American, the man of intense but vaguely directed ambition. To the extent that he had a goal in life before 1842, it was simply to become a "great engineer," whatever that might mean.

It was Benton who awakened the lieutenant to the West. Forty-five years later, Frémont recalled that his first talk with the senator, full of Benton's rosy visions of an American Hesperides, "was pregnant with results and decisive of my life."

Yet that modest expedition up the Platte to the head of the Sweetwater might well have passed into the limbo of a historical footnote to the Americanizing of the West. By 1842, three and a half decades' worth of far more extraordinary journeys beyond the Mississippi had been performed by Americans unknown to the eastern public. Those ephemeral but epic voyages began with John Colter, who, after almost three years of privation and adventure in the employ of Lewis and Clark, decided that he craved more of the same, begged leave of his bosses on the Missouri, and headed back into the wilderness in August 1806. During the next few years, Colter made the Anglo discovery of the geysers and hot springs of Yellowstone (Colter's Hell, his scoffing auditors dubbed this landscape of a crazed loner's fantasy) and miraculously survived his execution at the hands of the Blackfeet.

Colter, Manuel Lisa, Jedediah Smith, Joseph Reddeford Walker, Thomas Fitzpatrick, Old Bill Williams, Joe Meek, Jim Bridger—these, and many another mountain man, including Kit Carson, prosecuted journeys all over the West that made Frémont's 1842

outing look like a milk run. Indeed, no part of the itinerary on Frémont's first expedition—except his probe into the Wind Rivers—
covered ground that was new to Americans. South Pass, the key to
the Oregon migration, had been discovered by Anglos as early as
1812; Benjamin Bonneville had taken wagons across it in 1832; and
six years before Frémont came along, the first white women (missionaries' wives named Narcissa Whitman and Elizabeth Spalding)
successfully traversed the divide.

Yet, as Allan Nevins writes of the mountain men, "Though they
were the true pathfinders, their knowledge was relatively useless, for
it could not be diffused." The cardinal contribution of Frémont's
first expedition, as well as the pedestal of his fame, lay in the map
his expedition produced (the best yet drawn beyond the Mississippi)
and the report he published (at the time, the most stirring, romantic, and influential narrative of the western frontier to appear in
English).

Around St. Louis, Frémont had recruited the personnel for his
expedition. Nearly all were French voyageurs who already knew the
Great Plains. Frémont's own father was French, an itinerant painter
and womanizer who had drifted to Tidewater Virginia; the future explorer grew up fluent in French and comfortable with his paternal
culture. Though Kit Carson would become Frémont's most trusted
scout, at first on the 1842 expedition, "my favorite man" was one of
the voyageurs, Basil Lajeunesse. It was Lajeunesse to whom the lieutenant turned for onerous errands and dangerous missions, which
the Frenchman performed without stint. We know very little about
this worthy, who, at the outset of the journey, had only four years to
live: on Frémont's third expedition, in 1846, an ax wielded by an Indian in southern Oregon would split his skull as he slept by the
campfire.

From the start, however, Frémont was impressed by Carson's
quiet competence and savoir-faire. In an oft-quoted passage in his
official report, Frémont observed his new friend with admiration
tinged perhaps with envy: "Mounted on a fine horse, without a saddle, and scouring bare-headed over the prairies, Kit was one of the
finest pictures of a horseman I have ever seen." For if there was a
single quality the vain and impetuous lieutenant hankered after, it
was the kind of unconscious grace Carson exuded. Kit was, more-

over, a better buffalo hunter than the mountain man (Lucien Maxwell) Frémont had hired to be the expedition's meat hunter.

Carson's salary for the three-month journey was $100 a month. This may not seem a princely stipend, on a frontier where inflated prices held sway: at Chouteau's Landing (near present-day Kansas City), Frémont laid in such supplies as tea at $1 a pound and linseed oil at $2 a gallon. But the salary was more than three times as much as Carson had made the previous year, as a meat hunter for Bent's Fort on the Arkansas. Basil Lajeunesse, in contrast, was paid only 75 cents per day.

For all his enthusiasm about the journey west, Frémont found crossing a thousand miles of prairie an ordeal by tedium. Though his report would eventually help sell the Great Plains to several generations of emigrants, Frémont could not help recording "the same dreary barrenness" day after day, "the same naked waste." Of the view from a marly ridge in what is today western Nebraska, he wrote, "I had never seen anything which impressed so strongly on my mind a feeling of desolation."

On July 8, on the North Platte, while Frémont himself was absent on a reconnaissance to the south, the main body of his team crossed paths with an entourage of trappers led by the already legendary mountain man Jim Bridger. Returning from the very headwaters toward which Frémont's party was aimed, Bridger was full of dire alarms. The Sioux to the west and north, he reported, were on the rampage, having "declared war on every living thing." Bridger was certain the exploring party could not continue westward without risking pitched battles against the maddened Indians.

Frémont's account of the 1842 expedition is an artful concoction. Beneath a veneer of modesty about his own deeds, the narrative pivots around uplifting instances of its leader's courage and resolve. Bridger's scare furnishes the first such exemplum.

That night around the campfire, with Frémont still off on his reconnaissance, the voyageurs chew the fat of their fears, muttering, "*Il n'y aura pas de vie pour nous*" (in western movie lingo, "We're goners now"). Even Carson has dark thoughts, agreeing with Bridger about the certainty of warfare, and going so far as to make out his will.

Frémont, returning a few days later (if we can believe his own account), gives not a moment's thought to turning back down the

Platte. Instead, he gathers his men, declares his intention to march
forward, and offers to discharge with full pay any "who were disposed to cowardice, and anxious to return." Only one voyageur
seizes this humiliating escape clause. "I asked him some few questions," Frémont smugly reports, "in order to expose him to the
ridicule of the men, and let him go."

On Lewis and Clark's landmark journey almost four decades before, the men had been encouraged by their leaders to keep journals,
in hopes of compiling the richest possible record of their pioneering
odyssey. In 1842, Frémont forbade the keeping of diaries among his
own expeditioners. The only account that would emerge from his
survey of the Oregon Trail would be Frémont's own.

This precaution might have seemed all but moot, for most of the
voyageurs were illiterate—as was Kit Carson himself. But Frémont
had failed to calculate for the clandestine disobedience of the only
other well-educated member of his team, the man who was, by any
reckoning, the least likely adventurer in the lot: his German cartographer, Charles Preuss.

Frémont had met the mapmaker the previous December, when a shy
supplicant bearing a letter of introduction had arrived at his home
in Washington one evening as Frémont sat with Jessie before the
fireplace. Years later, Frémont recalled his first sight of the man—"a
shock of light curly hair standing up thick about his head, and a face
so red that we attributed it to a wrong cause instead of to the cold
and the nervousness and anxiety which turned his speech into stam-
mering."

A less generous man might have sent Preuss packing; but Frémont quickly saw that the diffident German was a superb draftsman
and topographer—and that he was destitute. He gave Preuss menial
work reducing astronomical observations from the 1838–39 survey,
then, as soon as he was put in charge of the western expedition,
hired Preuss as his cartographer.

Born in western Germany in 1803, Preuss was a decade older
than his employer. Since 1834, when he had emigrated to the
United States, he had puttered away at a series of desk jobs, most of
them with the U.S. Coast Survey, whose superintendent was a fel-

low expatriate German. But when a congressional appropriation failed to come through, Preuss, his wife, and young daughter (a son had died in childhood two years earlier) faced virtual starvation.

Preuss would eventually accompany Frémont on three expeditions, including the lieutenant's disastrous fourth, when both men were lucky to get out of the San Juan Mountains in Colorado alive. But in June 1842, as the party left Chouteau's Landing on the Missouri, Preuss was an utter greenhorn. Thirty-nine years old, he had never ridden a horse before; it is possible that he had never camped out.

Preuss kept his secret diary in German, which language Frémont did not read. It is a completely private document, with no pretensions to a wider audience than that of his wife, Gertrud, whom he addresses by the diminutive Trautchen. Lost in family attics for more than a century, the diary was rediscovered by a scholar in 1954 and published in an English translation four years later.

In the absence of any other account of the expedition besides Frémont's suave and self-congratulatory report, Preuss's unvarnished diary supplies a corrective viewpoint. The narrative also sparkles with accidental comedy, as Preuss plays an unwitting Sancho Panza to Frémont's Don Quixote.

Yet the German must have been a trying companion on the trail. Compulsively gloomy, homesick not only for his ménage outside Washington but for his native Germany, a hopeless bumbler about camp, an egregious know-it-all despite his shortcomings, contemptuous of the rough-hewn voyageurs who were his comrades, Preuss grumbles his way from St. Louis to the Wind Rivers and back again.

A bit of a toady to Frémont's face, Preuss delights in lampooning his commander in his private pages. Already, on the first day out from Chouteau's Landing, the leader is "that simpleton Frémont" and "a foolish lieutenant." Without stating his grounds, Preuss derides Frémont's astronomical observations, his botanizing, and his mineralogy. Carson fares a little better, though from the first pages on, Preuss nicknames him Kid Karsten.

Like many another tenderfoot dragged half-willingly along on a difficult journey, Preuss obsesses about food. After an ox was slaughtered, "Some of the men tried to eat the liver raw. I was satisfied with bread and coffee." Preuss's squeamishness about trail food intersects with his dudgeon against the French cook. "Have trapped a large turtle, which is being prepared for soup tonight. If our cook, the rascal, will only know how to fix it." One day later: "A prairie chicken was shot. If the cook cannot prepare it any better than the turtle, let him gulp it down himself." In his famished funks, Preuss retreats to smoke a solitary pipe on the edge of camp.

Proving himself an incompetent horseman, on only the fifth day out Preuss is relieved of the chores of grooming, saddling, and feeding his mount. Remarkably indulgent of the eccentric German's foibles, Frémont wins no gratitude in Preuss's diary. After a sleepless night among clouds of mosquitoes, Preuss grouses, "The others lay safely under their nets; mine had been forgotten because of Frémont's negligence." Unable to get used to wearing the same clothes day after day, Preuss hires a voyageur to do his laundry. The cartographer joins Frémont's splinter party for the reconnaissance of the South Platte, but, incapable of keeping up, is sent back with a single companion. Having regained the main trail, Preuss sits under a juniper and smokes his pipe, while his partner sets off on muleback to look for the rest of the team. Late in the afternoon, the companion returns, bearing a hamper of beef, buffalo tongue, bread, and brandy. "What a joy, what a delight!" Preuss crows in his diary. Yet in the next breath: "When I was eating, I thought that those people could have sent along a little salt if they had had anything of a cultured taste."

Frémont's initial fear that the man was a serious drinker, when he met the red-faced Preuss the previous December, may have hit the mark. At one point, Preuss reassures himself "that I am not such a bibbler as I believed at times." Yet his thoughts are constantly on ardent spirits. "I wish I had a drink," he blurts out the night of the failed turtle soup. A few evenings later: "If only I had a bottle of wine. . . ." Meat hung from the wagons to dry reminds Preuss of red curtains in the windows of a German tavern. "Oh, if there were a tavern here!" he sighs. Preuss lives for the keg of brandy Frémont taps on special occasions, cursing the "miserable red wine" that the lieutenant serves up for breakfast to celebrate the Fourth of July.

Nor is the topographer much interested in the landscape. "Nothing but prairie. Made twenty miles. Very hot," he natters early on. And near the end of the expedition, with the Missouri almost in

smelling distance: "I find it quite impossible to say anything interesting about this trip and about the country. I see nothing, I know
nothing, I think only of wife, child, bread, and coffee. Also, a little
drink passes through my thoughts from time to time. . . ."

Even the Indians fail to engage the dyspeptic traveler. Crowding
around camp, they are "irksome, pesky as children." In the face of
Jim Bridger's warning about Sioux on the warpath, Preuss is all for
going home. When Frémont announces his decision to press on,
Preuss, too humiliated to back out in front of his colleagues, bitterly
regrets having joined the expedition in the first place. Anticipating
his death by a Sioux arrow or knife, he proclaims, "I see no honor in
being murdered by this rabble."

Yet Preuss's iconoclastic mutterings puncture the chivalric idyll
that emerges in Frémont's report. A stirring typical passage in the
latter details the lieutenant's part in a buffalo hunt at full gallop: "I
fired at the distance of a yard, the ball entering at the termination of
the long hair, and passing near the heart. She fell headlong at the
report of the gun. . . ." In Preuss's telling, Frémont regularly returns
from such chases with no quarry more tangible than a boast: " 'I
knocked down one, and that fellow will not get much farther,' etc."

To cover the hiatus in his main party's progress while he is off on
his South Platte reconnaissance, Frémont pretends to transcribe entries penned by Preuss in his absence; these are plainly the lieutenant's compositions, based perhaps on notes by the German.
After Jim Bridger warns the team about the Sioux rampage, the
mountain man reluctantly offers to guide them to the headwaters of
the Sweetwater; "but the absence of our leader, which was deeply regretted by all," writes the "Preuss" of the report, "rendered it impossible for us to enter upon such an arrangement." At the moment,
the real Preuss was confiding in his diary, "I feel better because of
Frémont's absence."

The flip side of Frémont's considerable charisma as a leader was his
grandiose belief—or is it merely a literary conceit?—that all his
teammates' hearts beat in sympathy with his. When his third and last
barometer breaks in the Wind Rivers, writes Frémont, "The loss was
felt by the whole camp. . . . Their grief was only inferior to my own."

But Preuss views Frémont as a kind of mad tinkerer and gad-
geteer, more interested in his instruments than his men. "Our big

chronometer has gone to sleep," he writes almost gleefully on June 19. "That is what always happens when an egg wants to be wiser than the hen." Frémont had brought along a daguerreotype camera, with which he labored in vain to expose a single plate (successful photographs from a western voyage of discovery would not be taken for another eleven years). Having failed in this effort, Frémont neglects to mention the daguerreotype in his report.

Not so Preuss: "Frémont wasted the morning with his machine. . . . [H]e spoiled five plates that way. Not a thing was to be seen on them. That's the way it often is with these Americans. They know everything, they can do everything, and when they are put to a test, they fail miserably."

Frémont's ultimate gadget was an inflatable boat made of india rubber. On the journey out, he had used this dubious contraption to try to ferry supplies across the Kansas River, only to watch it capsize. Two men nearly drowned, and the expedition lost much of its sugar and coffee.

Unfazed, on the descent of the Platte two months later, Frémont launched the boat with a crew of seven and, inexplicably, the expedition's books and records. Provisioned for a twelve-day float, the raft bounced through a rapids-thronged canyon for some three hours before flipping. This time, three men almost drowned, a good part of the records was lost, and the navigators had to perform an arduous forced march—Frémont with one foot clad only in a stocking—to catch up with the rest of their party. Among this bedraggled band of survivors was the German cartographer, who later scolded in his diary, "It was certainly stupid of the young chief to be so foolhardy where the terrain was absolutely unknown."

Upon reaching the Wind Rivers in early August, however, it is Preuss's turn to grow grandiose. Apparently on the strength of a single walking tour in Switzerland, performed at the age of twenty-six, during which, suddenly turning a rocky corner, "I saw in front of me the entire range of the Alps from Mont Blanc to the Alps of Tirol" (a geographical impossibility), he styles himself the expedition's mountaineering expert. In this role, at first he sneers at the Wind Rivers. An earlier traveler had guessed that the range towered to 25,000 feet above sea level; Preuss doubts that the summits reach 8,000. Comparing the blissful memory of his Swiss prospect with a distant view of the Winds, he laments that "it is as though I were to turn my eyes from the face of a lovely girl to the wrinkled face of an old woman."

Preuss's alpine snobbery seems to affect Frémont. The lieutenant's report asserts that the prosaic divide of South Pass has "nothing of the Great St. Bernard and Simplon passes in Europe" about it, that the charm of the Wind Rivers has little to do with "the splendor of far off views, which have lent such a glory to the Alps." Having never been to Europe, Frémont must have dredged up his comparisons from books and from the stream of condescending prattle with which his German topographer annotated the New World landscape.

Once again, however, Preuss's uncensored version of events reveals the tensions and follies of the Wind River thrust, which Frémont's more polished narrative glosses over. "The leader, Carson, walked too fast," writes Preuss of the morning of August 13, the day the team hoped to reach the summit. "This caused some exchange of words. Frémont got excited, as usual, and designated a young chap [probably Basil Lajeunesse] to take the lead. . . ."

As the team leaves the mules in a grove and sets out, foodless and coatless, to bag the peak, Preuss calls on his alpine wisdom: "[O]nly I, a more experienced mountaineer, stuck a piece of dried buffalo meat in my pocket." According to the topographer, it is Frémont's throbbing headache that dictates an early halt. In camp, the lieutenant and Carson patch up their quarrel. On his bed of hard stone, Preuss struggles fruitlessly to sleep: "The night was very cold, the wind violent, and, as always, the best spots were already taken by others."

In the morning, according to Preuss, the team starts off deeply dispirited. "No supper, no breakfast, little or no sleep—who can enjoy climbing a mountain under these circumstances? Moreover, all the men, with perhaps two exceptions, would have much preferred to stay in camp."

One of those two is Preuss himself. For all his griping, for all his disdain for these humdrum American mountains, the German has caught summit fever. Though he knows that, at thirty-nine, he is not the man he was on his Swiss tour at twenty-six, Charles Preuss is determined not only to reach the top of the highest peak in the Rocky Mountains, but to be the first man to get there.

* * *

Why, exactly, did Frémont want to climb his mountain? His report is oddly circumlocutory on the matter, except when the tragedy of the barometer causes the lieutenant to agonize over the loss to science his inability to measure the height of the Wind River Range will bode. (Frémont ingeniously jury-rigged the barometer in camp and was able to take remarkably accurate altitudes.) Nothing in his formal expedition orders, of course, hinted at alpinism.

There is instead, in Frémont's gutsy determination to penetrate the contorted range and ascend its highest point—which would furnish not only the dramatic zenith of the first expedition, but one of the proudest moments of the Pathfinder's life—that modern note of exploration for its own sake. Today, Fremont Peak is not a difficult climb; by its southwest slopes, the mountain amounts, in the modern alpinist's dismissive phrase, to "a walk-up." By 1842 in the Alps, technical wizards were making the first ascents of such redoubtable peaks as the Gross Venediger and the Finsteraarhorn. By the same date in the American West, where the sheer remoteness of the mountains added much to their intrinsic difficulty, no one (except certain Indians, whose names and feats are lost to history) had yet climbed a summit as challenging as Fremont Peak.

In 1806, Zebulon Pike, making the Anglo discovery of the mountain that would bear his name, set out to climb it. Like Frémont and Carson, he radically underestimated the scale of his objective. Anticipating a one-day ascent, he and his men found themselves wallowing through waist-deep snow three arduous days later. Topping one of the mountain's innumerable false summits, he saw that the true apex still lay fifteen or sixteen miles away. Pike quit in disgust, declaring that "no human being could have ascended to its pinical."

Only fourteen years later, Edwin James, a young botanist on Stephen Long's expedition, led the first ascent of Pikes Peak, which required an ordeal rivaling Pike's. The huge but gentle Colorado mountain, however, is a far easier climb than Fremont Peak, as evidenced by the fact that an auto road was built to the top in 1915.

Frémont was not the first Anglo explorer to reach a Wind River summit. In 1833, looking for a direct route across the range, mountain man Benjamin Bonneville headed up one of the forks of the

Popo Agie River from the east, near present-day Lander. Crossing "fearful precipices" and "rugged defiles," forced at last to "clamber on hands and knees," Bonneville's small team topped out on some Wind River summit; but the account the pioneer left is so sketchy that no historian today can ascertain which peak he climbed.

Aside from these isolated deeds, no serious mountaineering had been performed in the American West before 1842. Frémont's own account of his team's plunge into the Wind Rivers, with their "gigantic disorder of enormous masses," makes this wilderness sound so forbidding that one would think the explorers were the first human beings ever to enter its labyrinthine heart.

A stray remark in Preuss's diary reveals otherwise, and hints at one of the beguiling mysteries of the prehistoric West. At Island Lake, scene of the party's frigid, hungry bivouac,

> we found remains of Indian lodges, but this did not disturb us. Kit, who otherwise makes a great to-do about such things in order to make himself important, said that the lodges were those of a weak, miserable tribe of Snake Indians. They were called "root-eaters" because they subsist chiefly on all sorts of roots and small game—squirrels, rats, beavers, etc. They have no horses and therefore frequent these regions.

As it turned out, Jim Bridger's warning had proved a false alarm: Frémont's party encountered only a handful of Sioux on their journey up the Platte and Sweetwater—harmless, demoralized men near starvation in the wake of a drought that had seized the Plains. Frémont knew that Crow Indians ranged east of the Wind Rivers, Shoshone to the west; but it was Blackfeet he feared most, claiming to have discovered signs of their encampments on the fringe of the range.

Whether or not Carson had a penchant for "making himself important," as Preuss carped, his résumé of the "root-eaters" was dead right. Carson, with his vast experience in the beaver country, was almost surely the only member of the party who could recognize the "lodges" of the ephemeral mountain people who had camped at Island Lake.

The "root-eaters" or Root Diggers, better known as the Sheepeaters, were indeed a Snake or Shoshone tribe. In their own tongue, they were called Tukuarika or Tukudeka, which translates as "sheep-eaters." Their range at the time of first contact by the mountain men was limited to the mountains of central Idaho, southern Montana, and northwest Wyoming. In all likelihood, they had been pushed into such marginal domains by the more aggressive tribes surrounding them, including their cousins the Shoshone proper. All early accounts of the Sheepeaters agree that they were a diminutive folk, peaceful and timid, who had never domesticated the horse. (The Shoshone, in contrast, had horses by the end of the seventeenth century.)

To explorers in the early 1800s, catching fugitive glimpses of these elusive people, the Sheepeaters invariably looked wretched and pitiful. Bonneville himself, in 1834, ran into a hundred families of Tukudeka near the mouth of the Powder River, a fork of the Snake in present-day Idaho. "They are, in general, very poor," Bonneville is paraphrased by Washington Irving, in the writer's vivid "digest" of the mountain man's manuscript diary; "destitute of most of the comforts of life, and extremely indolent: but a mild, inoffensive race." The women and children hid in the cliffs above to stare at the white intruders, but the men entered camp, where they "importuned Captain Bonneville and his companions excessively by their curiosity. . . . [A]ny thing they could lay their hands on underwent the most minute examination." Bonneville visited a Sheepeater village, where he was appalled by their half-starved dogs and their flimsy three-foot-high sagebrush shelters.

Yet viewed through the lens of the cultural relativism of our own day, the Tukudeka seem to have perfected their adaptation to a harsh environment with the same canny skill as the Inuit in Alaska or the Yaghan in Patagonia. Where Victorian travelers saw near-naked savages grubbing for roots, we might discern the "aboriginal affluence" of natives who had turned the subalpine flora of the West into a cornucopia of mushrooms, berries, nuts, wild onions, and other edible plants. The Tukudeka hunted not only sheep, but rabbits, prairie dogs, deer, and antelope. They had become without doubt the most virtuosic hunters of bighorn sheep the West has ever seen: their six-foot-long bows made of sheep's horn are museum pieces today.

Even Bonneville had to admire the Root Diggers' practical ingenuity. The mountain man marveled at the people's use of a twisted
cord made of sage bark, kept always lighted as a slow match; at the
hedgelike traps women built to capture antelope; at their water-
tight jars made of plaited wood smeared with wax; at sturdy ropes
they wove from weeds, and a flour they ground from native seeds.

Indeed, along with the common perception of the Sheepeaters as
"destitute" and "impoverished," one finds a remarkable vein in
nineteenth-century accounts attributing dignity and happiness to
these mountain nomads. One starry-eyed early traveler called them
"the proudest race of Indians that ever lived on earth." The trapper
Osborne Russell, bumping into a group of twenty-three Sheepeaters
in 1834 in what is today Yellowstone National Park, admired their
"beautifully wrought" bows, their "dressed deer and Sheep skins of
the best quality," and their knack at starting fires by rubbing two
sticks together. He concluded that, despite being "the only Inhabi-
tants of this lonely and secluded spot," the people "seemed to be
perfectly contented and happy."

Alas, the Tukudeka were destined for extinction. In 1875, what
remained of the tribe was given a joint reservation with the Lemhi
Indians near the Salmon River in Idaho. Wrote Frederick Webb
Hodge in 1910 in his magisterial *Handbook of American Indians
North of Mexico*, "They numbered 90 in 1904, but are no longer sep-
arately enumerated."

One of the strangest and most suspect of eyewitness accounts of
the Tukudeka is a forgotten book by one William Alonzo Allen,
called *The Sheep Eaters*. Writing in 1913 about events three decades
in his past, this Montana pioneer and dentist claimed that somewhere in a canyon on the Bighorn River he had once found the last
surviving member of the tribe, a woman who was 115 years old.
"She had outlived all her people and had wandered away from her
home in the mountains into the valleys, living on berries and wild
fruit as she wandered," writes Allen. "She alone could read the
painted rocks and tell their meaning. . . ."

These "painted rocks" Allen identifies as petroglyphs carved by
the Sheepeaters on certain granite walls in Wyoming and Montana,
which he was sure recorded the unknown history of the woman's
people. Allen conducts a long conversation with the "old squaw" in

sign language, uncovering the romantic saga of her love affair with one of the last Tukudeka chiefs, Red Eagle. Yet several aspects of the woman's rambling tale ring plausible: a great battle against the Sioux won long ago by prying loose booby-trapped boulders from the heights, which crushed the attackers from the plains; an illness that ravaged the people after they took in a solitary lost white man (many of the western tribes were in fact decimated by smallpox contracted from the Anglos).

In former Sheepeater country, Allen claimed to have come across stone blinds, sheep pens, and moldering lodges, the mute ruins left by the doomed people. The editor of Osborne Russell's diary claimed in 1914, "[T]races of them can still be found in isolated glens where their crude, conical shelters, made of small poles stood on end, resist decay very well."

By now, thanks to a century's stampede of hikers, hunters, climbers, and fishermen into such ranges as the Sawtooths and the Wind Rivers, almost no vestiges of the Sheepeaters can still be found, though no doubt their finely shaped obsidian arrowheads still lie scattered across unvisited timberline plateaus. Yet for all we know, as Frémont's men roused themselves on the morning of August 14, 1842, and trudged off toward the mountain of the young lieutenant's ambition, the Tukudeka watched them from their hiding places in the nearby cliffs.

Stiff and hungry after their bedrock bivouac at timberline, the dozen-odd men in the advance party (neither Frémont nor Preuss gives the exact number) set out early on the morning of August 14 to climb the peak. Carson, forgiven by his commander for the fault of walking too fast the day before, was put in the lead once more. The mountain man guided the party out of the valley that led to the upper lakes and, as Frémont would write, "took to the ridges again; which we found extremely broken, and where we were again involved among precipices."

Soon all semblance of an orderly ascent disintegrated; the mountaineers ran into a series of permanent snowfields, "among which we were all dispersed, seeking each the best path to ascend the peak." Preuss, the veteran of the Alps, tackled one of these snowfields, inclined at the modest angle of twenty degrees. Kicking steps into the upper edge of the field, the cartographer was unprepared when the snow abruptly turned (as is its August wont) to crusty ice. "I slipped," he confessed to Trautchen in his diary, "sat on my pants, and slid downhill at great speed." As Frémont watched, Preuss tumbled 200 feet, "turned a couple of somersets," and landed in the rocks below. "I . . . got away with two light bruises," wrote the chastened alpinist, "one on my right arm and one on my arse. The pain made me sit still for a few minutes; then I dragged myself to my feet, found my book, and climbed on slowly." The book Preuss clutched in his hands was the ledger in which he hoped to record Frémont's summit observations with compass and patched-up barometer, an exercise that still served as the official justification for the ascent. The climb, for which Frémont had originally allotted only two days from Boulder Lake all the way to the top and back, was already in its third day; though the lieutenant never mentions the dozen men left guarding camp on the fringe of the range, they must have been growing anxious.

Meanwhile the climb was turning into a debacle. Two altitude-sick voyageurs prostrated themselves on the rocks, ready to give up. Then Frémont was abruptly stricken "with headache and giddiness, accompanied by vomiting, as on the day before." A pair of loyal companions sat with the lieutenant and waited to see if his state might improve. Carson had charged off in the lead, oblivious to the laggards behind, and Preuss, bruised but still ambitious, plodded upward. "After about half an hour I had climbed so high that I could look over all the lower peaks," he later wrote. "On one of them I saw a part of the company sitting down, among them Frémont. I began to shout, and they recognized me."

This free-for-all parody of ascent continued. Having decided that he could not go on, Frémont sent Johnny Janisse, a voyageur who was half-French, half-Negro, to carry the precious barometer up to Preuss so that the topographer could make the summit observations. Seeing two men start to climb toward him, however, the ever-competitive Preuss took off, as his diary candidly admits, "in order to be the first on top, ahead of all the others." Thinking the summit only a few hundred feet above, Preuss climbed into a cul-de-sac. Foreshortening had once more taken its toll: "Nothing but vertical rocks, which naturally looked low to me from below but which were so steep that it was impossible for me to climb them."

Vexed and discouraged, the German descended, plagued by the thought that "the others had probably reached the peak by an easier route." Finding himself alone on an unfamiliar slope, Preuss "began to halloo," but got no answer. At last he found footprints in the snow and followed them.

The footprints were Janisse's, who had charged up another couloir with the barometer, bent on catching the elusive cartographer. By this point, Frémont had turned back toward Island Lake, ordering all his other companions to retreat with him.

Finally, Janisse saw Preuss trailing him, and stopped to confer. The voyageur was nervous about the hard snow he had encountered, unwilling to climb it carrying the fragile barometer. For Preuss, this "changed the situation; all ambition left me." At his highest point, he took his observations, hoping "that Frémont would be satisfied with the altitude I had established and would add five or six hundred feet in order to fix the assumed highest point."

It is doubtful that Preuss was so close to the summit. Meanwhile, Carson plugged on, somewhere out of sight above. It seems entirely likely that Kit could have soloed Fremont Peak, but—whether or not on the lieutenant's orders, as conveyed by Janisse—Preuss now told the voyageur to fire off his gun, presumably as a signal to Carson to descend at once. Frémont's report concludes vaguely that Carson "succeeded in reaching one of the snowy summits of the main ridge," from which the top appeared to be 800 to 1,000 feet higher.

So the grand alpine campaign of August 14 degenerated into something like farce—though in all truth the party was lucky not to sustain a serious injury during its every-man-for-himself assault. Severally the climbers stumbled back to Island Lake; Preuss found himself "quite exhausted" on reaching treeline.

But the eternally stubborn Frémont had not yet thrown in the towel. Even before regaining Island Lake, he had sent his favorite man, Basil Lajeunesse, off on a Herculean errand: to return all the way to the Camp of the Mules and bring back blankets, food, and mounts, preferably before nightfall. The next morning, altitude-sick or not, the lieutenant would lead a second attempt on the mountain of his dreams.

* * *

Today, Island Lake, just below timberline, is a favorite campsite for backpackers and fishermen, few of whom know anything about Frémont's grim bivouacs there more than a century and a half before. On the northeast shore, a number of boulders fit the lieutenant's description of a "broad flat rock, in some measure protected from the winds by the surrounding crags," where the mountaineers had struggled vainly to sleep on the gale-torn night of August 13.

From Island Lake, most hikers follow the trail north into Titcomb Basin, where three turquoise lakes strung end-to-end fill a craggy chasm: on the right, the west face of Fremont Peak rises more than 3,000 feet in less than a mile. A careful reading of Preuss suggests, however, that on August 15 the climbers veered east, climbing to a high cirque now called Indian Basin. Gaining this cirque, the team would have stood a mile and a half directly south of Fremont Peak.

Even today, relatively few parties choose to camp in Indian Basin, 500 feet above timberline. A patchwork of shallow, fishless ponds fills the stony floor of the basin, through which meanders a faint trail that leads to 12,100-foot Indian Pass, the only escape on the east. Across the pass, the miniature Knife Point Glacier nestles beneath the Continental Divide. All the cirques and valleys on the east side of the divide lie on the Wind River Reservation, seldom visited by Anglos.

Indian Basin is walled in by handsome peaks that would only be named in the 1920s, when mountaineers first tackled their challenging ridges with rope and piton: blocky Elephant Head; the soaring, pyramidal north face of Ellingwood Peak; lofty Jackson Peak, connected to Fremont by a crenellated ridge. All in all, the basin is a lonely place, its perpetual snowfields carved by the ceaseless west wind. Conies scuttle among the talus, carrying tufts of grass in their mouths; marmots pierce the silence with their shrill warning whistles; and squadrons of rosy finches swoop overhead.

Directly north, Fremont Peak dominates the basin. The southwest shoulder, self-evidently the route by which to climb the mountain, rises in a single, clean sweep from lower left to the sharp summit.

Refreshed by food and sleep, Frémont and five teammates left

their camp on the broad, flat rock at Island Lake early on the morning of August 15, 1842. On the specious pretext of preparing for the
long retreat homeward, the commander had ordered Carson and
the remaining men to head back at daybreak toward the Camp of
the Mules. One need not read between the lines of Frémont's report
to detect the lieutenant's fear that the sure-footed Carson might
beat him to the coveted summit.

Frémont had learned his lesson from the chaos of the preceding
day. Now the six men climbed methodically upward together. By
late morning, they were among the cliffs and ledges of the southwest
shoulder. The party traveled light, "having divested ourselves of
every unnecessary encumbrance." Frémont insisted that the six men
stick together, and that whenever someone got winded, the whole
team stop for a breather. Among the cliffs, the lieutenant donned a
light pair of leather moccasins, "as now the use of our toes became
necessary to a further advance." He was pleased to discover that
"with the exception of a slight disposition to headache, I felt no remains of yesterday's illness."

According to Preuss, it was Basil Lajeunesse who performed the
route finding, not Frémont. Higher up, as the team kicked steps in
a dangerous snowfield, another voyageur took the lead; named
Couteau or Descoteaux, he has all but escaped the documentary
record, failing to appear on Frémont's roster of the expedition.

For the modern mountaineer, the southwest shoulder of Fremont
Peak is a straightforward scramble. Small cliffs bar the way here and
there, but they are easily turned. So vaguely defined is the broad
crest of the ridge that perhaps half a dozen different lines offer non-
technical routes to the summit. But for the nervy explorers in 1842,
this high waste of rock and snow teemed with terrors none of them
had previously countenanced.

Frémont's report is full of harrowing obstacles that the modern
climber is hard put to locate: "a sort of comb of the mountain,
which stood against the wall like a buttress"; an overhang that had
to be circumvented; "a vertical precipice of several hundred feet";
and what one would call today the crux of the route, a crack that
Frémont conquered only by "putting hands and feet in the crevices
between the blocks."

Sometime after 1 P.M., as Frémont later wrote, "I sprang upon the summit, and another step would have precipitated me into an immense snow field five hundred feet below." As he had hoped and schemed, the lieutenant became the first human being to set foot on what he believed to be the apex of the Rocky Mountains. So precarious did Frémont find the summit block ("which it seemed a breath would hurl into the abyss below") that he allowed his partners to ascend it only one at a time. In turn, Charles Preuss, Basil Lajeunesse, Johnny Janisse, Clément Lambert, and the shadowy Descoteaux clambered up to the highest point.

Here, at the heart of his savage sublimity, Frémont's rapture was complete, as he basked in "a stillness the most profound and a terrible solitude. . . . It was a strange place, the icy rock and the highest peak of the Rocky Mountains, for a lover of warm sunshine and flowers."

Frémont unfurled his American flag, which he would later give to Jessie as a memento of his conquest. The men fired off pistols and shouted "hurrah" several times. Then they settled down to make observations with the compass, while they stared at the Tetons in the northwest, the endless plains far to the east: "Around us the whole scene had one main striking feature, which was that of terrible convulsion."

The temperature was 44° F. Preuss took a barometer reading that Frémont later rendered as an altitude of 13,570 feet—remarkably close to the peak's true height of 13,745 feet. Even here, on his proud summit, Preuss found reason to grumble about being hurried through his readings: "When the time comes for me to make my map in Washington," he scolded Frémont in his diary, "he will more than regret this unwise haste."

As the men lingered just below the top, they were startled to see a bumblebee fly by, coming to rest on the knee of one of the men. Frémont later mused, in a characteristic conceit, "that he was the first of his species to cross the mountain barrier, a solitary pioneer to foretell the advance of civilization." (In fact, bumblebees are common on Rocky Mountain summits in August.) The lieutenant squashed the bee between the pages of a book: one more specimen to bring back to the learned savants in the East. Then the team headed down.

As Frémont would later congratulate himself, "We had accomplished an object of laudable ambition, and beyond the strict order of our instructions. We had climbed the loftiest peak of the Rocky Mountains, and . . . standing where never human foot had stood before, felt the exultation of first explorers."

From the top, Frémont could see, only four miles to the north, the broad summit snowfield of another mountain, which would come to be known as Gannett Peak. Gannett, in fact, is 59 feet higher than Fremont; and although its greater height cannot be verified with the naked eye, there is no avoiding the suspicion. Yet Frémont never admits the slightest doubt that he stands atop the Wind River Range.

Fremont Peak, it turns out, ranks only third in height in Wyoming, after Gannett and the Grand Teton. It does not come close to being the highest peak in the American Rockies, which the Hayden Survey would prove to be Colorado's Mount Elbert, at 14,431 feet. In Colorado alone, there are 126 summits higher than Fremont Peak.

Nonetheless, for its time, Frémont's ascent was a bold feat of exploration, the hardest climb yet performed by Americans in the West. His conquest on August 15, 1842, must have seemed to Frémont a mere youthful harbinger of a glorious career to come. Yet in a sense, he would never surpass that moment of unalloyed triumph. Never again would he reach a pinnacle of accomplishment with quite so untroubled a spirit, so blithely beyond the reach of critics and second-guessers.

Whether Kit Carson was miffed at missing his chance to share in the lieutenant's summit glory, we cannot know. In the memoir the mountain man dictated late in life, he does not even mention the 1842 foray into the Wind Rivers.

2

ONE-CENT REWARD

WHO were these two men, Christopher Carson and John Charles Frémont, driven to know the West for such different reasons, attacking the unfathomed landscape in such different fashions? As they withdraw from the Wind River Range that long-ago August, still traveling in the innocence of their obscurity in the world, just entering the prime of life (Carson was thirty-two, Frémont twenty-nine), they invite us to wander back along the branching paths that led them to their twinned destiny in the Rocky Mountains.

To plumb Frémont's essential nature, one must peel away layer upon layer of autobiographical rumination that camouflages it. The man not only wrote—or, more properly, dictated—the reports that would make both Carson and himself famous, but, late in life, he penned a nostalgic and incomplete *Memoirs* that casts a subtly different light on his career. Complicating the matter, the Pathfinder's wife, Jessie, was a skillful yarn spinner who embroidered her own gaudy tapestry of prose around her husband's deeds.

By the late 1880s, having gained and lost a fortune dug out of the California goldfields, the elderly Frémonts were reduced to a state of near destitution. Jessie in effect turned herself into a freelance writer, earning small checks from such magazines as *Land of Sunshine* and *Century* by recycling deeds of derring-do performed by "the

General" (his later rank in the Civil War) almost half a century before. She also cobbled together a pair of books full of edifying vignettes and stirring episodes from the Frémontian past, published as *Souvenirs of My Time* and *Far West Sketches*.

Jessie's hand in her husband's writing presents one of the thorniest problems in Frémont biography. Perusing the leaden specimens of prose found in the Pathfinder's letters and memoranda, historians conclude that the hairbreadth escapes, purple-tinted landscapes, and nuggets of moralizing anecdote that made the public so avid for Frémont's reports can almost all be ascribed to Jessie. By his own admission, the explorer found writing painful and awkward; he chose, instead, to stroll about his study "dictating" the reports to the imaginative amanuensis who would turn these chronicles of adventure into bestsellers. As she did so, she wove a Victorian veil about her husband's visage that it would take the iconoclastic diaries of a dozen Charles Preusses to pull aside.

The problem of knowing the essential Kit Carson is quite the opposite: we have too little from the man himself. The only autobiography Carson attempted is the sketchy and unreliable *Memoirs* he dictated to a lieutenant in the army at the age of forty-six. (This fugitive document nearly vanished altogether. Discovered in Paris in 1905, in a trunk full of old papers that was about to be thrown out, it was first published in 1926.)

Looking back in 1856 almost with impatience on his long odyssey in the West, Carson could not even be troubled to get the dates of his adventures right. Having grown ashamed of his illiteracy, he may have thought himself unworthy of a book; and by nature he was an extraordinarily modest and taciturn man. Of the climax of the 1842 expedition, culminating in the bold jaunt into the Wind Rivers to climb Fremont Peak, he reported only: "We continued on our march [and] arrived at the South Pass. Fremont accomplished all that was desired of him and then we returned."

The *Memoirs* is, moreover, such a dry recital of campaigns and travels, so barren of introspection, that the reader must squeeze it like a dry sponge to make even the smallest drops of Carson's character trickle out. In consequence, the mountain man's biographers have time and again resorted to the lame device of paraphrasing around the lacunae: e.g., "If Kit, at sixteen, was fascinated by the black-eyed señoritas of Santa Fe, he made no mention of it thirty years later." And they have padded their lives-and-times of Carson with inert chunks of "times"—long disquisitions on the lonely trade of beaver trapping; evocations of trails and battles borrowed from other, literate voyagers.

Perhaps a dozen comrades of Kit Carson left portraits of him in their own books, but these lean toward the anecdotal or the lapidary. So Carson himself, within his relatively short lifetime, became more myth than man. By the age of thirty-eight—only six years after the first Frémont expedition—Carson had become a fictional western hero, with the appearance of "An Adventure of Kit Carson: A Tale of the Sacramento," in *Holden's Dollar Magazine*, published in New York. The next year, two novels cast the scout as an Indian-killing, damsel-rescuing knight of the plains: *Kit Carson: The Prince of the Goldhunters* and *The Prairie Flower*.

Dime novels, invented before the Civil War, quickly seized on Carson as an archetypal figure. In books such as *Kiowa Charley, The White Mustanger; or, Rocky Mountain Kit's Last Scalp Hunt*, the former scout emerged as the peerless scourge of redskins across the West: "A keener eye was not to be found in the Indian lands of America; a deadlier rifle never rested upon a saddle."

In a stunning instance of art parodying life, one day in 1849 Carson discovered his celebrity. Apaches had ambushed a wagon on the Santa Fe Trail in northeastern New Mexico, killing several emigrants and taking a Mrs. James M. White captive. With a company of dragoons, Carson set out in pursuit. After ten days of trailing the Apaches, Carson spotted their camp. He urged an immediate charge, but the commander delayed, to plan an attack. The Indians got away.

Riding into the hastily abandoned camp, Carson and the dragoons found Mrs. White's body, still warm, with an arrow through her heart. Before death, she had been tortured. Among her belongings scattered around the camp, to his shock Carson came upon "a book, the first of the kind I had ever seen, in which I was made a great hero, slaying Indians by the hundred." Though illiterate, Carson by now could write (and therefore recognize) his own name; some of the dragoons no doubt summarized the novel for him. In an uncharacteristic moment of rueful irony, Carson records the sudden reflection that would plague him for years: "that as Mrs. White would read the [book], and knowing that I lived near, she would pray for my appearance and that she would be saved."

The problem for the modern reader, then, is to disentangle the dime-novel hero from the real man. It is far easier to imagine Kit Carson as played by Clint Eastwood than by the historical Christopher Carson.

In his *Memoirs*, Carson breezes through the first sixteen years of his life in eight laconic sentences. Then, to explain why he ran away from his apprenticeship to a saddler in Missouri, he allows the first hint of feeling to creep into his narrative. The recollected account frames a pithy definition of adolescent wanderlust:

> The business did not suit me and, having heard so many tales of life in the Mountains of the West, I concluded to leave [the saddler]. He was a good man, and I often recall to my mind the kind treatment I received from his hands. But taking into consideration that if I remained with him and served my apprenticeship I would have to pass my life in labor that was distasteful to me, and being anxious to travel for the purpose of seeing different countries, I concluded to join the first party for the Rocky Mts.

If there are two qualities that center Carson's character, that restlessness is the foremost. The urge to head off for some new campaign or frontier would seize him throughout his days, despite the several occasions on which he tried to settle down and lead a quiet, sedentary life. The other linchpin of Carson's nature is that, in some fundamental sense, he was a loner. Not a hermit or a recluse: he liked a social evening, he had many friends, and he would marry three times. But at the core, he had a private soul. No other human, one suspects, ever knew Kit Carson intimately.

Biographers have ransacked the records of frontier counties to flesh out the details of Carson's youth. His forebears were Scottish-Irish emigrants who came to America in the early eighteenth century. In Pennsylvania, where Kit's great-grandfather first landed in the New World, the Carsons fell under the sway of that charismatic pioneer Daniel Boone. During the next several decades, Boone led an entourage that included various Carsons as they wandered from

Pennsylvania through North Carolina and Kentucky, ending up shortly after 1800 in what would soon become the Missouri Territory.

Of Kit's father, Lindsey Carson, we know only a few facts. He sired five children by a first wife; after she died, he married Rebecca Robinson (of whom we know even less); with her, he had ten more sons and daughters. The sixth of Rebecca's offspring, Christopher Carson (whose middle name may or may not have been Houston) was born in Kentucky on December 24, 1809. At the age of one and a half, presumably mounted on horseback in front of his mother, Kit rode west with his burgeoning family to homestead near Boon's Lick, some 170 miles beyond St. Louis.

Lindsey was a diligent farmer and cabin builder, a soldier in the War of 1812, and a fearless fighter who had two fingers of his left hand shot away in a battle with unspecified Indians on the frontier. When Kit was eight years old, his sixty-four-year-old father was killed while laboring to clear a field, when the limb of a burning tree fell on him. Rebecca somehow managed single-handedly to raise at least eight children (the two eldest having reached adulthood) for four years before remarrying.

Family records indicate that the Carson men tended to be large and robust; half-brother Moses, who would become a mountain man before Kit, stood six feet one and weighed over 200 pounds. Kit himself, however, may have been, in the phrase of the day, "the runt of the litter," weighing perhaps 135 pounds and standing not more than five feet eight inches tall (some say five-six). Later, when his fame as scout and mountain man was fixed, a number of travelers, meeting him for the first time, would record their surprise at how mild-mannered, soft-spoken, even effeminate he seemed.

In the absence of richer biographical detail, these two things— Carson's diminutive and unimpressive stature, and the loss of his father at age eight—tempt the pop psychologist toward facile theories about wounds and compensatory drives that may have fed his life of wandering and struggle. But on the American frontier in his day, many a man lost a parent at an early age, and nothing in the patchy record of Carson's life even hints that he bore his size or his apparent meekness like a chip on the shoulder.

In their homestead on the Missouri frontier, the Carsons and their neighbors lived in constant wariness against an Indian attack. The memory of that childhood vigilance was burned deep in Carson's soul: in the fourth sentence of his *Memoirs*, in the only words he bothered to lavish on the home where he lingered from age two to sixteen, he recalls, "For two or three years after our arrival, we had to remain forted and it was necessary to have men stationed at the extremities of the fields for the protection of those that were laboring."

Like most of his youthful companions in Boon's Lick, Kit spent much of his time in the drudging work by which a family wrung a living from the wilderness: felling trees; planting and harvesting corn, wheat, and potatoes; building cabins and sheds; hunting and foraging. It is not surprising that Carson never learned to read. Many years later, he told Jessie Benton Frémont, "I was a young boy in the school house when the cry came, 'Indians!' I jumped to my rifle and threw down my spelling book, and there it lies." (So Jessie's fable-mongering memory insisted: the aphoristic recital bears her stamp rather than Carson's.)

Many biographers have shied at the suggestion that Kit Carson was illiterate, but the evidence is irrefutable. As late as the 1860s, when he was required as an army officer to file regular dispatches, he dictated them to a scribe, signing with his laboriously rehearsed "C. Carson." On surviving documents, the signature is penned in a manifestly different hand from that of the competent bureaucratese of the texts. Earlier, at the time of Frémont's first expedition west, Carson apparently could not even print his name: the voucher for his $340 salary as scout that summer of 1842 is signed with his mark and witnessed by the signature of a St. Louis clerk.

In the 1820s, Boon's Lick lay on the well-beaten path that, some 120 miles farther west, bifurcated to become the two storied trails, the Oregon and the Santa Fe, along which restless American settlers had already started trudging to seek their destiny beyond the Mississippi River. Among the cabins in the rough-hewn village where Carson grew up, there was much talk of Stephen Long's expedition, which had passed this way in 1819; and some pioneers still gossiped about Zebulon Pike's dangerous foray into the Spanish Southwest in 1806 (Pike and his men had in fact been arrested and briefly held prisoner in Chihuahua). By 1825, two of Kit's half-brothers and his oldest brother had served on trading and surveying expeditions into the great unknown; Moses Carson had come to treat the route up and down the Missouri as a familiar highway.

During that year, however, the fifteen-year-old Kit continued to languish in the tedious servitude of his apprenticeship to the saddler, David Workman. He stuck it out for another year, until, in August 1826, as he dryly puts it in the *Memoirs*, "I had the fortune to hear of a party bound for that country to which I desired to go." But it took more than fortune to liberate Kit from the saddlery. A Carson family tradition has it that Kit asked his mother's permission to light out for the territories, but she insisted that he serve out his contract under Workman first. Rather than submit to further incarceration in his trade, Kit ran away from home.

In the local newspaper, Workman posted the pro forma appeal for the boy's return that law required. That fugitive document contains the first published description of Kit Carson, as well as the famously ironic last line that biographers read as Workman's slap on the boy's back and hearty bon voyage (Workman himself would head west the next year):

> Notice is hereby given to all persons, THAT CHRISTOPHER CARSON, a boy about 16 years old, small of his age, but thick set; light hair, ran away from the subscriber, living in Franklin, Howard county, Missouri, to whom he had been bound to learn the saddler's trade, on or about the first of September last. He is supposed to have made his way towards the upper part of the state. All persons are notified not to harbor, support or assist said boy under the penalty of the law. One cent reward will be given to any person who will bring back the said boy.

The reward went unclaimed. Kit Carson would not return to his boyhood home for another sixteen years. When he did, in 1842, at the age of thirty-two, not a single building of the village still stood in the clearing where he had passed nearly all his youth.

With the same maddening verbal economy that dismissed his childhood in eight sentences, in the *Memoirs* Carson hurries impatiently past the events of his next three years—from ages sixteen to nineteen, years as formative as any in his life—in four dry paragraphs.

Once again, the biographers are forced to resort to scenic and historic padding to bulk up their accounts of Carson's novitiate in the West.

After 1821, with Mexico's independence from Spain, the land first penetrated by Coronado became far less perilous for Anglo-Americans. Spaniards in Santa Fe had sometimes put to death the vagabonds and treasure hunters from the States who blundered into their realm; Mexicans welcomed the Americans for their trade. By the time Carson rode it at the age of sixteen, the Santa Fe Trail had become, if not a milk run, at least a well-traveled thoroughfare across the prairie.

Yet that dusty path across the Kansas plains, up the Arkansas River, and over Raton Pass into New Mexico must have unfolded as a landscape of wonder and adventure to the sixteen-year-old. By the time, however, that Carson sat down to tell his life's story, the Santa Fe Trail had indeed become a milk run. Of that initial trek into the Southwest, Carson saw fit to recall only a single event—albeit a dramatic one.

As one of the members of the caravan, a man named Andrew Broadus, took his rifle out of a wagon to shoot a wolf, it discharged, shattering his right arm. In hideous pain, Broadus traveled on with the expedition, but his arm turned gangrenous; to save his life, one of his companions had to amputate the limb on the spot. Remembered Carson:

> The doctor set to work and cut the flesh with a razor and sawed the bone with an old saw. The arteries being cut, to stop the bleeding he heated a king bolt of one of the wagons and burned the affected parts, and then applied a plaster of the tar taken from off the wheel of a wagon. The man became perfectly well before our arrival in New Mexico.

Carson's party reached Santa Fe in November 1826. Within days, Kit journeyed northeast to Taos, where he wintered over in the house of a mountain man who had also rambled west from Boon's Lick. Taos would become Carson's favorite place on earth, and though he did not die there, he lies buried in the town's small cemetery, only a few blocks from the low adobe dwelling where he spent the happiest of his years in later life.

We know nothing whatsoever about how Carson fared during that first winter in the Southwest. Perhaps at seventeen he found life on the Mexican frontier a little daunting; perhaps he even grew homesick, for in the spring of 1827 he headed back to Missouri. It was his restlessness that saved him from the sedentary obscurity to which the companions he had left behind at Boon's Lick would be consigned. As he descended the Arkansas River, heading east toward his family, he ran into a new caravan of westbound emigrants; without hesitation he joined them and headed back toward Santa Fe. One year later, he would perform an identical U-turn on the Arkansas. If guilt or family feeling tugged at the young adventurer, the lust to see new places overwhelmed the homing urge.

For two years in the Mexican Southwest, Carson scrounged a living as a teamster and a cook. The first hint that he might possess exceptional talents comes in the *Memoirs* as Carson lets drop that in 1828 he was hired as an interpreter for an Anglo trading expedition down to Chihuahua. At the age of eighteen, illiterate or not, Kit had learned Spanish better than men of greater age and longer experience among the Mexicans.

But in the 1820s, the romance of the frontier lay centered not in trading jaunts to Mexico, not in setting up stores and saloons in Santa Fe and Taos, but in the beaver trade. In Taos, Carson had befriended Ewing Young, a southerner some seventeen years Kit's elder, already one of the foremost trappers in the West. Finally, in August 1829, Young invited Carson to join his team of forty Americans, Canadians, and Frenchmen on a long and ambitious trapping expedition. To add spice to the venture, it was illegal under Mexican law, and thus had to be carried out under the cloak of subterfuge.

At age nineteen, Kit Carson was about to become a mountain man.

Carson's first mentor in the West was an impressive figure. In his late thirties at the time of the 1829 expedition, Ewing Young hailed from Tennessee, but had already trapped and prowled across the western wilderness for seven years. He would die in Oregon in 1841 of a mysterious "dyspepsia," still a relatively young man. Yet during his two decades of rambling, Young saw more country than nearly all his rivals in the fur trade. Claims one of his biographers, "Only Jedediah Smith and [Hudson's Bay Company agent] Peter Skene Ogden can be said to have surpassed Ewing Young in terms of penetration of wide areas of the Far West and sheer distance covered."

Young left no record of his travels except a patchy series of vivid but barely literate letters. The cursory sketch of the 1829 expedition in Carson's *Memoirs* remains the primary source for that jaunt. Kit had gotten to know Young in Taos by hiring on as the mountain man's cook: free board was his only compensation. Evidently the veteran saw potential in the greenhorn, for from the start of the journey, among Young's forty adventurers, the nineteen-year-old Carson was entrusted with some of the most crucial tasks.

Only one physical description of Young survives: an Oregon missionary remembered him as "a large finely built man six feet and perhaps two inches in height." Carson makes no comment about his leader's qualities, but at the outset of the journey he must have been in awe of Young. Another contemporary considered Young "a candid and scrupulously honest man . . . , thorough going, brave and daring."

To circumvent a new Santa Fe law, which forbade trapping by Anglos on Mexican rivers, Young's party headed north out of Taos that August, pretending to head toward the beaver streams of central Colorado, within the territory of the Louisiana Purchase. In the San Luis Valley, well beyond the sight of any Mexican officials, the team abruptly took a left turn and marched southwest across Zuni and Navajo land, arriving at the head of the Salt River in Arizona.

So began a monumental journey of some twenty months, during which Young's men often traversed, according to Carson, "country never explored." Their wanderings took the team north across the Colorado River just below the Grand Canyon, west across the Mohave Desert and the Sierra Nevada Range, and north within the fertile inland valleys of California all the way to the Sacramento River. Though he does not mention the fact, in all likelihood, somewhere near either present-day Los Angeles or present-day San Francisco, Kit saw the ocean for the first time.

Along the way, Carson mastered the laborious and dangerous craft of beaver-trapping. From Ewing Young, he learned much else, such as how to go four days across a desert without water and survive. But of all the disciplines his teacher schooled him in, the most important, in view of Carson's subsequent fame, was the art of killing Indians.

It is likely that Kit Carson shot his first native at the age of nineteen, on the Salt River. Ewing Young had trapped the Salt three years earlier, under a legal Mexican license. During that previous expedition, he had exacted a stern revenge on a band of Papago Indians (known today as the Tohono O'odham).

In 1826, near the junction of the Salt and Gila Rivers in Arizona, Young's party had come upon the only three survivors of a thirty-man French-American trapping party under the leadership of Miguel Robidoux. Nearby, they found the mutilated bodies of the victims, which they buried. The following day, Young led an attack on a Papago village, killing a number of warriors. Whether the murdered Papagos were the same Indians who had attacked Robidoux's party, no one bothered to ascertain. Such was the code by which mountain men lived; such was the code Young taught Carson in 1829.

The year before, from his store in Taos, Young had sent a party of trappers out on more or less the same trail as he would follow in 1829. The team had turned back empty-handed, intimidated by Apache threats.

Now, at the head of the Salt, Young once more carried out his style of retribution. That his foe were Apaches (probably Coyoteros) was all he needed to know. Carson laconically describes the ambush:

> Young directed the greater part of his men to hide themselves, which was done, the men concealing themselves under blankets, pack saddles, and as best they could. The hills were covered with Indians and seeing so few, they came to the conclusion to make an attack and drive us from our position. Our commander allowed them to enter the camp and then directed the party to fire on them, which was done, the Indians losing in killed fifteen or twenty warriors and great number in wounded.

During the next year and a half, Young's party would twice again prosecute one-sided battles against Indian tribes. In California,

Young volunteered his men to help round up a band of "runaways," Indians pacified by the Spanish missions into an apathetic dependency which they could resist only by flight. The roundup turned bloody. In Carson's unapologetic telling, "The Indians were routed; [they] lost a great number of men. We entered the village in triumph, set fire to it, and burned it to the ground."

Carson's early reconnaissance of California would stand him in good stead a decade and a half later, on Frémont's second and third expeditions. There is a painful irony in Kit's memory of his first impression of the San Gabriel Mission, only a few miles from the fledgling Pueblo de los Angeles. With its livestock, fields, vineyards, one priest, and a thousand docile Indians, the mission seemed to Carson "paradise on earth." In 1846, as Frémont's right-hand man, Kit would be instrumental in dismantling that paradise.

On the return journey, as Young's trappers camped on the bank of the Colorado River, a huge band of Indians approached—perhaps Apaches, perhaps Yavapai. (Carson claims they numbered more than 500 warriors, but anxious Anglos always overestimated the sizes of enemy bands; the largest force the Apaches ever mustered for a single battle probably amounted to fewer than 200 men.) Just as carnage seemed once more to be on the verge of breaking out, it was discovered that one of the Indians spoke Spanish. Carson addressed him in that language, threatening to shoot any Indian who had not left the camp within ten minutes. Remarkably, despite their superior numbers, the Indians retreated.

Scrupulously honest Ewing Young may have been in dealing with fellow Americans, but he dispatched savages with an almost casual brutality, and for the Mexicans among whom he had chosen to live, he had formed an abiding contempt. His disdain had been deepened by the ill luck attending his 1826 expedition to the Gila. While he was off gathering beaver pelts, the colonial governorship in Santa Fe changed. The new governor at once promulgated the ban on Anglos trapping in Mexican territory.

Young returned to Santa Fe with his horses bearing a fortune in beaver pelts; some chroniclers estimate their value at $20,000. But rather than selling them on the open market, Young had to watch as Mexican officials confiscated his prize. When a partner escaped with two packs of pelts, Young was briefly clapped in jail.

This time, in April 1831, he pulled off a foolproof dodge. Returning to Santa Fe via the Rio Grande with a ton of beaver pelts in his
possession, and no hope of pretending that they had not been illegally trapped, he deposited the booty with an Anglo crony at the
Santa Rita copper mines in southwestern New Mexico. In Santa Fe,
he applied for a license to trade with the Santa Rita Indians, went
back and loaded up his pelts, then sold them "legally" back in Santa
Fe.

Thus, Kit Carson came into the first fortune of his life—"several
hundred dollars," as he recalled a quarter-century later. In one of the
few passages in the *Memoirs* that hints at humor and wry self-knowl-
edge, he soliloquizes on the libertine spree that inevitably followed:

> [W]e passed the time gloriously, spending our money freely—
> never thinking that our lives were risked in gaining it. Our only
> idea was to get rid of the dross as soon as possible but, at the same
> time, have as much pleasure and enjoyment as the country would
> afford. Trappers and sailors are similar in regard to the money that
> they earn so dearly, daily being in danger of losing their lives. But
> when the voyage has been made . . . , they think not of the hard-
> ships and danger through which they have passed, spend all they
> have and are ready for another trip.

Something like that formula might stand as a motto for Kit Carson's
whole life.

Thus began, for Carson, twelve years of almost continuous wandering through the West, trapping for beaver, hunting deer and buffalo,
and fighting Indians. After the Ewing Young expedition, Kit focused
his travels on a vast mountainous quadrangle stretching from Taos
to southern Idaho, from the upper Missouri River to the Great Salt
Lake. The pull of home and family, which had launched him east on
the Santa Fe Trail twice as a teenager, all but lost its force on the
self-contained mountain man those years perfected.

As he trapped across the West, Carson sometimes joined up with
other mountain men who would themselves become legends: most
notably, Jim Bridger, Thomas Fitzpatrick, and Joe Meek. Yet he

never forged a lasting partnership with any other trapper. Some years a group of mountain men would winter over in an improvised fort built for the purpose; in summer, starting in 1834, Carson regularly attended the annual rendezvous, a three-week orgy of trading, drinking, horseplay, and gossip. Of these intensely social gatherings that served so raucously to alleviate the loneliness that was a mountain man's lot, Carson has left us not one tableau.

Only in a single passage, inserted at the end of his account of those twelve years of vagabondage, does Carson somewhat ruefully recall the privation to which he became accustomed in the prime of his youth:

> The greater part of that time passed far from the habitations of civilized man, and receiving no other food than that which I could procure with my rifle. Perhaps, once a year, I would have a meal consisting of bread, meat, sugar, and coffee; would consider it a luxury. Sugar and coffee could be purchased at the rendezvous for two dollars per pint, and flour one dollar per pint.

At the heart of those years of toil and adventure was the ceaseless quest for beaver. In his *Memoirs,* Carson offers almost no details about his practice of this demanding art, taking it for granted in 1856 that his auditors had at least a nodding acquaintance with the discipline that made a mountain man. Now that trapping has become an all-but-lost craft, it is worth pausing to reconsider just how arduous and risky the business was in the 1830s.

A mountain man thought nothing of crossing hundreds of miles of forest, foothills, and desert, in any season; yet the sheer bulk and weight of his impedimenta made travel cumbersome. His clothing was a hodgepodge of European and Indian fashions: typically, a cotton or flannel shirt, buckskin trousers, deerskin moccasins (with a dry spare pair carried in a bag), wool or otter- or beaverskin cap, buffalo-skin mittens in winter, and a heavy buffalo-robe coat. He carried his long-barreled, muzzle-loading rifle, which weighed eleven or twelve pounds, across his saddle, ready for use. The rifle required a whole kit to reload and care for it—powder, shot, patch box, ramrod, flint, steel, and cleaning rod. Usually, a mountain man carried a pistol for backup, as well as a tomahawk and a long butcher knife.

Other necessities, kept close at hand, were pipe and tobacco, needles and awl, and possibly a razor.

For camping, the mountain man needed a bedroll of several blankets and/or robes, as well as his indispensable iron cooking kettle. In addition, he toted a ration of food, often in the form of pemmican, the greasy congelation of buffalo fat, dried lean meat, and berries. In a separate sack, he carried his beaver traps: no fewer than six, as many as twenty, each weighing several pounds. Finally, he carried a prized box of castoreum, the oily yellow excrescence of the beaver's sex glands, with which he baited his traps.

Thus laden, even before he secured his first pelt, the trapper had more baggage than a single horse could haul: with a season's catch to transport, he needed a packtrain. Mountain men tended to favor mules over horses as beasts of burden for three reasons, each of which, as tale after campfire tale established its pedigree, enriched the folklore of the West. Mules, the mountaineers averred, were more affectionate critters than horses, hence more docile. They were also, so the oldtimers swore, hypersensitive to the presence of skulking Indians, snorting and raising their ears long before their owners had any inkling of unwelcome visitors. Last, in the pinch of starvation, mule meat was far more palatable than horseflesh.

As onerous as traveling the trackless West in 1830 might seem to the modern backpacker, with his streamlined, lightweight gear, the mountain man had whittled the essentials of trapping and survival down to an absolute minimum. In the empathic phrase of Carson's early biographer, Edwin L. Sabin, "Taking him by and large, the mountain trapper was intensely practical. Beaver, buffalo and Injuns—fur, meat and ha'r: these were the chief matters occupying his mind. To find the fur and meat he would risk the hair and many a peril besides."

Unlike buffalo hunting, beaver trapping was not a regimen widely practiced by the Indians. Before the white men came, the animals could be killed in winter with clubs or spears as they emerged from their lodges or swam streams beneath a skin of ice. Various tribes had perfected snares for small land animals, but not for the amphibious beaver. The hand-forged metal trap that made the whole life of the mountain man possible was an eighteenth-century European invention.

In the Rocky Mountains, beavers build lodges on slow-flowing streams in stands of cottonwood, aspen, and willow, soft-wooded trees easily felled by the insatiable gnawing of strong, sharp teeth; the logs are then hauled into the stream to create beaver dams. The trapper would look for a "slide," a beaver trail from stand to stream. In a few inches of water, he would spread open the jaws of the trap, securing it with a pole plunged into stream-bottom mud. Then he took a peeled stick, dipped one end in castoreum, and planted it between the jaws so that some four inches of baited twig protruded above the water.

Scenting the essence of desire, the animal swam near the twig. As he stood on hind legs to reach his nose toward the bait, he triggered the trap. Struggling vainly to free himself, he exhausted his strength, sank to the bottom, and drowned. Often, however, the beaver's death throes pulled the trap loose: to retrieve it, the mountain man had to wade or even swim.

Mountain men were convinced that beavers were preternaturally intelligent. Many an anecdote documented a trapper's comeuppance at the paws of a beaver who deliberately used a stick to trigger a trap, or who turned it upside down, rendering it harmless. Veterans of the mountains swore that beavers had their own watery language with which they communicated with each other.

Constantly wading in and out of freezing mountain streams, the trapper was an inevitable candidate for hypothermia, rheumatic pains, even death by drowning. Moreover, once he had claimed his beaver, the toil had only begun. There on the riverbank, he skinned his prey, keeping the meat (the tail was a favorite delicacy), stretching the hide on a willow hoop to dry. Properly prepared, each dried beaver pelt weighed about a pound and a half. The pelts were conventionally amassed in packs of sixty, a good mule load per pack, worth in the 1830s from $300 to $600 at the trading post.

Rather than haul their pelts from hither to yon, trappers often cached them. This, too, was a tricky business, for not only might predators and natural spoilage ruin a season's labor, but Indians and unscrupulous trappers were known to poach whole caches. In the spring of 1833, at the end of a bountiful trapping season, Carson's team cached some 400 pounds of beaver pelts beside the Arkansas River, digging a deep hole in the topsoil, then covering the booty with dirt, leaves, and brush. A few days later, two men deserted with the party's three best horses. Carson and another man trailed the runaways back to the cache, where they found all the pelts looted. The poachers had made their getaway by canoe.

The raison d'être of the whole beaver industry lay in a fashion craze that held sway for decades among the haut monde of Paris, London, New York, and other glittering, faraway cities, where raw pelts were turned into the most exquisite men's high hats money could buy. Year after year, styles came and went: the d'Orsay, the Beau Brummel, the Paris bear, the Wellington. It was the shiny sheen that only beaver pelts possessed that lent these foppish concoctions their glamour. At the time Kit Carson launched his career as a mountain man in 1829, perhaps some 600 Americans pursued the trade across the West, with another 600 British venturing out from Hudson's Bay Company posts in western Canada. In its heyday, the beaver trade claimed about 100,000 pelts per year.

Kit Carson attended his first rendezvous in the summer of 1834. The annual gathering had been invented in 1825 by the tireless trader William Ashley. Before that date, whenever a trapper wished to sell the pelts he had spent a year or more amassing, he had to ride all the way to St. Louis to exchange his booty for the goods that would see him through another year of lonely labor in the wilderness; alternatively, he might trade the pelts, for less than their market value in St. Louis, to intermediaries at the makeshift forts and posts that sprang up along the Missouri and Platte Rivers after 1807.

Ashley realized that everyone would benefit if he could send a supply train west to a prearranged campsite and somehow spread word to the mountain men to meet there at a given date to trade their beaver. Thus the trappers could stay in the mountains year-round, and Ashley might claim a one-man monopoly on the trade.

The first rendezvous was held in July 1825, in a spot whose exact location scholars still debate, somewhere in the southwestern corner of what is today Wyoming. According to Ashley, 120 men attended, including such luminaries as Jedediah Smith and Étienne Provost, as well as twenty-nine "deserters" from the Hudson's Bay Company. Although the actual event may have lasted but a single day, this first rendezvous was a great success, in no small part be-cause the men so craved the riotous celebration that it inevitably set loose—not to mention the coffee, sugar, tobacco, liquor, fishhooks, scissors, blankets, and buttons that their hard-won pelts earned them.

For the next fifteen years, the midsummer rendezvous brought hundreds of men together at an agreed-upon site in northern Utah, southeastern Idaho, or western Wyoming. The time and place of the gathering were spread throughout the West by word of mouth, but so effective was this "bush telegraph" among mountain men that few trappers ever inadvertently missed a rendezvous. As one modern historian puts it, "You were considered dead until you did show up."

The 1834 rendezvous took place at the junction of the Ham's and Black's Forks, tributaries of the Green River. The site lies not far north of today's Interstate 80, in a region little traveled today, near the dusty hamlet of Granger (population ca. 125). The town sur-vives only because of the trona, or soda ash, mines nearby, and the desultory ranching the older local families still carry on.

A rutted mud track leads from town down to the confluence of the two streams. The grassy bottom where the mountain men as-sembled in 1834 is a forlorn, forgotten place. The streams run clear, meandering through tall stands of grass; small gray birds sit in strings on a nearby telephone wire, while a giant silo looms in the east. Away from the river, the land looks barren, clumped here and there with sagebrush. In all directions, shapeless chalky hills fill the hori-zon. There is not a tree in sight.

Carson mentions his first rendezvous in a typically dry paragraph in the *Memoirs*. He recalls that about two hundred trappers came in. (In addition, by now, sizable bands of Indians joined the throng.) But Carson's most vivid memory is of the prices at which he bought his staples for the next year: "Coffee and sugar [were] two dollars a pint, powder the same, lead one dollar a bar, and common blankets from fifteen to twenty-five dollars apiece." During the years of the rendezvous, prices paid the trappers for their pelts varied from about $2 to $5 per pound. A simple calculation makes it clear why no mountain man ever got rich from his arduous profession.

Since 1825, other entrepreneurs had jumped on Ashley's band-wagon. One of the most ambitious was Nathaniel Wyeth, an ice merchant from Boston who first took a supply train west in 1832. At his third rendezvous in 1834, he still managed to be shocked by the rude behavior of the mountaineers. "[A] collection of Scoundrels," he described them in a letter to a friend; "every exertion is made to debauch my men in which they have had some success. . . ."

It was the drinking that, to eastern eyes, turned the celebrations so ugly and frenetic. A captain traveling in Wyeth's party judged the trappers "as crazy a set of men as I ever saw." A delicate-tempered naturalist with Wyeth complained about the daily hijinks: "These people, with their obstreperous mirth, their whooping, and howling, and quarrelling, added to the mounted Indians, who are constantly dashing into and through our camp, yelling like fiends, the barking and baying of savage wolf-dogs, and the incessant cracking of rifles and carbines, render our camp a perfect bedlam."

In 1834, for the first time, Christian missionaries came to the rendezvous. Needless to say, they made few converts among these profane, hard-living men.

Eighteen thirty-four also marked a subtle turning point in the beaver trade, which would ultimately doom the whole profession of the mountain man. Through that year, the demand for pelts had seemed limitless, just as the supply of beavers appeared inexhaustible. But by 1835, the first silk hats came into fashion in Paris and London; and for the first time, the mountaineers began to notice that certain streams were in danger of being trapped out.

Some sixty miles north of Granger lies the most favored rendezvous site of all, just west of Pinedale, an appealing frontier town starting to gentrify in response to the tourism the nearby Wind River Range generates. Here, in a fertile, open valley, where Horse Creek flows into the Green River, no fewer than six rendezvous were held, of which Carson attended three, in the years 1835–37.

For decades, Pinedale has made a fuss about its proximity to mountain-man history. The Green River Rendezvous, held on Main Street every summer the weekend after July 4, unfolds as a carnival of vendors, booths, competitions, and parades. It is, in fact, the biggest event in the town's year, outstripping even the high school football homecoming game.

The federal government has likewise made a fuss about the rendezvous site, declaring it a National Historic Landmark. From a small bluff known as Trappers Point, the idyllic basin unfurls below, with the Green River winding placidly among rich green fields, Horse Creek joining it from the far left. Here and there stand groves of stately cottonwoods. It is easy to sense why the mountaineers chose such a spot for their summer spree.

On the bluff a large, rustic-lettered National Park Service bill-board announces: RENDEZVOUS: BIRTH OF AN EMPIRE. Its text lists many of the famous mountain men who camped in the valley below, while deftly skirting the vicissitudes of manifest destiny:

> Trappers, traders and Indians from throughout the west here met the trade wagons from the east to barter, trade for furs, gamble, drink, frolic, pray and scheme. . . . The warring Blackfeet did not participate. . . . [The mountain men's] trails became the highways of an empire at the cost of many a violent death.

In a roadside pullout a few miles west, where Route 189 crosses the Green River, the Sublette County Historical Society has erected its own memorial to the mountain men, worded less am-bivalently than the Park Service's: "It is a tribute to the brave men, both red and white, who blazed the trails for culture and progress, and to the lowly beaver who gave it impetus."

From the rendezvous site in 1835, Carson enjoyed almost the same view of the Wind River Range, spreading snow-capped and majestic along the eastern horizon, that seven years later would in-spire John Frémont to try to ascend what he was sure was the apex of the Rocky Mountains. In 1837, one Alfred Jacob Miller would at-tend the rendezvous, under the employ of a knighted Scot who headed west for hunting and adventure. Miller's mandate was to capture the rendezvous on canvas. Some of the finest and most ro-mantic paintings from the American West show the teepees of the trappers and Indians ranged in the foreground beside Horse Creek, the jagged Wind Rivers seemingly only a stone's throw beyond.

Carson's first Green River rendezvous in 1835 was particularly memorable for two reasons: here he fought the only duel of his life, and here he may have met and wooed the Arapaho woman who would become his first wife. (The two events appear to be interre-lated.)

Carson's account of the duel embodies one of the few passages in his *Memoirs* where the habitual deadpan recital lapses into real passion. Yet the episode emerges in an oversimplified and misleading form. According to Carson, one of the French voyageurs in camp was a loudmouth bully: "He made a practice of whipping every man that he was displeased with, and that was nearly all." Carson does not even name the miscreant, observing merely that he was "large," "overbearing," and "very strong." The taciturn Missourian takes it upon himself to play David to the voyageur's Goliath.

> One day, after he had beaten two or three men, he said that for the Frenchmen, he had no trouble to flog, and as for the Americans, he would take a switch and switch them. I did not like such talk from any man, so I told him that I was the worst American in camp. Many could t[h]rash him, only [they did not] on account of being afraid, and that if he made use of any more such expressions, I would rip his guts.

"Rip his guts"—after pages of Carson's homely Victorian locutions, his phlegmatic accounts of epic journeys, the phrase leaps from the text.

> He said nothing but started for his rifle, mounted his horse, and made his appearance in front of the camp. As soon as I saw him, I mounted my horse and took the first arms I could get ahold of, which was a pistol, galloped up to him and demanded if I was the one which he intended to shoot. Our horses were touching. He said no, but at the same time drawing his gun so he could have a fair shot. I was prepared and allowed him to draw his gun. We both fired at the same time; all present said but one report was heard. I shot him through the arm and his ball passed my head, cutting my hair and the powder burning my eye. . . . During our stay in camp we had no more bother with this bully Frenchman.

In his whole life, no one ever questioned Carson's bravery. Yet by 1834, having been in the mountains for five years, Kit had learned prudence. A point-blank horseback duel, pistol against rifle, simply to put a bully in his place, seems uncharacteristic of the canny mountain man.

Fortunately, Carson's is not the only account of this showdown. Rev. Samuel Parker, a missionary bent on converting the Nez Percé and Flathead Indians, was also present. In his journal, he recorded that the voyageur's name was Shunar (most likely an Anglicized spelling of Chouinard). The bully "challenged any Frenchman, American, Spaniard or Dutchman, to fight him in single combat. Kit Carson, an American, told him if he wished to die, he would accept the challenge." Parker's version of the outcome of the duel accords with Carson's, except that he insists that as Carson "went for another pistol, Shunar begged that his life might be spared."

Three years later, when Parker published his diary as *Journal of an Exploring Tour Beyond the Rocky Mountains*, Kit Carson's name appeared in print for only the second time—the first having been David Workman's wanted poster for the sixteen-year-old runaway. Many years later, Jessie Frémont wrote that Carson "could never tell the story without showing marked resentment for Shunar."

From a relatively fugitive source comes the clue that makes deeper sense of Carson's reckless duel. Writing in 1914, Carson's thoroughgoing biographer Edwin L. Sabin claims (without attribution) that Captain Smith H. Simpson, who later served under Carson and knew him in Taos, "had it from Carson's own lips that the quarrel rooted in a rivalry for the favors of an Arapaho girl in camp."

It was a common practice for a mountain man to take an Indian wife; Jim Bridger would successively marry three native women. Even more common was for a trapper to live and travel in an unformalized alliance with an Indian woman who cooked and sewed for him and kept him warm at night. Yet Carson's first marriage has all but escaped the documentary record. He makes no mention of the Arapaho woman in his *Memoirs* (nor of a short-lived, comically misguided second marriage to a Cheyenne woman). By the time he dictated his life story, Carson was married to a well-born Hispanic woman in Taos. And he had confessed to Jessie Frémont that he feared having been a "squaw man" might disqualify him from civilized society.

Many a mountain man took an Indian bride for purely selfish reasons: she served not only his sexual needs, but as a domestic servant. Given the inevitable linguistic and cultural barriers, one imagines very little in the way of real communication between, say, an Indian girl in her late teens and a grizzled, uneducated trapper in his forties.

Yet there is good evidence that Carson found genuine love and companionship with the Arapaho woman he met around 1835. We know that her name was Waanibe, "Singing Grass" or "Singing Wind." Despite his public reticence, Carson later confessed to close friends that, long after Waanibe's death, he was loyal to her memory. At some point, Carson learned to speak a passable Arapaho. And rather than abandon the couple's only surviving child, a daughter he named Adaline, he went out of his way to secure a stable life for her.

The argument that Carson met Waanibe at the 1835 rendezvous hangs by a scholarly thread—essentially Captain Simpson's recollection as recorded by Sabin. There is no independent evidence, in fact, that any Arapahos were camped by Horse Creek that summer; the rendezvous took place far from the people's homeland on the plains of eastern Colorado and western Kansas.

Whenever it did take place, however, the marriage between Carson and Waanibe had a major significance for the Arapahos, whose oral tradition preserves its legacy today. At about the same time, trader William Bent—later to become Carson's friend and boss at Bent's Fort on the Arkansas—had married a Cheyenne chieftain's daughter. The Arapahos and Cheyennes were sometime enemies, sometime allies. In the words of a leading Arapaho ethnographer, Virginia Cole Trenholm, "These marriages of policy in a broad sense included the women, their extended families, and the bands to which they belonged, as well as those commonly associated with them. In short, Bent and Carson formed a strong alliance with bands of both tribes." These bands in turn served to smooth trading with Cheyennes and Arapahos at Bent's Fort, where Carson went to work as a meat hunter in 1841.

It is a symptom of Carson's impatience with the task of setting down his life's story that in the *Memoirs* he glosses over the various rendezvous so hurriedly. Only the fight with Shunar fully occupies his attention. The 1836 rendezvous, at which Carson camped for twenty days, is dispatched in a single sentence. The 1837 rendezvous, so lavishly limned in Alfred Jacob Miller's canvases, Carson forgets to mention altogether: in fact, his sketchy memory folds two years into one, so that he jumps seamlessly from the spring of 1837 to the spring of 1838 like a traveler in a time machine.

Yet those three rendezvous at the junction of Horse Creek and the Green River were full of extraordinary deeds and vivid pageants. Thanks to the witness of other participants—chiefly the impressionable eastern traders and missionaries—we have a patchy record of what transpired during those uproarious summer get-togethers.

In 1835, either just before or just after Carson had settled Shunar's hash, a missionary doctor removed a three-inch-long arrowhead that had lodged for three years in Jim Bridger's shoulder —evidently without anesthetic. The wide-eyed Reverend Parker captured the surgery:

> [T]he arrow was hooked at the point by striking a large bone, and a cartilaginous substance had grown around it. The doctor pursued the operation with great self possession and perseverance; and his patient manifested equal firmness. The Indians looked on meanwhile, with countenances indicating wonder, and in their own peculiar manner expressed great astonishment when it was extracted.

Eighteen thirty-six marked the first rendezvous attended by women, the wives of two missionaries. Their presence so excited the mountain men that on arrival they charged the party at full gallop, firing their rifles over the missionaries' heads. Many years later, Joe Meek recalled that "wild brigade . . . , riding with that made speed only an Indian or a trapper can ride, yelling, whooping, dashing forward with frantic and threatening gestures; their dress, noises, and motions, all so completely savage that the white men could not have been distinguished from the red."

The Indians were even more nonplussed by the presence of the white women. Osborne Russell, whose *Journal of a Trapper* is one of the most reliable memoirs written by a mountain man, recalled that "the two ladies were gazed upon with wonder and astonishment by the rude Savages they being the first white women ever seen by these Indians and the first that had ever penetrated into these wild and rocky regions."

The "bashful trappers," in Meek's phrase, adopted the daily ritual of parading in their fanciest dress before Narcissa Whitman's tent: "Should they succeed in catching her eye, they never failed to touch their beaver-skin caps in their most studiously graceful manner, though that should prove so dubious as to bring a mischievous smile to the blue eyes of the observant lady." Meek managed to win a private audience with the lovely Narcissa, who asked him if he envisioned a future home. Meek shyly allowed that he planned to settle in Oregon's Willamette Valley after he gave up "bar fighting and Injun fighting."

The three Green River rendezvous attracted huge congregations. Alfred Jacob Miller insisted that no fewer than 3,000 Indians attended the 1837 gathering. Along with trading, drinking, and gambling, fights frequently broke out. In 1837, a dispute between Nez Percé and Bannock Indians over stolen horses turned into a three-day pitched battle, costing several lives.

That summer a missionary named William Gray watched the goings-on with a scandalized disapproval he managed to suppress well enough to record many lively vignettes—of, among other antics, a scalp dance performed by twenty-five "mostly naked" Delaware Indians. (Because of their skill and courage and their readiness to fight other Indians, Delawares often accompanied western parties as mercenary soldiers.) Gray also learned "that Indian women are a lawful commerce among the men that resort to these mountains." He noted instances of mountain men who had gambled away their "squaws," traded them for horses, or sold them for a hundred dollars. One wonders whether Gray observed the partnership of Kit Carson and his Arapaho wife, Waanibe.

At the 1837 rendezvous, gloomy tidings circulated. The country was in the grips of a financial panic; in St. Louis, for the first time, the price of beaver had substantially dropped. Even more ominously, the beaver were getting scarcer. As one veteran trapper noted in his diary, "[T]imes is getting hard all over this part and low all peltries are on the decline." It was the beginning of the end of a way of life.

One reason Kit Carson remains elusive is that we cannot hear him talking. The stiff, hard-earned periphrases of his dictated memoir, like the dutiful prose of his later army dispatches, emerge from the pens of his amanuenses like some foreign language Kit had only half-mastered. Yet here was a gifted, a natural linguist: his most perspicacious modern biographer, Harvey L. Carter, concludes that eventually "he had a working vocabulary in the Navajo, Apache, Comanche, Cheyenne, Arapaho, Crow, Blackfoot, Shoshone, Piute, and Ute languages." Few if any other mountain men ever attained a comparable command of alien tongues.

With Frémont, we do not have this problem. When his report on the 1842 expedition paraphrases his morale-boosting speech to his men, worried about rampaging Sioux on the prairie, we can hear the lieutenant's voice: "Still I was unwilling to take with me on a service of some certain danger, men on whom I could not rely; and as I had understood that there were among them some who were disposed to cowardice, and anxious to return, they had but to come forward at once and state their desire, and they would be discharged with the amount due to them for the time they had served." Charles Preuss relates that at dawn on August 15, 1842, as the summit team left its bivouac for their second try at Fremont Peak, the lieutenant said, "Well, Mr. Preuss, I hope we shall, after all, empty a glass on top of the mountain." It is the same voice, slightly pompous, striving for understated eloquence, conscious always of its speaker's pose before eternity.

Born in the boondocks of Kentucky, raised on the Missouri frontier, Carson no doubt spoke a strong southern vernacular. Harvey Carter is convinced that Kit "said 'thar' and 'whar' and 'hyar' " and " 'fit' for 'fought' and 'done' for 'did.' " One acquaintance memorably recalled, "Kit never swore more'n was necessary." Another reported that by 1850, Carson's "language was forcible, slow, and pointed, using the fewest words possible. He talked but little, was very quiet, and seldom used immoral or profane language."

One auditor tried to capture verbatim a Carson outburst upon hearing about the Sand Creek Massacre in 1864:

"I tell ye what; I don't like a hostile Red Skin any better than you du. And when they are hostile, I've fit 'em—fout 'em—as hard as any man. But I never yit drew a bead on a squaw or papoose, and I loathe and hate the man who would. 'Taint nateral for brave men to kill little women and little children. . . ."

By 1864, of course, Carson's speech had been homogenized by years of government service and Taos society. Even so, the utterance rings somehow inauthentic, like the conventional piety it expresses.

We cannot disentangle the way a mountain man like Carson spoke from the stylized heroic vernacular that dime novels first minted. Studiedly colorful, defiantly ungrammatical, that fictive style of speech has come down to us (much modified by the influence of Hemingway) as the hard-bitten colloquial pithiness of gunslingers in Western movies. Robert Redford playing the mountain man "Jeremiah Johnson" sounds more like John Wayne heading the cattle north than, in all likelihood, anything Redford's prototype, the historical Jedediah Smith, ever uttered.

There is, however, a backdoor entry into this question. Just as the eastern merchants and missionaries were scandalized by the hell raising of mountain men at the rendezvous in the 1830s, so were they flabbergasted by their speech. The usual response was to deplore the vulgarity and blasphemy of these hard-drinking wild men, but the sharp ear of Samuel Parker, the reverend who recorded Carson's duel with Shunar, caught something more interesting:

> They disdain the commonplace phrases of profanity which prevails among the unpious vulgar in civilized countries, and have many self-phrases, which they appear to have manufactured among themselves, and which, in their imprecations, they bring into almost every sentence and on all occasions. By varying the tones of their voices, they make them expressive of joy, hope, grief, and anger.

It is thanks to the equally talented ear of George Frederick Ruxton, an itinerant Englishman who died at the age of twenty-seven, that we have a generous sampling of what that mountain-man patois really sounded like. Ruxton spent four months in 1846 and 1847 traveling among what was left of the fraternity of mountain men, hunting and trapping as he went. A fictionalized account of his experience ran in *Blackwood's Edinburgh Magazine* from June to November 1848. By the time the last installment was published, Ruxton was dead in a St. Louis hospital, apparently from internal injuries suffered in the Rockies in a fall from muleback.

Life in the Far West remains a unique, classic account of mountain-man culture, nowhere more intriguing to the modern reader than in its reproduction of 1840s dialogue. Ruxton's heroes, La Bonté and Killbuck, banter thus, after a near-fatal fight with Indians:

"Is the top-knot gone, boy?" asked Killbuck; "for my head feels queersome, I tell you."

"Thar's the Injun as felt like lifting it," answered the other, kicking the dead body with his foot.

"Wagh! boy, you've struck a coup; so scalp the nigger right off, and then fetch me a drink."

A cranky old scout, trailing Indians, soliloquizes:

"Do 'ee hyar now? This niggur sees sign ahead—he does; he'll be afoot afore long, if he don't keep his eye skinned—*he* will. *Injuns* is all about, they ar': Blackfoot at that. Can't come round this child—they can't, wagh!"

A voyageur speaks broken French-English:

"Enfant de Gârce, me see bout honderd, when I pass Squirrel Creek, one dam war-party, parce-que, they no hosses, and have de lariats for steal des animaux. May be Yutes in Bayou Salade."

Here are the "self-phrases" Reverend Parker marveled at. As these passages suggest, the mountain men not only conventionally referred to Indians as "niggers," but alluded to themselves in the third person as "this nigger," "this coon," "this hos," or "this child." "Wagh!" was their expletive of choice. French and Spanish phrases and epithets larded their speech, and they strove for the vivid turn of phrase: "Well, Dick was as full of arrows as a porkypine"; "If them Spaniards wasn't born for shootin', why was beaver made?"

Ruxton makes it clear that mountain men scalped their enemies as gleefully as any Indians, and that a favorite pastime was boasting of their kills: "He counted a coup did St. Vrain. He throwed a Pueblo as had on poor Bent's shirt. I guess he tickled that niggur's hump-ribs." This callous recital adumbrates, moreover, a frontier pragmatism of which Ruxton approves. Of his hero, La Bonté (and of mountain men in general), he says: "[W]hen in the midst of Indian fight, it is not probable that any tender qualms of feeling would allay the itching of his fingers for his enemy's scalp-lock, nor would any remains of civilized fastidiousness prevent his burying his knife again and again in the life-blood of an Indian savage."

To imagine Kit Carson immersed in the world Ruxton celebrates is to hear him narrate his adventures with an almost Shakespearean indulgence in far-fetched conceit and homespun hyperbole. No doubt Carson spoke as his fellow mountaineers did; and, taciturn or not, he had his own special gift for language.

Ruxton allows us to imagine Carson stripped of the chivalric pieties of the dime novels, cleansed of the moral didacticism of the late-nineteenth-century hagiographers who first chronicled his stirring life, loosened even from the stodgy chronological plod of his own dictated memoir. Even more valuably, Ruxton gives us a central insight into the single question that has most perplexed the mountain man's latter-day apologists: just what Kit Carson thought and felt about Indians.

3

INDIAN KILLER

BY the 1860s, no higher praise wreathed Carson's brow than the claim that he had become a master at slaying redskins. In the dime novel *Kiowa Charley*, it is observed of an aging Kit that "[h]e had ridden into Sioux camps unattended and alone, had ridden out again, but with the scalps of their greatest warriors at his belt."

After the Sand Creek Massacre in eastern Colorado in 1864— one of the most brutal and unprovoked of all atrocities in the American West—its perpetrator, Colonel John Chivington, boasted, "I have eclipsed . . . Carson, and posterity will speak of me as the great Indian fighter."

As early as 1846, when George Frederick Ruxton traveled in the West, Kit Carson had become, thanks to Frémont's reports, something of a legend. Though he never met Carson, the Englishman pauses in his narrative to celebrate that "paragon of mountaineers":

> Small in stature, and slenderly limbed, but with muscles of wire, with a fair complexion and quiet, intelligent features, to look at Kit none would suppose that the mild-looking being before him was an incarnate devil in Indian fight, and had raised more hair from head of Redskins than any two men in the western country.

One hundred and fifty years later, his zeal as an Indian fighter has come to seem Carson's greatest moral failing, and his biographers and apologists scramble to rationalize it. In the Kit Carson Museum in Taos, installed in the scout's restored adobe house, a mounted plaque today baldly proclaims CONTRARY TO POPULAR BELIEF, CARSON WAS NOT AN INDIAN KILLER.

To get at the murky question of Carson's attitude toward Indians, it is necessary to read his own memoir attentively, without importing the bias of hindsight. It is clear that that attitude evolved over time, that the crude law of reprisal taught him as a teenager by Ewing Young was not a code Carson was comfortable with by the 1860s. No doubt his marriage to Waanibe, sometime around 1835, softened the stern and pragmatic mountaineer's opportunism that Ruxton championed.

Although Carson did not dictate his memoir until 1856, one of the virtues of its straightforward telling is that the author resists the temptation to add a retrospective gloss to the deeds he performed two decades before. One senses that the views Carson espouses as he narrates his dozen years of Rocky Mountain vagabondage were the views he had at the time, not the pondered judgments of reflection. (One cannot say the same of Frémont's reports, sugar-coated as they are with Jessie's editorial glazes.)

Most of the close calls and narrow escapes Carson endured during those twelve years as a trapper came at the hands of Indians. Yet what he later told his niece was his "worst difficult experience" came one day in 1834, when he was out hunting elk alone. Hearing a noise behind him, "I turned around and saw two very large grizzly bears making for me." Without time to reload, Carson dropped his gun and ran for a tree. From ten or fifteen feet up among its branches, he watched as the more inquisitive of the two bruins made swipe after swipe at the tree, along with uprooting nearby aspen saplings. "He finally concluded to leave," dictates Carson in his homely way, "of which I was heartily pleased, never having been so scared in my life." It was dark before Carson regained camp.

The duel with Shunar—a point-blank rifle bullet creasing his hair—must also be accounted a close call. Yet virtually all the other "'scapes and fixes" (to use Ruxton's vivid phrase) during Carson's twelve years of trapping came in Indian battles. The closest call of all may never have happened.

The episode was told by Carson's crony, Joe Meek. In the spring of 1833 or 1834, Meek insisted, he, Carson, another trapper, and 3 Delaware Indians were abruptly attacked by 200 Comanches, somewhere south of the Arkansas River. The men resorted to a desperate strategy: they maneuvered their mules into a circle, slit their throats, then lay behind their carcasses in a makeshift "fort," firing at the Comanches. Three men shot while the other 3 reloaded.

The Indians, armed mainly with lances and bows and arrows, kept getting picked off by the sharpshooters' bullets; their horses, maddened by the scent of mule blood, balked at charging. The attack, Meek claimed, was led by medicine men, 3 of whom were killed; each time, the Comanches retreated to elect a new shaman.

The battle lasted all day till dusk, at which point the trappers had killed 42 Comanches without injury themselves. At last, the Indians abandoned the futile fight. The parched, exhausted trappers kept up a dog-trot all night, reaching water only after they had covered seventy-five miles.

Meek recounted this epic struggle only in 1870, at the age of sixty, when he dictated his own life's story to Frances Fuller Victor, whose *The River of the West* became a wildly popular account of mountain-man days. By then, Meek had perfected his fabulist delivery, even while his memory had turned erratic. Many scholars doubt whether the Comanche attack ever happened. If it did, Carson's participation remains doubtful. No trace of such an encounter appears in Carson's own memoir, and it seems hardly likely that he could have forgotten it. Nonetheless, Carson's perspicacious early biographer Edwin L. Sabin credits the story without the blink of an eye.

The summary plainness of Carson's frequent accounts of Indian troubles veils some extraordinary adventures, and one must read between the lines to appreciate the scout's acumen as a warrior. In the winter of 1833–34, for instance, an Indian employed by the trader Antoine Robidoux stole six of the Frenchman's finest horses and headed for California. Robidoux asked Carson to track the renegade. Carson pursued the thief for 130 miles before overtaking him. In his most laconic vein, Carson narrates what ensued:

> Seeing me by myself [he] showed fight. I was under the necessity of killing him, recovered the horses, and returned on my way to our camp and arrived in a few days without any trouble.

Carson offers no apologies for the eye-for-an-eye law of revenge to which he and other mountain men subscribed in the 1830s. One night in January 1833, a party of Crow Indians stole nine horses that had been turned out to graze. Kit and eleven colleagues tracked them through the snow, discovered their camp, and crawled undetected to within a hundred yards of the campfire, around which the Crows were dancing their triumph. After the Indians had retired for the night, Carson and five others succeeded in crawling up to the tethered horses and releasing them without attracting the notice of any sentry.

What followed—as well as Carson's unabashed recollection of it—gives us a vivid glimpse of the man's character at age thirty-two:

> We then held council taking the views of each in regard to what had best be done. Some were in favor of retiring; having recovered their property and received no damage, they would be willing to return to camp. Not so with those that had lost no animals. They wanted satisfaction for the trouble and hardships they had gone through while in pursuit of the thieves. Myself and two more were the ones that had not lost horses and we were determined to have satisfaction, let the consequence be ever so fatal.

That trio bent on harsh punition won the day. As the trappers marched on the Indian "fort," a barking dog woke the sleeping Crows. "We opened a deadly fire," Carson remembered, "each ball taking its victim. We killed nearly every Indian in the fort." That evening, the party regained its winter camp. "During our pursuit for the lost animals we suffered considerably but, in the success of having recovered our horses and sending many a redskin to his long home, our sufferings were soon forgotten." As remarkable as the deed is Carson's tone—as close to a jaunty boast as he ever allowed himself to express. (And the sentiment itself comes as near as Carson ever got to endorsing General "Little Phil" Sheridan's infamous apothegm, "The only good Indian is a dead Indian.")

At the Green River rendezvous of 1837, which hundreds of Indians attended, a fight broke out between Bannocks and trappers. As usual, this murky episode has come down to us only in versions derived from the mountain men who took part in the battle. According to them, an aggressive band of thirty Bannock warriors galloped up to Jim Bridger's tent to demand the return of some horses that (so said the Bannocks) the Nez Percé had stolen and delivered over to Bridger for protection. Some recalled that in the previous weeks, Bannocks themselves had stolen horses and killed two trappers. Once more, the question of whether those Indians were the same as the ones who now confronted Bridger seems never to have been asked.

In any event, the Bannock leader, speaking his own language, declared, "We came here to get horses or blood and let us do it." Trapper Osborne Russell understood the vaunt, and translated it to his comrades. As Bridger held the bridle of one of the disputed horses, the Bannock leader boldly seized it, only to be shot dead by Bridger's allies. The rest of the Bannocks wheeled on their horses and fled. At least twelve warriors were shot in headlong flight. With grim tenacity, the mountain men trailed and harried the rest of the fugitives for three days, until they pleaded for mercy. According to Joe Meek, an old squaw advanced from the Bannock village, peace pipe in hand, to cry, "You have killed all our warriors. Do you now want to kill the women?"

Unlike the case of Meek's extraordinary account of six men lying behind their slaughtered mules to hold off 200 rampaging Comanches, there is no doubt that this battle with the Bannocks really took place. But did Carson play a part in its stern vengeance? His memoir makes no mention of the episode—although by 1856, perhaps all the Indian fights he had engaged in had been stitched in his memory into a seamless tapestry short on details. By 1837, Carson had become a close friend of Bridger. It is hard to imagine him standing by as the Bannocks threatened the peace of the rendezvous. Two years earlier, in the same camp, Carson had fought his duel with Shunar upon a far slighter provocation.

Yet by 1837, in all likelihood, Carson was camped on the Green River with Waanibe. Would he have left his Arapaho wife to trail and kill Bannocks? We cannot know: but such a turnabout would have been second nature to the typical mountain man, who had no qualms about distinguishing good Indians (such as Arapahos) from bad (Bannocks).

The worst of all Indians, in the mountain men's view, were the

Blackfeet. Six months before the skirmish with the Bannocks, in a winter camp along the Yellowstone River, Carson and some sixty other trappers under Jim Bridger's leadership had withstood an all-out Blackfoot effort to annihilate them. This assault Carson well remembered, though in his memoirs he misdated it by two years, placing the event in January 1839 rather than January 1837. Almost two decades later, the drama remained so fresh in his mind that he lavished an uncharacteristic four long paragraphs (550 words spilling from the mouth of this most laconic memoirist!) on its recital.

Just after New Year, some men out hunting stumbled across a party of Blackfeet. A brief and inconclusive exchange of gunfire ensued. Several days later, forty men from Bridger's camp, including Carson, rode out and drove the natives onto an island in the Yellowstone River. After an all-day battle, the trappers had suffered the loss of only one man, a Delaware Indian from east of the Mississippi. The next morning, the trappers gained the abandoned island and reckoned the damage they had wrought, as they found the snow stained with blood and strewn with brains; a trail leading to a hole in the ice revealed how the Blackfeet had disposed of their dead.

Bridger knew that the main Blackfoot village was nearby, and he told his men what they could expect. "Now, boys, the Indians are close," Carson heard him say. "There will in a short time [be] a party of five or six hundred return to avenge the death of those we had slain. . . ." With a will, the trappers set to work building a makeshift fort out of brush and poles; when it was done, it stood six feet high and enclosed a 250-square-foot camp. Fifteen days later, a sentinel saw the advance guard of a huge Blackfoot army approaching. Carson insists that in this climactic encounter, the mountain men were outnumbered 1,500 to 60. (It is not possible that 1,500 Blackfeet ever assembled for a single battle, but even 200 would have been a formidable force.)

It was so cold that February day, Osborne Russell recalled, that trees popped as their sap froze. Around 10 P.M., brilliant sheets of aurora borealis swept the northern sky. The besieged men heard the Indians singing war chants and saw them dance for victory. But the next day, the fort proved impregnable. As Carson put it, "They fired a few shots, but done no execution." He bragged that the trappers longed for an attack, so sure were they of the invincibility of their bastion. In the end, the frustrated Blackfeet rode off without having made a significant charge. Surprised at the Indians' refusal to join battle, the trappers concluded that they had taken the display of northern lights to be an ill omen.

As he narrated all his Indian fights during his mountain-man years, Carson told this tale with matter-of-fact panache. It was taken for granted that the Blackfeet were bad Indians; to shoot them whenever he could was a mountain man's instinct and duty. Three years before the siege on the Yellowstone, in another winter battle, Carson had been badly wounded. This time, the odds were more even: 30 Blackfeet versus 12 trappers. Carson and another man, Mark Head, were in the scouting vanguard as they trailed the withdrawing Indians. They approached a pair of Blackfoot men hiding behind trees. Each trapper picked his victim, but Head, reported Carson, "was not paying sufficient attention." Just as one warrior took aim at his comrade, Carson shot him dead.

This gave the other warrior the opening he needed. "He was sighting for my breast," recalled Carson in 1856. "I could not load in time so I commenced dodging as well as I could. He fired; the ball grazed my neck and passed through my shoulder."

Nearly a century of Western movies has imprinted in our minds the image of cowboys charging on horseback as they fire volley after precise volley at doomed Indian opponents. In the 1830s, however, the repeating rifle had yet to be invented: thus Carson's quandary. In the days of muzzle-loaders, every shot had to be carefully weighed against the vulnerable interval of recharging one's rifle. Having fired his precious .50-caliber ball from his Hawken, a mountain man had to pull the plug from his powderhorn with his teeth, pour a measure of gunpowder into the muzzle, tear off a square of cloth to use as a patch, wet the patch in his mouth, insert the patch in his barrel with the ball on top, tamp it down with his "short starter" (a small wooden mallet), then ram the ball home with his ramrod, before he was ready to shoot again. Astoundingly, an expert could perform the whole process in a matter of seconds.

Carson's wounding by the Blackfoot warrior was one of his closest calls. That night was bitter cold; Head and Carson dared not build a fire, for fear of giving away their bivouac. They lay in the snow, covered only with saddle blankets. "I passed a miserable night from the pain of the wound," recalled the stoic veteran, "it having bled freely, which was frozen."

The next summer, Carson survived another close call at Blackfoot hands, when the Indians set fire to the brush surrounding his camp in a grove of pines and aspens near the Gallatin River. "Death seemed almost inevitable," wrote Osborne Russell later. But the wind shifted and the fire doubled back on the Indians, driving them from their commanding position on a high bluff. "I cannot account for our miraculous escape from the flames," Carson would insist. "It was the hand of Providence over us that was the cause."

Given the fierce and unvarying enmity between trappers and Blackfeet, one can imagine the delight of Bridger's men in the spring of 1838 when they learned of a new development from a party of Crow Indians. These longtime enemies of the Blackfeet reported that they had warily entered several villages, only to find the teepees abandoned. An epidemic of smallpox had struck the Blackfeet. Unable to comprehend its cause, they had fled the plague as they seldom fled the white man. What all the rifle power in the West had failed to accomplish, an invisible virus was about to wreak, decimating one of the proudest native peoples in North America.

For four years already, eastern missionaries who had showed up at the rendezvous had been preaching compassion for and peace with the Indians. Vast numbers of "friendly" natives had assembled in recent summers to share in the merrymaking on the Green River. The Blackfeet, however, remained beyond the pale of white sympathy. For the mountain men, a smallpox epidemic among their most inveterate enemies was an occasion not for leniency but for rejoicing.

That attitude emerges plainly in Carson's account of the last battle he fought with the Blackfeet. In the late spring of 1838, still traveling with Bridger's company of mountain men, Carson ascended the Madison River in what is today Montana. The party struck a Blackfoot trail and followed it. They came to an abandoned teepee, inside which lay the dead bodies of three victims of the smallpox. Wearied perhaps of his decades of Indian fighting, Bridger urged his men to turn aside from the Blackfoot trail and get on with their trapping; but a number of the younger men—Carson was among the most avid—would not hear of avoiding a battle with the despised foe.

Six men, including Carson, pushed the trail to within four miles of the Blackfoot village. "[A]s we were determined to try our strength to discover who had right to the country," Carson baldly recounted, "I with forty men started for the village—sixty men being left to guard the camp—and we soon reached the village, attacked it, and killed ten Indians."

The Blackfeet fought back with a desperation born of their helplessness. As the trappers started to run short on ammunition, the Indians charged, sending the forty sharpshooters scurrying toward their own camp. In the midst of this retreat, Carson suffered yet another very close call. Near him, the horse carrying Cotton Mansfield, a longtime Bridger man, stumbled and fell, pinning the trapper beneath it. (According to Joe Meek, in what he assumed would be his last moments, Mansfield yelled, "Tell old Gabe [Bridger] that old Cotton is gone!") But Carson, with his fearless sense of loyalty, intervened. "Six Indians made for him for the purpose of taking his scalp," Kit recalled in his usual deadpan manner. "I dismounted, fired, and killed one Indian. The balance run."

Mansfield used the diversion to free himself from his thrashing horse, mount it, and flee. In the pandemonium, however, Carson's own horse galloped off. Kit called out to a comrade who, with a kindred sense of loyalty, risked his own life to ride into the fracas, allowing Carson to jump onto the back of his mount. The two men rode a single horse to safety.

The battle waxed on, with the Blackfeet holed up in a pile of rocks 150 yards from the mountain men's front line. Carson recalled seeing pairs of antagonists not ten feet apart on opposite sides of a boulder, "each dodging and trying to get the first shot."

At last, the Blackfeet were routed. No one counted the number of dead they left among the rocks. A few days later, as the insatiable pursuers prepared to attack another village of Blackfoot lodges, the Indians, demoralized by disease, surrendered without a shot fired, pleading with the mountain men to trade goods instead of wage war. "This proceeding conquered the bravest in our camp," testified Osborne Russell.

But if anything like pity filled Carson's breast as, in his twenty-ninth year, he beheld the ravaged camp of the Blackfeet, he did not bother to remember it. Of the battle on the Madison and his own narrow escape, he commented in 1856, "It was the prettiest fight I ever saw."

That the Blackfeet were the worst of all western Indians, the ones most bent on exterminating the encroaching white man, was an ax-iom for the seasoned mountain man. He did not waste effort won-dering why this might be so. Blackfoot treachery was simply part of the lore he absorbed from his elders in the beaver-hunting trade, a taxonomic distinction he lived by, like the situations in which it was most dangerous to run across a grizzly bear or the kinds of clouds that portended a winter blizzard. The trappers' wisdom about Black-feet even assumed a kind of circular logic, so that if word of Indian atrocities reached Americans' ears, they assumed that the miscre-ants must be Blackfeet.

Yet for fifty years before Kit Carson killed his first Blackfoot, those people had traded harmoniously with another set of white men on the frontier—Canadian voyageurs and explorers. Indeed, the Blackfeet had made fruitful contact with Canadians some two decades before they saw their first American. By Carson's time, in one of those rueful ironies of cross-cultural perception, the Black-feet had learned to distinguish between good and bad Anglo-Amer-icans—between the "Northern White Men" north of the border and the "Big Knives" to the south.

Thanks to the survival of the Blackfeet, for whom more than one learned nineteenth-century observer predicted extinction, and to the deep and diligent researches of such ethnographers as George Bird Grinnell, Clark Wissler, and John C. Ewers, we are in a posi-tion at the close of the twentieth century to understand how these nomads of the prairie comprehended the twin invasions of white traders and trappers two hundred years ago.

The Blackfeet are an Algonkian people, related thus to such other Indians as the Cheyennes, Arapahos, Crees, and Gros Ven-tres. Sometime before the eighteenth century (and perhaps as early as the fifteenth), they became the first Algonkians to leave the shel-ter of the midwestern forests and edge out into the Great Plains.

There they encountered hostile Shoshone and Sioux, yet carved out their own niche.

Before the Blackfeet saw their first white men, they learned from rumor of these interlopers from the east. The stories must have emphasized the powerful magic these strangers wielded. The Blackfeet called their creator Napi, or Old Man; now they named the whites Napikwan, or "Old Man People." It was not until around 1730 that the Blackfeet had first seen horses, bizarre beasts ridden by Shoshone whom the Blackfeet met in battle. They named these apparitions *ponokamita,* or "elk dogs," for the horses were as big and swift as the lordly elk, yet served men as dogs did.

The first Blackfoot contact with a white man may have come only after 1780, somewhere along the Saskatchewan River. For two decades agents of the Hudson's Bay Company had been striving to find and trade with the elusive Indians, about whom in turn they had heard many provocative rumors.

Yet disease traveled faster than the swiftest trader. Sometime in 1781, a group of Blackfoot warriors scouted a large Shoshone village they planned to attack. From a high hill nearby, they watched the camp all day, puzzled by the fact that not a single Shoshone made his appearance. Fearing a trap, the Blackfeet waited till the next morning to charge. When they did so, ripping open the teepees with their knives, they found only dead bodies inside, along with a few Shoshones in their last throes. Delighted at their good fortune, which they attributed to divine intervention, the Blackfeet seized all the horses and booty they could carry away. With them on their triumphant march they also carried the deadly virus.

Two days later, smallpox broke out among the Blackfeet. Their medicine men were helpless in the face of this calamity; to no avail, the Blackfeet sacrificed feathers and grasses to appease the spirit they assumed had brought them ill. Maddened by the plague, warriors plunged into the river and drowned. By the time the epidemic had run its course, half the Blackfoot nation had perished.

We know of this catastrophe thanks to the *Narrative* of the first white man to make lasting contact with the Blackfeet—a Hudson's Bay Company agent named David Thompson, who in 1787 wintered over with the people on the Bow River in what is today Alberta. It was Thompson who set the course for decades of peaceful

trading with the Blackfeet, inculcating among the Algonkians a benign image of the white-faced Napikwan who had come into their
country with all their strange and wonderful belongings.

Despite the plague of 1781, by the turn of the century the Blackfeet, armed with rifles traded from the British, had routed their
longtime enemies on the south and west, the Shoshones, the Flatheads, and the Kootenays. In the words of ethnographer John C.
Ewers, "the Blackfeet had become masters of the northwestern
plains. . . . [They] talked of their old Shoshoni enemies as miserable
old women whom they could kill with sticks and stones."

The Shoshone hatred of the Blackfeet was no less fervent. Father
Pierre-Jean De Smet, the first Catholic priest to celebrate a mass
among the mountain men, described the preparations of a Shoshone war party setting out against their foe, which he witnessed in
1840:

> If they take any women prisoners on these expeditions, they carry
> them to camp and hand them over to their wives, mothers, and
> sisters. These women immediately butcher them with their hatch-
> ets and knives, vomiting upon the poor wretches, in their frantic
> rage, the most crushing and outrageous language. "Oh, Blackfoot
> bitches," they cry: "If we could only eat the hearts of all your young
> ones, and bathe in the blood of your cursed nation!"

By 1800, the Blackfoot lifeway was firmly based on the buffalo. In
the long run, the people's dependence on that animal would prove
to be a liability; but before the advent of the mountain men, Blackfoot skill at hunting the bison and resourcefulness in using every
scrap of bones and carcass amounted to a cultural virtuosity of the
highest order. With horses specially trained for endurance runs,
Blackfoot men chased a herd across the plains, each hunter singling
out a beast. At close range, he shot it dead with bow and arrow,
since it was too difficult to recharge a muzzle-loader on horseback.
(As Ewers points out, each hunter could determine which buffalos
he had slain by retrieving his own distinctive arrows, whereas there
was no telling whose rifle ball had killed a given beast.)

A hunter's wife joined him in the process of butchering his prize;
working quickly with sharp knives traded from the British, the pair

could finish the job in a single hour. Every edible part of the animal was consumed. The Blackfeet regarded as a special delicacy not only marrow, but a kind of sausage made of intestines filled with blood. Dried meat and fat were rendered with berries into a portable pemmican. Buffalo hides were tailored by the women into cloaks, leggings, belts, moccasins, mittens, headdresses, bedding, lodge covers, tobacco pouches, food containers, and horse bridles, whips, and shoes. The women also turned sinew into sewing thread, horns into powder flasks, tails into fly whisks, ribs into arrowshaft straighteners, hipbones into paint brushes, dung into firewood, and penises into glue.

By 1806, the Blackfeet lived in a state of what anthropologists call aboriginal affluence. Two decades of profitable trade with the British had only strengthened their culture. They had cowed their enemies; they lived in fear of no one. And then they met their first Americans.

Returning from their epochal journey across the continent, Meriwether Lewis and William Clark divided their party to explore tributaries of the Missouri River. With only three other men, Lewis pushed north toward the source of the Marias River in what would become Montana, hoping to fix precisely the northern boundary of the Louisiana Purchase. On July 26, 1806, he climbed a low hill to look westward, only to see eight Indians of a tribe he did not recognize coming steadily toward him.

Wary, but determined to impress on these equally wary strangers his peaceful intentions, Lewis camped with them that night, shared his tobacco and pipe, and tried to converse in sign language. At dawn, one of the Blackfeet seized a pair of rifles that Lewis's night guard had recklessly left on the ground. Another man struggled with the Indian for possession of one of the firearms, crying out, "Damn you! Let go my gun!" The Blackfoot ran away, but Reuben Fields chased him and stabbed him in the heart. Later, as the Indians tried to seize the Americans' horses, Lewis opened fire, shooting a Blackfoot in the stomach. Leery of reprisals, intensely vulnerable, the four explorers at once headed south to rejoin Clark and the rest of the expedition.

This, in any event, was Lewis's version of the unfortunate contretemps. What the Blackfeet thought had provoked the fight, we do not know. Yet this single fracas fixed in the Blackfoot mind the image of another kind of Napikwan from the Canadian trader—a treacherous, southern white man who brought danger and death into the people's homeland. Later, as the mountain men swarmed into Montana, the Blackfeet would label these intruders with the ominous epithet the Big Knives. For decades, the people remembered the name of the martyr whom Reuben Fields had stabbed to death: He-That-Looks-at-the-Calf.

Only a month later, one of Lewis and Clark's men, John Colter, asked to be dismissed from the returning expedition and headed back toward the Yellowstone River, becoming in some sense the first of the American mountain men in the far West. Colter would also be the first to taste the bitter enmity against the Big Knives that Reuben Fields's quick thrust had unleashed.

To add to the fault of his white skin, Colter made the mistake of joining a party of Crow Indians that pushed west into Blackfoot country. On the Shoshone River, Blackfeet attacked the Crows and sent them running, every man for himself. Colter found himself deserted by his fickle comrades, and would later learn that the Blackfeet had taken careful note of his presence among their longtime Indian enemies.

To make his way back to the safety of a fort on the Bighorn River, Colter traversed the sources of the Yellowstone alone in winter, making the Anglo discovery of the fairyland of hot springs and geysers that would be derided as "Colter's Hell" until their outlandish reality could be verified. Undaunted by his tribulations, with a man named John Potts, also a veteran of the Lewis and Clark expedition, Colter set out in the spring of 1808 to trap his way into the Blackfoot country.

To forestall detection, Potts and Colter hid by day and trapped at night. They were not careful enough—nor, perhaps, could any white men have passed through the Blackfoot homeland unnoticed. One morning, Potts and Colter awoke to find themselves surrounded by Blackfeet. The legend sets their number at "five or six hundred"; twenty or thirty would have sufficed. The Indians killed Potts at once, riddling his body with arrows. Then they devised a crueler end for the Big Knife who had fought for the Crows. They stripped Colter naked, considered using him as a human target for their archery, then tauntingly asked him if he was a fast runner. Colter apparently had picked up a smattering of Blackfoot language, for he managed to reply "that he was a very bad runner." The chief gave the naked Napikwan a three- or four-hundred-yard head start on the prairie; with a "horrid war whoop," the race for his life began.

The Blackfeet had underestimated their adversary. Colter took off running, six miles barefoot through prickly pear. Halfway across the plain, he turned to see the swiftest Blackfoot closing in on him, spear in hand. Suddenly, Colter stopped and spun around. The surprised Indian fell as he tried to throw his spear, which broke as it stuck in the ground. Colter seized the pointed shaft and plunged it through his fallen pursuer's body.

Meanwhile the rest of the Blackfoot band approached. Colter had reached the banks of the Jefferson Fork. Now he jumped into the river, swam downstream, and surfaced amid a "raft" of downed timber that had drifted against the point of an island. The raft, overgrown with brush and weeds, offered Colter a hiding place. All day and night he stood neck-deep in the stream, listening to the yells and screeches of the Blackfeet, who searched within a few feet of him without locating their prey.

The next morning, Colter set off again. Incredibly, the mountain man arrived seven days later at a trading post on the Yellowstone, still naked, having survived by eating roots he knew were "much esteemed by the Indians of the Missouri."

Thus, Colter escaped an all but certain death. By 1811, however, the Blackfeet had taken such a toll among trappers that for the next decade mountain men scrupulously avoided entering that people's homeland, beaver-rich though it was. The discovery of South Pass in Wyoming, the key to the Oregon Trail (through which Carson and Frémont would pass on their way to the Wind Rivers in 1842), was made in 1812 by a party doing its level best to stay far to the south of the fatal Blackfoot domain. As late as 1837, Alfred Jacob Miller, the skillful painter at the Green River rendezvous, estimated that forty to fifty trappers each year were still being killed by Blackfeet.

That Kit Carson, then, had hardened his heart against these Algonkian warriors to the point where he not only gleefully seized any opportunity to kill them, but might rejoice in the people's decimation by smallpox, should be seen not as the defect of a character short on sympathy but as one more linchpin of a mountain man's pragmatism. The Blackfeet were bad Indians: it was as simple as that.

One odd lacuna in the American perception of the Blackfeet persists. By 1837, the yearly rendezvous included quite a number of Canadians, "deserters," as they were sometimes called, from the Hudson's Bay and North West Companies. Surely during many a grog-fueled evening parley, the talk turned to the Blackfoot scourge, and surely any Canadian with the dimmest grasp of history would have pointed out that the British experience of these Indians north of the border was a long record of fruitful trade and peaceable relations. Did this discrepancy give American trappers pause? If so, no record of such a feeble stirring of ethnographic curiosity has come down to us.

In reconstructing the smallpox epidemic of 1837, anthropologist John C. Ewers relied on the still undimmed memories of his informants in the 1940s. Ewers's canny book, *The Blackfeet: Raiders on the Northwestern Plains,* captures the full horror of the inexplicable plague that fell upon the people that year. The catastrophe was presaged, Blackfoot shamans later realized, by a total eclipse of the sun and an unprecedentedly brilliant meteor shower in 1833. Ewers believed the epidemic was spawned by some infected blankets traded up the Missouri, some of which ended up in Blackfoot hands. Within ten days, the plague was running rampant through the people's lodges. Rather than waste slowly away, as they saw their brethren doing, many men committed suicide by stabbing themselves or throwing themselves into rivers. Curiously, the only group of Blackfeet spared by the plague were those elders who, having survived the 1781 epidemic, had developed a resistance to the terrible disease. By the time the epidemic ran its course, Ewers estimates, 6,000 Blackfeet, a full two-thirds of the people, had died.

The desperate, weakened men whom Carson picked off among the rocks in "the prettiest fight I ever saw" were the epigones of a tribe of fearless warriors who only two decades before had ruled the northern plains.

*   *   *

The last rendezvous we can be sure Kit Carson attended was the gathering in the summer of 1838. The original plan for the annual get-together of trappers, traders, and Indians was to meet again at the favored junction of the Green River and Horse Creek, where the rendezvous of 1833, 1835, 1836, and 1837 had been held. At the last minute, however, the site was changed, ostensibly to brush off the Hudson's Bay Company men, whose competition the burgeoning American Fur Company hoped to eliminate.

To notify the far-flung mountain men of the change, a note was tacked to the door of a storehouse on Horse Creek: "Come to Popoazua on Wind River and you will find plenty trade, whisky, and white women." In this offhand manner, the veteran wanderers were directed to another river junction 120 miles away, on the opposite side of the Wind River Range. (The white women of whom the note boasted were the unapproachable wives of missionaries. The whiskey, however, was every bit as accessible as promised.)

The former grassland where the Popo Agie runs into the Wind River is occupied today by the middling village of Riverton, Wyoming. So thoroughly has the modern town turned its back on the streams that first gave it its reason for being that it is difficult to make one's way either by car or foot to the rendezvous site. (Many lifelong residents of Riverton have no idea the mountain men gathered there in 1838.) The promisingly named River Lane dead-ends in a dilapidated trailer park festooned with KEEP OUT signs. Only a devious meander along the rutted dirt track of Oberg Lane leads to the triangle of river bench where the trappers cavorted more than a century and a half ago. Across the site today sprawls a marshy sheep ranch. In July, the mosquitoes are fierce.

The insects were just as bothersome in 1838, for more than one attendee complained about them. The intimations of the decline in the beaver trade that had put a gloomy edge on the 1837 rendezvous were deepened this summer: silk hats were becoming all the more fashionable in London and Paris, the price for pelts in St. Louis had dropped again, and the beaver themselves were getting harder to find. The sense that a way of life was coming to an end may have lent a compulsive frenzy to the proceedings. Some men squandered as much as a thousand dollars each in booze and gambling within a day or two. The missionaries preached salvation to the jaded mountain men, but, as one minister complained, "there is little hope of benefitting them."

Jim Bridger's entourage, which included Carson, struck the missionaries as particularly "rude & savage." The horde of a hundred scruffy trappers, some sixty Indian women, and "a great number of half breed children," wrote one observer, came to the rendezvous "painted in a most hideous manner . . . [T]hey looked like the emissaries of the Devil worshipping their own master." The "white men acted like Indians," scolded another. The missionaries were shocked by the unalloyed glee with which the mountain men talked of the smallpox devastating the Blackfeet. One member of Bridger's party flaunted a Blackfoot scalp that he carried in his hand. Another described a recent battle with the Blackfeet to the Reverend Asa Smith:

> The Indians made no attack on B[ridger]'s party but this party attacked them & shot 15 of them dead without excuse but to please their wicked passions. Thus sending 15 souls to eternity & to the bar of God unprepared. A man . . . [s]aid that one they shot and wounded but not killed. Said that this Indian grasped the limb of a white man who stood near & made signs begging that his life might be spared while others dragged him away & cut his body in pieces regardless of his groans & entreaties. This fellow seemed to exult in it.

In his usual fashion, Carson glossed over his last rendezvous in a few sentences, none illuminating his own part in the merrymaking. From a roundabout but reliable source, however, we learn that the Swiss entrepreneur John Sutter, on whose land in 1848 would be made the strike that launched the California Gold Rush, bought an Indian boy from Carson for $130 at the Wind River rendezvous. The practice of buying and selling orphaned Indian children was more common among mountain men than most historians have recognized, but we know no further details about this venture of Carson's into the trade. Five years later, however, in the midst of Frémont's second expedition, somewhere in the Utah mountains, that iconoclastic grumbler Charles Preuss would record in his secret diary a transaction that neither Carson's memoir nor Frémont's official report saw fit to mention:

Kit bought an Indian boy of about twelve to fourteen years for forty dollars. He is to eat only raw meat, in order to get courage, says Kit, and in a few years he hopes to have trained him, with the Lord's help, so that he will at least be capable of stealing horses. He actually eats the raw marrow, with which Kit supplies him plentifully. He belongs to the Paiute Nation, which subsists only on mice, locusts, and roots, and such a life as the present must please him very much.

After the 1838 rendezvous, Carson trapped desultorily through the autumn, then settled in for the winter at Brown's Hole, a refugium of relatively mild climate on a bend of the Green River in the northwest corner of Colorado, where entrepreneurs had built a stockade called Fort Davy Crockett. It was becoming evident to the mountain men that, to survive, they must diversify their options. One inventive solution to their plight came in the form of a grand horse-stealing expedition into Mexican California. On this journey rode some of the toughest veterans of the beaver trade, including Carson's lifelong friend Dick Owens; the erratic and alcoholic Old Bill Williams, who would play a fateful role in Frémont's disastrous expedition of 1848–49; and Peg-Leg Smith, who, having some years before received a bullet wound that shattered his ankle, cut off his own lower limb with a butcher knife and a meat saw, then whittled his own prosthetic stump.

Carson, who had illegally taken beaver along the Gila on his first trapping expedition nine years before, had nothing against stealing Mexican horses, but he declined to join his friends on the jaunt to California. Instead, his prowess as a hunter earned him a job shooting game for the fort. "I had to keep twenty men in venison," he recalled drily many years later.

The last rendezvous of all took place at the idyllic Green River camp in 1840. A mood of despair hung over the forced gaiety of the midsummer spree. "Times was certainly hard no beaver and everything dull," wrote one trapper. In a valedictory mood, Jim Bridger spoke to his assembled confederates, saying that he believed he was the only trapper present who had also been at the first rendezvous in 1825; nearly all his other comrades from those lusty, optimistic days were now dead. "Come," said Robert Newell to his old friend Joe

Meek (in a moving panegyric perhaps improved by Meek's 1870 as-told-to autobiographer, Frances Fuller Victor),

> we are done with this life in the mountains—done with wading in beaver dams, and freezing or starving alternately—done with Indian trading and Indian fighting. The fur trade is dead in the Rocky Mountains, and it is no place for us now, if ever it was. We are young yet, and have life before us.

The years 1839–41 remain the single period in Kit Carson's adult life during which it is hardest to trace his movements. While lingering at Brown's Hole in 1839, he joined his cronies in at least two more memorable Indian fights, against the Sioux and the Snakes. In his memoirs, Carson mentions neither battle. He went on a mule-trading expedition all the way to the Navajo country. And he trapped on with Bridger and Dick Owens, pushing hard to the heads of obscure streams in quest of the few beaver that still survived.

Yet so vague is Carson's own narrative of these years, so muddled the chronology, that his careful modern biographers, Thelma S. Guild and Harvey L. Carter, pondering one passage, comment: "[T]he remainder of this account appears to be filler, or camouflage for events Carson had no wish to relate."

Those events, in all likelihood, involved his Arapaho wife, Waanibe, with whom he surely lived at Fort Davy Crockett. Sometime, perhaps late in 1838, she gave birth to a daughter, whom Carson named Adaline, after the niece who had been his favorite childhood companion back in Missouri. Perhaps two years later, Waanibe gave birth to a second daughter, who was destined for a short life, for she would perish in 1843 in Taos in a domestic accident, when she fell into a kettle of boiling soap.

Then—perhaps of a fever, conceivably during childbirth—Waanibe herself died. (Guild and Carter tentatively place her demise in 1841.) Because of his subsequent marriage to a highborn Hispanic woman in Taos, and his fear that having been a "squaw man" might exclude him from polite society, Carson never admitted in print to having taken an Indian wife. There is every reason to believe that he loved Waanibe, however, and mourned her passing. And by 1841, he was preoccupied with ensuring that his daughters find some refuge from the vagabond life that by now was the only kind Kit Carson knew how to lead.

That a man who could blithely buy and sell an Indian orphan might be so protective of his half-Indian daughters may seem incongruous. But the code of personal loyalty that drove Carson unthinkingly to ride to the aid of a comrade in an Indian battle extended just as unthinkingly to his young progeny.

By the fall of 1841, Carson and five companions, among them Old Bill Williams, had made their way to the Arkansas River in southeastern Colorado. "Beaver was getting scarce," he recalled in 1856, "and, finding it necessary to try our hand at something else . . . , [we] concluded to start for Bent's Fort." There Kit was "kindly received" by Céran St. Vrain and William Bent, who gave him the job of meat hunter for the fort at a salary of one dollar per day. Carson remained grateful to these men the rest of his life, pausing in his memoir to offer a rare encomium: "I can only say that their equals were never in the mountains."

Bent's Fort had been built in 1834 on the north bank of the Arkansas, well out on the plains, six miles east of today's town of La Junta. It lay right on the border of Mexican territory, which stretched south from the opposite shore of the river. At the time of its construction, remarkably enough, the spacious private fort may have been the grandest building raised by American hands anywhere in the vast expanse between the Great Plains and the Pacific Ocean. It quickly became a prime focus not only for the beaver trade, but for barter with Mexico.

Born near St. Louis seven years before Carson, the offspring of Flemish nobility and Louisiana settlers, Céran St. Vrain had been one of the earliest and most ambitious of the mountain men before settling into his partnership with William Bent. Carson had almost surely met him during his first winter in Taos, at age seventeen. Bent, too, hailed from St. Louis. The same age as Carson, he had come to the Southwest along the Santa Fe trail in 1829, with his brother Charles, who would become Carson's brother-in-law. Unlike his partner, St. Vrain, William Bent only dabbled in trapping before deciding that fort building was his true métier.

By the time Carson arrived, looking for work, in 1841, Bent had taken a Cheyenne bride named Owl Woman. This linkage proved vital for the fort's trade with Plains Indians—not only Cheyennes, but Arapahos. And it may have encouraged Carson to make what would turn out to be an embarrassing mistake. Sometime during the winter, still (we presume) mourning Waanibe, Carson married a Cheyenne woman whose name translates as Making-Out-Road. The liaison lasted only a few months before she removed Kit's belongings from her lodge, effecting what Indians recognized as a legal divorce.

Almost nothing is known about this woman, although historian David Lavender, without making clear his sources, paints an unflattering portrait of "the belle of the southern Cheyennes":

> The girl was spoiled. She had put most of the Cheyenne bachelors and half the white men at the fort in a slow burn, and they had showered her with gifts. Now that she was married she expected Kit to keep her in expensive foofaraw. She ignored her household chores and neglected little Adaline. . . .

Built as they were of such perishable stuff as wood and adobe, virtually all the forts that buttressed the beaver trade have vanished altogether. At the site of Fort Bonneville, for instance—erected in 1832 and crucially linked to the six Green River rendezvous that unfurled only six miles away (though glad to avail themselves of the post, the trappers nicknamed it "Bonneville's Folly" and "Fort Nonsense")—nothing remains today except a stand of willows and sagebrush behind a white granite boulder affixed with a commemorative plaque.

But Bent's Fort was professionally excavated in the 1960s, then rebuilt by the National Park Service in 1975. It stands today not only as the most accurate replica of an 1830s trading post in the West, but as one of the nation's triumphs of historical reconstruction. Even today, the fort thrusts out of a stark prairie isolation, gentled only by the line of nearby cottonwoods that follows the sleepy Arkansas. Built as a two-story hollow square with corner watchtowers, the stockade with its defensive shape proclaims the evident comfort and security it offered, where on the coldest winter days each room was cheered by a fire in a pot-bellied stove.

Wandering through the fort today, one gains an intensely visceral sense of Kit Carson's daily round that winter of 1841–42, when he was not out on the prairie shooting deer and bison and antelope. Even the furnishings of the trader's store, researched from company ledgers, reveal the very goods that Kit might have pondered spending his hard-earned daily dollar on: Bent's Water Biscuits (2 cents a box); Havana sugar, in sacks; clay pipes; Japanese porcelain; "Beans—19 cents a pound"; "English Gun Flint—$1.00 doz." Across the dirt courtyard, Carson would have strolled to visit the blacksmith's shop, or purchase a U.S. Army blanket from the warehouse, where he also bought .54-caliber cartridges for his pistol and, on occasion, brandy straight from the cask. Through the mica windows, he must have squinted for signs of the Comanches who regularly threatened the fort. We can even imagine him taking his turn at the billiard table in the low-roofed second-floor game room.

But we cannot imagine Carson lapsing into sedentary content at Bent's Fort: the wanderlust was too deep in his soul. He served eight months as meat hunter for Messrs. Bent and St. Vrain. In April 1842, he joined a wagon train headed east. For the first time in sixteen years, Carson would return to the Missouri homestead where he had grown up. Even now, his journey was prompted not so much by homesickness as by the need to give his four-year-old daughter a stable life.

Carson's memoir details what must have been a memorable, emotional homecoming with his usual dry impatience:

> It had been a long time since I had been among civilized people. I arrived at the States, went and saw my friends and acquaintances, then took a trip to St. Louis, remained a few days and was tired of remaining in settlements. . . .

What Carson in his reticence neglects to report is that, somewhere in Howard County, Missouri, he found his sister Mary Ann, and delivered Adaline over to her to raise. She was subsequently schooled in a female seminary. Despite their years apart, her father never forgot Adaline. When she was about fourteen, Carson returned to Missouri to bring his daughter out to New Mexico, where he had chosen to live. The next year, a man named Louis Simmons asked Carson for Adaline's hand in marriage. She was perhaps fifteen, Simmons some two decades older, but Kit consented.

Adaline remains one of the most shadowy of presences in Carson's life. The few known facts hint at a tragic denouement. Not long after the marriage, Simmons left or divorced her; according to a family friend, the rupture came about because "she was a wild girl and did not behave properly." Adaline made her way to the gold-fields of California during the rush of 1859, where she got involved with a man named George Stilts, about whom nothing else is known. She died the next year—at the age of about twenty-two. Her nickname in California was Prairie Flower. She was buried on the shore of Mono Lake, but a monument that was planned in 1930 for her grave was apparently never erected.

Having tired of St. Louis in only a few days that spring of 1842, Kit Carson boarded a steamship that was headed up the Missouri River. Only thirty-two years old, he was truly at loose ends. The art he had spent sixteen years perfecting had evaporated before his eyes. Even such low-paying sinecures as his job as a meat hunter for the forts belonged to a world of doomed professions (for all its grandeur, Bent's Fort would be abandoned in 1849). And the fact that Carson could neither read nor write further limited his professional options.

Many a mountain man who had not succumbed to a Blackfoot cartridge or a winter blizzard was destined for a sorry end, like Carson's first mentor, Ewing Young, dying of dyspepsia in Oregon while still in the prime of life. William Sublette, an erstwhile partner of Jedediah Smith who may also have trapped with Carson, tried to retire into a health spa he concocted in Missouri; the resort failed, and the ex-trapper died of tuberculosis at the age of forty-five. Peg-Leg Smith drank himself to death in San Francisco in 1866.

In an aimless funk on the Missouri steamer, Carson stumbled upon the pivotal opportunity of his life, in the person of another passenger on board, a young lieutenant in the U.S. Topographical Corps. Carson had never heard of John Charles Frémont, but when he learned that the green explorer needed a scout to lead him across the great West, he "informed him that I had been some time in the mountains and thought I could guide him to any point he would wish to go." (One can easily hear the laconic understatement of Carson's self-assessment.) In his officious way, Frémont was not about to take the ex-trapper at his word; instead, as Carson recalled,

"He replied that he would make inquiries regarding my capabilities of performing that which I promised. He done so."

Yet in Frémont's own retrospect, the meeting with Carson was esteem at first sight. In his *Memoirs* dictated late in life, the Pathfinder insisted, "I was pleased with him and his manner of address at this first meeting. He was a man of medium height, broad-shouldered and deep-chested, with a clear steady blue eye and frank speech and address; quiet and unassuming."

Frémont offered Carson the job. On no chance meeting in the long history of the American West would more doings of high consequence depend.

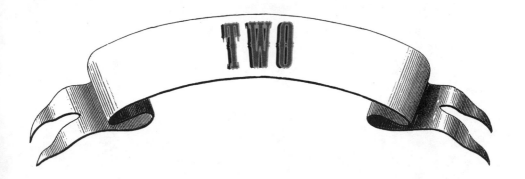

THE CONQUEST OF
CALIFORNIA

4

CHILDE HAROLD'S

PILGRIMAGE

FEW explorers of the American wilderness have seen so many detractors crawl out of the underbrush as did John C. Frémont. Some of his most vituperative critics were former comrades whom Frémont had managed to alienate.

Kit Carson, however, was not one of them. So far as we know, Carson never uttered a public aspersion against his erstwhile commander. By 1856, when he dictated his autobiography, the old scout had drifted out of contact with the lieutenant. Word had reached him, though, of the fortune Frémont had gained in the California goldfields:

> I have heard that he is enormously rich. I wish to God that he may be worth ten times as much more. All that he has or may ever receive, he deserves. I can never forget his treatment of me while in his employ and how cheerfully he suffered with his men when undergoing the severest of hardships. His perseverance and willingness to participate in all that was undertaken, no matter whether the duty was rough or easy, is the main cause of his success.

Perseverance, indeed, was Frémont's strongest suit—turning, at its worst, into the pigheaded obstinacy that time and again threatened to derail his career. In Carson's eyes, Frémont's character was uncomplicated, a born leader's amalgam of loyalty and resolve. But the Pathfinder's biographers have struggled to comprehend the contradictions that drove the man's erratic behavior.

Allan Nevins, whose magisterial but overadmiring life of Frémont first appeared in 1928, hailed his subject as having "explore[d] more of the West than any other single man." (The claim is unprovable, for we shall never know just how much territory such nonliterate adventurers as Jedediah Smith, or Ewing Young, or, for that matter, Kit Carson covered.) Yet Nevins emphasized the "almost melodramatic alternations of good and bad fortune" that marked Frémont's life. After 689 lucid pages devoted to chronicling that life, Nevins would insist on the "psychological mystery" at the core of his hero's soul. "How could the man who sometimes succeeded so dazzlingly at other times fail so abysmally?" asked Nevins, without venturing a definitive answer. "Fortune came bearing her amplest gifts on a golden platter, and as he touched them they turned to the apples of Sodom."

Half a century after Nevins, Ferol Egan's *Frémont: Explorer for a Restless Nation* added much richness to our understanding of some of the explorer's most enigmatic doings, in the course of his various campaigns in California. Like Nevins, Egan puzzled over the wild vagaries of Frémont's path: "[H]e climbed the peaks of glory only to endure the deserts of despair." But, like Nevins, Egan let admiration cloud his critical faculties, summing up his subject as "[h]andsome as Lord Byron, mysterious as Sir Richard Burton, a figure of dash and romance."

In 1991, Andrew Rolle published *John Charles Frémont: Character as Destiny*, a far darker biography than either Nevins's or Egan's, which profits from sources previously unplumbed. Rolle leapt straight at the throat of Nevins's "psychological mystery," constructing his portrait of the man along psychoanalytic lines. The result is a fascinating—if ultimately procrustean—account of an ambitious adventurer constantly striving for greatness, but thwarted by compulsions and obsessions, born of childhood trauma, over which Frémont had no control.

Better than any of his biographers, that acute historian Bernard De Voto, in *The Year of Decision: 1846*, sized up the fundamental paradox in Frémont's character. Writing in 1943, De Voto also saw the explorer as a Byronic hero, but in this case as a self-styled Childe Harold. Following Frémont on his vainglorious errands up and down the length of California, De Voto brilliantly played "the Conqueror" as a comic figure, strutting and posing, often more preoccupied with the picture his deeds ought to compose than with the efficacy or justice of the deeds themselves. Without resorting to psychoanalysis, De Voto pierced to the heart of what may have been Frémont's fatal flaw: a self-conscious preoccupation with how everything he did would look in the view of history, which precluded the kind of thoughtless performance that, at its purest, defines true heroism. (Kit Carson had that quality in his very blood.)

De Voto was far from fair to Frémont: he either overlooked or ignored the explorer's flashes of genuine greatness. But in one delicious vignette after another, *The Year of Decision* captured the grandiose pomposity that was always just beneath the Pathfinder's surface—which Nevins, Egan, and Rolle alike, in their biographical earnestness, tended to miss.

Thus: "Frémont brought his force southward with a wariness that would have prevented a surprise by overwhelming numbers of the enemy, if there had been any." Or: "So, summing up these phantom dangers to assuage his hurt, he . . . dragged northward toward Oregon, a bedraggled knight with some tail feathers plucked, through chilly rain." After California, judged De Voto, "from then on to the end of his life he was to go, always subtly, astray. Nothing came out quite the way it should have done. Lord Byron, who imagined him, could not make him rhyme."

In retrospect, the trajectory along which Kit Carson rode to his destiny in the West seems all but inevitable, the only possible outcome for a youngster so restless he ran away at sixteen from his first job. In contrast, there is little in Frémont's childhood and youth that even hints at the five dramatic voyages that would crown his maturity and fix him as an American hero. Given the aimless, even feckless meanderings of his first twenty years, it seems a wonder that history should have accorded John Charles Frémont even a footnote.

He was born in Savannah, Georgia, on January 21, 1813, the offspring of a most improbable union. His mother, whom Frémont idealized with fierce partiality all his life, was Anne Pryor, born into a leading Virginia family that had fallen on lean times. Anne was, claims Nevins, "a spirited and beautiful young woman." To improve her prospects (Anne was the youngest of twelve children), she was married without her consent at age seventeen to a sixty-two-year-old veteran of the Revolutionary War. John Pryor, according to Rolle, "was described as stuffy, short, fat as butter, and very rich and very gouty."

Needless to say, the marriage was a deeply unhappy one for Mrs. Pryor. Into the Richmond beau monde that she detested (and to which her husband, she later complained, was "addicted") came, sometime around 1810, a shadowy bon vivant who called himself Charles Frémon. The story he handed out was that he was a well-born Frenchman hailing from Lyon, a Royalist forced into exile during the Revolution. On his way to the West Indies, his ship was captured by the British. Frémon spent several years imprisoned on an unspecified Caribbean island, where he charmed his jailers with his skill at making cabinets and baskets and painting frescoes.

Flat broke, he eventually fetched up in Norfolk, where he was, in Nevins's bland phrase, "promptly taken into the best circles in Tidewater Virginia." By the time he met Anne Pryor in Richmond, Frémon was scrounging a living as French teacher, fresco painter, and dancing master. He was also a noted seducer, who had defied local mores by openly living with an unmarried woman. (Without citing his source, Nevins describes the charismatic foreigner as "a dark, slender man, with fine features and much distinction of manner.")

Anne Pryor started taking French lessons from the dancing painter. They fell in love and began an affair. When her outraged husband confronted Anne with her betrayal and threatened to kill her, she threw his dudgeon back in his face and eloped with her paramour the next morning.

For the next few years, the lovers, having chosen ostracism over comfort, wandered about the South, landing briefly not only in Savannah but in Williamsburg, Norfolk, and Nashville. At some point, Anne Pryor must have been divorced by her gouty husband, for he, an upstanding member of the Virginia gentry, eventually remarried. But when she gave birth to the child who would become the famous explorer, she was still married to John Pryor.

When Frémont ran for president in 1856, as the first candidate of the newly formed Republican Party, Democratic muckrakers pried into his origins. Campaign broadsides set out to prove not only that Frémont was a bastard, but that he was a closet papist and that he had been born abroad. The first two allegations were damning enough; the third, if true, would have disqualified him from the presidency.

Although scandalous at the time, the passionate tryst between the unhappy young wife and the vagabond French painter glows with a romantic aura in the pages of biography. So Nevins played it, taking at face value Charles Frémon's myth of himself, seeing only a man whose "life had been packed with adventure." Yet by 1928, when Nevins wrote, assiduous Canadian scholars had already demonstrated that "Charles Frémon" was actually Louis-René Frémont, born in Quebec City, a failed small-time politician who sailed for Saint-Domingue (today's Dominican Republic) not as an exiled Royalist fleeing the guillotine, but probably as an opportunist hoping to freeload off an aunt who lived there. The capture of his ship by an English frigate, and his subsequent imprisonment, seem actually to have happened. "Charles Frémon," however, newly arrived in Norfolk, may have been an escapee from British authorities hoping to start life over in a new land with a new name.

By 1818, the mysterious Canadian had died, leaving Anne Pryor with three illegitimate children (John Charles's younger brother and sister), struggling to make ends meet by renting out rooms to boarders. What Frémont knew and thought about his father, we cannot guess; though he would cherish his idealized memory of his mother all his life, the Pathfinder never wrote a single word about the Canadian dancing master who sired him.

Rolle sees the loss of his father at the age of five, and the taint of uncertainty and illegitimacy hovering over his boyhood, as the central fact in Frémont's life, inflicting an Oedipal wound he spent the rest of his life compensating for, "struggl[ing] for self-validation." In certain respects, Frémont would recapitulate his father's deeds and character in classic Freudian fashion. Like Charles Frémon, John C. Frémont would elope with the woman he loved, defying (in this case) her father's stormy opposition. Like the Canadian progenitor he hardly knew, Frémont would grow skillful at cloaking his failures

in secrecy. And like the itinerant fresco painter, Frémont would become a habitual womanizer. (The discovery of numerous infidelities
later in Frémont's life, of which previous biographers seem to have
been unaware, is one of Rolle's contributions.)

We know considerably more about Frémont's childhood than
about Kit Carson's, but much of what has come down to us has an
anecdotal patness shaped by the nineteenth-century hagiographers
who first published "lives" of the Pathfinder full of moral exempla
(not the least effective of this company being Jessie Frémont herself). Handed down by family tradition, a very curious happenstance
in 1814, which may or may not have taken place (though both
Nevins and Rolle accept it as fact), reeks of the heavy foreshadow-
ing via pregnant coincidence so favored by bad Hollywood direc-
tors. We do know that on September 4 of that year, in a tavern in
Nashville, Thomas Hart Benton—destined to become not only Frémont's father-in-law but the senator most ardent in promoting
American expansion in the West—had angry words with Andrew
Jackson, fated to become the seventh president. Words escalated
into pistol shots; a ball fired either by Benton or his brother shattered Jackson's left shoulder. The family legend has it that, along
with his parents, John Charles Frémon[t], a babe of one-and-a-half
years, slept through the melee in a room upstairs, despite the errant
bullet that passed through the walls of their chamber.

By 1819, the impoverished widow with her three illegitimate
children had landed in Charleston, South Carolina. Here John Frémont would spend his seventh through his twentieth years. For all
its antebellum charm, no town in the United States was steeped in
a more thoroughgoing racism than Charleston. Slaves were routinely auctioned in the marketplace, runaways severely punished.
As Rolle points out,

> Blacks were not allowed to follow military units, to bathe horses
> in public, or to walk on the Battery. [Frémont] watched them by
> the hour and saw them arrested, and sometimes beaten, for fight-
> ing or being out after the warning tattoo sounded.

One apparent paradox of Frémont's nature is that a boy brought
up immersed in such a social climate should turn into a man com-

pletely free of racial prejudice—indeed, as staunch an abolitionist as the most adamant Massachusetts minister. His biographers have facilely attributed that tolerance to an infancy gentled by the loving care of a series of black nannies; but many another southerner nursed by loyal Negro women matured into a diehard defender of slavery.

Nevins, determined to narrate Frémont's youth in the vein of a nineteenth-century Bildungsroman, sees only auspicious glimmerings in Charleston:

> He grew up wonderfully agile and hardy of body, active of mind and, with his dark hair, olive skin, penetrating blue eyes, and chiseled features, a very handsome lad. Charleston had no more attractive youngster than "Charley" Frémont. Every one befriended him.

Yet in quixotic conjunction with the active mind and the hardy body, a streak of listless indolence ran through Frémont's character. Years later, his first schoolmaster would recall that "intelligence beamed in his dark eyes," and would single out for praise Frémont's precocity in Greek and Latin: "Whatever he read he retained." If so, he must have forgotten most of that early learning, for the reports and memoirs he eventually dictated to Jessie are virtually barren of classical allusions.

He was admitted to the College of Charleston at the early age of sixteen, but soon found himself in trouble because of cutting classes. Often he used his truant freedom to explore the surrounding woods and marshes; at an early age, his deep love of nature had surfaced. But Frémont also spent many an evening at the Tivoli Gardens (recalled by a classmate as the habitual hangout of Charleston's "lowlifes"), sometimes carousing through a weekend-long drunk. This, too, seems odd, for in later life Frémont never had a weakness for alcohol.

Then, at seventeen, "Charley" fell in love. We know very little about Cecilia, except that she was a Creole girl whose French-speaking parents had fled Saint-Domingue during a slave revolt. Decades later, convinced by his worldly success that the dire warnings of his teenage mentors had been misguided, Frémont looked back on the affair with Cecilia as "the bit of sunshine that made the glory of my youth." Wandering the meadows with his true love, staying out late, murmuring to her in French, he so neglected his studies that the college dismissed him for "habitual irregularity and incorrigible negligence." In his *Memoirs*, Frémont smugly gazed back at this rebuke as a blessing in disguise: "I smiled to myself while I listened to words about the disappointment of friends, and the broken career. I was living in a charmed atmosphere and the edict only gave me complete freedom."

It is hard to believe that at the time the young hedonist was quite so insouciant. To supplement his mother's meager income, Frémont wangled a part-time job teaching mathematics at a private secondary school. Nearing the age of twenty, the handsome youth had no prospects of anything like a serious vocation. What he had instead—and would continue to have through his thirty-third year— was extraordinary good luck.

Arguing more from theory than from biographical fact, Rolle sees in these aimless teenage years the development in Frémont of a "grandiose selfhood." "One of his defenses was to distance himself from intimacy with others," the biographer goes on. The worm in the bud, a priori, must have been "the loss of a father who yet remained present in his life but as a painful memory."

There is a simpler explanation for Frémont's slow start toward fame and achievement. The young man was restless, passionate, and beguiled by the natural world; but his own libertine propensities undermined whatever ambitions glimmered in his soul. Frémont certainly wanted to amount to something; later, he would remember as his favorite adolescent reading the lives "of men who had made themselves famous by brave and noble deeds, or infamous by cruel and base acts." But until he discovered the West, his sense of destiny would remain vague and unfocused.

Oddly, given the semipoverty in which he grew up, and the scandal that surrounded his parents' union, Frémont seemed from an early age to behave as though the world owed him a living. That sense of entitlement, stiffened by an almost violent stubbornness of will, would cause him trouble again and again.

* * *

Just as it came naturally to the young Frémont to charm women, so he seems to have had the knack of gaining the good graces of important men. (If he were a job seeker in the year 2000, we would say that he "interviews well.") Frémont's first great break in life came in the person of Joel Poinsett, who returned to Charleston in 1830 from almost five years' service as the country's first minister to Mexico. Later, Poinsett would become secretary of war under Van Buren, and eventually have the scarlet poinsettia named after him (he had brought the plant back with him from Mexico).

We do not know when or how Frémont wriggled into Poinsett's orbit, but in 1833 the ex-minister used his influence to get the twenty-year-old an appointment as mathematics teacher aboard the warship *Natchez*. During a several-month cruise to South America, Frémont for the first time saw a world larger than the surroundings of Charleston. In Argentina, he fell "desperately in love" with a Miss Palmer, daughter of the American consul in Buenos Aires. Unlike the "bit of sunshine" Cecilia had cast into his life, Miss Palmer seems to have left little impression, for Frémont never acknowledged the relationship in writing. (We know of it only thanks to an acquaintance's obscure diary entry that Rolle uncovered.)

Later, Frémont would look back on his cruise as tedious and irrelevant to his fortunes, but the naval service helped him obtain his second important post—as an assistant engineer on a surveying expedition into the wilds of the Carolina mountains. Once again, Joel Poinsett gave the nudge that secured the young man his job. This journey, too, proved no great adventure, at least compared to the forays Frémont would lead in the 1840s. In his *Memoirs*, he recalled the jaunt as something of a lark: "The survey was a kind of picnic, with work enough to give it zest. . . ."

The hostile campaign biographers of 1856 dredged up an unsavory episode from Frémont's picnic. In Greenville, South Carolina, swore an eyewitness, the charmer seduced "a very pretty girl, in moderate circumstances. . . . He was engaged to her, and deserted her without a cause, and the family were very much distressed about the matter." Needless to say, Frémont himself left no more record of this passing infatuation than he did of his Argentine dalliance with Miss Palmer.

The Carolina survey, in turn, led to Frémont's first true expedition, a venture through the winter of 1836–37 into the Cherokee country along the border of Georgia and South Carolina. Once again, the young mathematician was charged with surveying the land, but for the first time he found himself exploring true wilderness—deep forest punctuated by scattered Indian villages clinging to the clearings. Frémont threw himself into this voyage with wholehearted zeal. Indeed, the laziness that had marked so much of his youth seemed by now to have sloughed away from his spirit. In later years, detractors would charge Frémont with many a fault, but laziness would not be one of them.

The Cherokee survey is of further interest because it marks Frémont's first real encounter with Indians. Given the times and his Charleston upbringing, the young explorer brought a surprising liberality and openness to that encounter. As Nevins puts it, Frémont concluded "that the Indians were capable of being civilized, that their culture depended upon their physical and social surroundings, and that the Washington authorities were too changeable, lax, and political-minded to be trustworthy agents for their care." Yet, as did many another man of his day, Frémont believed that converting the Cherokees to Christianity was a vital and noble mission, and that removing them from their homeland—the cultural tragedy that would go down in history as the Trail of Tears—was good not only for the whites who would usurp their territory but for the Cherokees themselves.

In these formative years, we get little insight into the development of Frémont's character. He still seems vaguely ambitious, without any true sense of aim or direction. His love of nature and of journeying deepened, but he might well, save for further good luck, have ended his days as an unheralded surveyor and teacher of mathematics.

Rolle discerns a pattern emerging in Frémont's twenties of "keeping a barrier between himself and others." He quotes a companion from the Cherokee survey: "I am mystified with regard to the character of my companion, Frémont. The most taciturn, modest man I ever met . . . not readily drawn into conversation, looking at times as if he were resolving some difficult problem in Euclid." The observation is puzzling, for the Pathfinder in his glory years was anything but taciturn or modest. (True taciturn modesty was what stamped

Kit Carson—not Frémont.) Yet the seeds of the habitual secrecy that would sprout in Frémont's maturity may have germinated on these early journeys.

In 1838, Poinsett, by now secretary of war, commissioned his favorite protégé as a second lieutenant in the Topographical Corps. That appointment led directly to the long expedition surveying the little-known plains between the upper Mississippi and the upper Missouri Rivers, on which Frémont was second in command to the brilliant but sickly Joseph Nicollet. On this far-ranging jaunt out of St. Louis, which occupied the better part of two years, Nicollet served in effect as a one-man graduate school in surveying and map-making. And on the James and Red and Minnesota Rivers, Frémont came to appreciate the skills of the hardened voyageurs who, though technically under his command, gave him another graduate education in hunting, navigation, and survival in the wilds. Among them was Basil Lajeunesse, who on the 1842 expedition to the Wind Rivers would function as Frémont's right-hand man.

Three years after returning from his grand tour of the Midwest, when Nicollet would prove too ill with cancer to lead the expedition along the Oregon Trail, Frémont would get the best of all the breaks that thrust him toward his destiny as the Pathfinder. By 1839, thanks to Poinsett and Nicollet's favorable reports, the adventurer, still only twenty-six years old, was gaining a good reputation in Washington. The last piece of the puzzle came in 1840, when Poinsett introduced Frémont to Thomas Hart Benton, the senior senator from Missouri, now one of the most powerful men in Congress. Benton took an immediate shine to the topographer, convoking with him endlessly about his favorite topic, the Great West.

Before Frémont could bask, however, in the mentorship of the architect of American expansionism, he very nearly wrecked everything—his future career, his hopes of fame, even his personal honor—by falling in love with Benton's fifteen-year-old daughter.

Jessie Benton, second of the senator's six children and his favorite, may have been a teenage beauty, for by the age of fourteen she had already received several offers of marriage. "[I]t was clear," writes her only modern biographer, Pamela Herr, "that she would soon have her pick of Washington." A portrait of Jessie painted when she was thirty-two reveals a conventionally pretty, round-faced woman with dark eyes; about her mouth lurks a hint of prissiness.

To safeguard her chastity, her parents sent her off to Miss English's Female Seminary in Georgetown. Jessie hated the school. At a concert at the seminary one day in 1840, John Frémont saw his future wife for the first time. Almost fifty years later, in his unreliable *Memoirs*, Frémont would reconstruct that first meeting:

> She was then in the bloom of her girlish beauty, and perfect health effervesced in bright talk. . . . Naturally I was attracted. She made the effect that a rose of rare color or a beautiful picture would have done.

At twenty-six, Frémont was unmistakably handsome: everyone who described him singled out for mention his "piercing" blue eyes; some added an "aquiline" nose to the portrait. He was five feet nine inches tall, and even in his twenties grew a full beard. Later paintings give his face a severe look, with the trace of a fixed, incipient frown. In the only known photo of Frémont with Kit Carson, taken in 1849, the seated explorer, all but hidden by his cape, his hat, and his extravagant beard, rests gloomily with his hand on a cane, a look not far from fanaticism in his eyes. A decade earlier, when he first met Jessie, no doubt his face was more open, the eyes less pained.

The pieties of nineteenth-century biography later gilded the romance that began to unfold between the lieutenant and the teenager as a dramatic tale of potentially star-crossed lovers who concoct a happy ending. For a Victorian audience, the story of John and Jessie served as the American equivalent of Elizabeth Barrett's startling elopement and partnership with Robert Browning. Jessie herself would emerge as that Victorian paragon, the staunch and loyal woman behind the great man. The virtues that her contemporaries found so admirable tend to cloy us today—as does the saccharine and homiletic prose of her late writings (and of so much of her husband's silently "improved" reports and reminiscences).

Despite the literary conventions of true love at first sight, one wonders whether John Frémont initially saw in the fetching girl at Miss English's school only another possible seduction, a successor to

Miss Palmer in Buenos Aires and the jilted damsel in Greenville, South Carolina. Like Frémont himself, Jessie is hard to disentangle from her own mythologizing. Her biographer would see her as a feminist before her time, "a heroine too spirited for her age, too gifted to be readily contained within the narrow image of proper Victorian womanhood." Such a pedestal is too grandiose for Jessie Benton Frémont: in many respects, she was as thoroughly Victorian as heroines came in the mid nineteenth century.

Yet she must have been an interesting child. At her family's country home in Virginia, a passionate tomboy emerged, a hoyden who climbed trees and hunted ducks with slave children. She was as strong-willed and quick-tempered as her father, and her intense identification with the senator made her eventual fealty to Frémont all the more unlikely. Long after his death, she would still ache for the closeness with her father she had lost, writing almost mystically of a tender moment when he had caught the three-year-old Jessie up in his arms, "Did he even then feel the germ of that instinctive sympathy which made us one?"

Another demonstration of that instinctive sympathy came in a tantrum during Jessie's sixteenth year. Fed up with the whirl of Washington, with the curriculum in genteel manners in which she was steeped at Miss English's Seminary, one day Jessie took a pair of scissors, cut off her long, curly auburn hair, burst into her father's study, and announced she was finished with "society." She would henceforth stay home "to study and be [her father's] friend and companion," she declared, following the example of Madame de Staël. Appalled at the demonstration, the senator sent his wayward daughter back to Miss English's with the admonition to grow her hair back and learn to be a lady.

Whatever the depth of John and Jessie's initial attraction to each other, they began to court. Wrote Frémont in 1887, "And so it came that there was no room for reason." The girl who had no use for society, who wished only to stay at home and be her father's helpmeet, suddenly and violently transferred her passion to the handsome surveyor. Jessie's biographer, Herr, glosses that transfer with a piece of facile psychologizing: "Perhaps she sensed that here was a man who could cross the rivers and mountains that were only words in her father's mouth. She may have dreamed that he would carry out, as she, a woman, could not, her father's vision of a nation stretching to the Pacific."

More plausibly, both Jessie and John had streaks of pure willfulness running through their hearts. Perhaps the very fact that the courtship was forbidden gave it a strong allure. For Jessie's parents quickly grew alarmed by the young lieutenant's ardor. They made her, at sixteen, promise to wait a year before marrying; implicit in the bargain was the hope, as Herr puts it, that she "could make a far better match."

On a day that both later considered a point of no return—April 4, 1841—Frémont invited the whole Benton family to view the funeral procession of President William Henry Harrison (who had died just after taking office) from his workrooms at the Topographical Corps. There the lovers managed to talk and to pledge their undying troth.

As Jessie later reconstructed it, at this point her father may have persuaded Secretary of War Joel Poinsett, Frémont's first mentor, to send the lieutenant off on a hasty survey of the Des Moines River that even Nicollet, Frémont's boss, opposed. The ruse served only to keep the lovers apart for six weeks.

At this crucial juncture in Frémont's life, it is worth pausing to ponder just what the surveyor thought he was up to. With his dark view of the lieutenant's character, his biographer Andrew Rolle sees at this point in Frémont's life the formation of a full-blown narcissist. Spinning his psychoanalytic web, as always, from the hypothesized wound of the death of the explorer's father, Rolle argues that the loss "deprived Frémont of the ability to trust others. This distrust was, in turn, linked to his inability to attain full commitment to anyone, even in marriage."

With his theoretical bias, quoting Otto Kernberg, Rolle insists, "For such narcissists 'trust goes inside.' "

More prosaically, one might ask whether in Jessie, Frémont truly felt he had met the love of his life. Or did his passion for her, perversely, have everything to do with the stern disapproval of her father, the kind of man Frémont absolutely needed on his side to win the fame he sought?

In any event, in October 1841, Jessie eloped with her lover. John desperately sought a clergyman who would perform a secret wedding ceremony. After a Protestant minister turned him down, he managed to get the deed done by a Catholic priest in Washington. The details are murky, for as the 1856 campaign would prove, when slandermongers tried to prove Frémont a papist, that clandestine Catholic wedding could have cost the lieutenant much in worldly terms.

And secrecy failed in the face of the gossip that spread all over Washington, turning the elopement into the scandal of the season. At last, the young couple decided to face Thomas Hart Benton's music.

In a family tradition that may have its roots in Jessie's incessant self-mythologizing, Benton confronted Frémont with a livid command: "Get out of the house and never cross my door again! Jessie shall stay here!" Frémont, alternatingly pale and flush, was speechless, but Jessie thrust herself forward, took her husband's arm, and quoted Ruth in the Bible, " 'Whither thou goest, I will go; and where thou lodgest, I will lodge; thy people shall be my people, and thy God my God!' "

So, in one rash stroke, Frémont might have condemned himself to a scrounging, wandering life not unlike that his parents led after their own elopement had scandalized Richmond. But the explorer's uncanny luck would still hold for another five years, no more surprisingly than at this juncture.

Benton was known as the Thunderer for his fiery speeches in the Senate. But he was, for all his temper, not the kind of man who held a grudge. By 1829, as he was inaugurated president, Andrew Jackson could count on Benton as one of his strongest supporters—despite the fight with pistols and knives in the Nashville tavern fifteen years before that well could have cost Jackson his life. Benton could even joke about the fracas, telling the curious, "Yes, I had a fight with Jackson. A fellow was hardly in fashion then who hadn't."

In like manner, seeing that his favorite child had made up her mind, Benton repealed his outrage. He even invited Frémont to leave his boardinghouse and come live with Jessie in the Benton household. By the next May, as he set off for the Wind Rivers, the son-in-law Benton had hoped to banish forever had become the senator's loyal protégé. As early as 1825, with a bill to establish an

American port at the mouth of the Columbia River, Benton had begun to envision a country spreading from the Atlantic to the Pacific. Now, together—Benton behind his desk, Frémont astride his
horse—the two men set out to win the West for America.

5

THE HOWITZER

IN THE SNOW

RETURNING from the Wind Rivers in September 1842, Kit Carson took his leave of Frémont's party at Fort Laramie and headed south. Guiding the expedition along the Oregon Trail, at the princely salary of $100 a month, had been the best job Carson ever had; but that autumn, he harbored no expectations that he would hook up again with a government survey, nor that his life would intertwine with Frémont's for most of the next decade.

From September to January, Carson may have resumed his duties as a meat hunter for Bent's Fort on the Arkansas. No record from those months has survived, other than Carson's habitually laconic "I went to Bent's Fort" in his dictated memoir. We do know, however, that for most of a year Carson had been in love with a young woman in Taos named Josefa Jaramillo. As preparation to marry her, he had been baptized in the Catholic church the previous January—four months before he would meet Frémont on the Missouri River steamboat.

Josefa was the daughter of a well-to-do Hispanic landowner and, as such, a member of what passed for Taos aristocracy. The illiterate scout and ex-trapper was thus marrying considerably above his station. This, despite the fact that Josefa was only fourteen. The wedding took place on February 6, 1843, a month before the girl's fifteenth birthday.

A description of Josefa has come down to us from Lewis Garrard, the lively chronicler of the Taos Trail, who met her in 1846: "Her style of beauty was of the haughty, heart-breaking kind—such as would lead a man with the glance of the eye, to risk his life for one smile."

Unlike Frémont, Carson was no womanizer. His first wife, the Arapaho woman Waanibe, had died at least a year before; his second, the incompatible Cheyenne, Making-Out-Road, had kicked him out of her lodge. For the rest of his life, Carson would show no interest in any woman other than Josefa. He would die, in fact, only a month after she did, as much from grief as from illness. They lie today side by side inside a wrought-iron fence in the diminutive cemetery not far from Taos's main square.

For his part, Frémont did not reach Washington until the end of October. During his absence, with no news from the frontier, Jessie had set a place for her husband at the Benton dinner table every night. Although the 1842 expedition seems tame by the standards of Lewis and Clark or Zebulon Pike, it was fraught with more peril than any of Frémont's previous surveying jaunts. Charles Preuss, the cranky German cartographer, wrote in his secret diary that upon reaching an American Fur Company post in Missouri, the expedition learned that "people had almost given us up [for dead]," thanks to Jim Bridger's alarms about a Sioux rampage.

As Frémont arrived in Washington, Jessie was more than eight months pregnant. Two weeks after his advent, she gave birth to a daughter whom the couple named Elizabeth. Many years later, Jessie would recall that as he beheld the newborn, Frémont spread a tattered U.S. flag over mother and child, reciting, "This flag was raised over the highest peak of the Rocky Mountains; I have brought it to you."

Yet Jessie was deeply disappointed to have given birth to a girl, weeping as she bemoaned her failure to present her husband with an heir who would carry on the Frémont name. John himself was perfectly sanguine about having a daughter, as he struggled to reassure his wife. Pondering this discrepancy, one wonders whether Jessie's bitterness stemmed from the pat Victorian notion that great fathers should produce boys who might follow in their footsteps to glory, or from her profound identification with the two important men in her own life—or for that matter from her unsquelched tomboy nature, convinced as she was that all things manly were preferable to all things feminine.

Soon after his return, Frémont sat down to begin work on the official report summarizing the findings of the 1842 expedition, the book that would, on its publication the following spring, finally bring him the fame he so desired. It was by far the most serious challenge he had yet faced as a writer—his previous tasks amounting to little more than cartographic notes for Nicollet. His response was to be seized with writer's block. Start after start came to nothing. The paralysis took the psychosomatic form of incessant nosebleeds.

Finally, Jessie made a suggestion: that he dictate the report to her, who would write it down. This sidestepping of the phobia worked a charm. Through the winter months, the report cohered as the result of a most peculiar process. For four hours at a time, Frémont would pace his study, notes in hand, pouring out his words. Jessie wrote them down as fast as she could. "The freedom of movement," she later noted, "was essential to his freedom of expression." Frémont himself would later excuse his block with an odd periphrasis: "I write more easily by dictation. Writing myself I have too much time to think and dwell upon words as well as ideas." So neurotic was Frémont's compositional fit that he could not bear for Jessie, seated at her desk, pen in hand, to make the slightest "restless motion."

For the explorer, then, writing was an agony; for Jessie, the collaborative effort became "my most happy life-work." (She had already tried her hand at editing her father's speeches.) Frémont's apologists have long been at pains to insist that despite Jessie's prettifying touches, the reports essentially stand as his writing. Allan Nevins sets the ratio of creative contribution as nine to one in Frémont's favor.

These claims can hardly withstand a scrutiny of style. Frémont's official letters abound in leaden pomposities like the following: "I had the gratification to receive on the 6th. your letter of the 3d. Inst; and the farther gratification to receive yesterday by the hands of Lieut. Hunter your favor of the 10th. conveying to me assurances of your disposition to do any thing within the scope of your instructions to facilitate the public service in which I am engaged." The 1842 report is seamed with romantic effusions that owe more to Sir Walter

Scott than to stolid American bureaucratese, such as this moment in a Cheyenne village: "It reminded me of the days of feudal chivalry; and when, as I rode by, I yielded to the passing impulse, and touched one of the spotless shields with the muzzle of my gun, I almost expected a grim warrior to start from the lodge and resent my challenge." The same man could hardly have written both sentences.

Jessie herself helped propagate the myth that she was a mere passive amanuensis. As she penned the last sentence of the report, she later recalled, she burst out in joy, "I have not put to paper one half the beauty and truth you have shown me, but I have done the best I could, my darling!"

In March, the book, infelicitously titled *A Report of an Exploration of the Country Lying Between the Missouri River and the Rocky Mountains on the Line of the Kansas and Great Platte Rivers*, was published as a Senate document. The two senators from Missouri, Thomas Hart Benton and Lewis Linn, intended that the report serve as the chief propaganda instrument in their cherished campaign of manifest destiny. The immediate aim was to seize Oregon from the British. To that end, Senator Linn introduced a motion to print, at government expense, an additional thousand copies for sale to the general public.

The effort was well calculated. Not only did every congressman devour the brief narrative, but the thousand copies quickly sold out. As popular interest burgeoned, newspapers began reprinting long passages. Far from the West, in his Cambridge, Massachusetts study, Henry Wadsworth Longfellow was so captivated by the report that he considered writing an epic poem based on Frémont's journey. "What a wild life, and what a fresh kind of existence!" he scribbled in his journal.

There were three reasons in particular why the report seized the country's imagination. Thanks to Jessie, the narrative was indeed vividly written, full of those chivalric vignettes that seem so mannered today, but which gratified the readers of 1843: "My horse was a trained hunter, famous in the West under the name of Proveau; and, with his eyes flashing and the foam flying from his mouth, sprang on after the [buffalo] cow like a tiger." (No matter how attenuated Jessie's formal education had been, she had grown up surrounded by books and by men of ideas.)

Second, with Preuss's superb maps illustrating the route, the report served as a virtual guidebook to the Oregon Trail. Careless historians have sometimes attributed the mass emigration of the 1840s to Frémont's book alone; in reality, the momentum had already gathered by 1842, and even in Indian territory the exploring expedition had crossed paths with homesteaders heading west. But Frémont gave that momentum a colossal boost, and the fine passages, broadcast by newspaper excerpt and well-thumbed copies passed from hand to hand, turned many a settler's visions toward the land beyond the Rocky Mountains.

Third, and more particularly, the report painted a picture of the Great Plains as fertile rather than arid, in stark contrast to the gloomy earlier reports of Zebulon Pike and Stephen Long. The latter, for instance, in 1823, had dismissed the plains as "almost wholly unfit for cultivation, and of course uninhabitable by a people depending on agriculture for their subsistence." To be sure, Frémont himself had felt oppressed by the "desolation" of the thousand miles of prairie he had crossed to reach the Rockies, but in the report he balanced that response with encomiums on the fertile soil of the river valleys and the acres of billowing grasslands on either side.

It was the report, then, rather than the expedition itself—as was not the case for Lewis and Clark, Pike, or Long—that brought Frémont, as he turned thirty, his first heady dose of celebrity. Bernard De Voto would later memorably remark that Frémont's reports "were far more important than his travels." The comment is unjust: Frémont's expeditions were significant not so much for crossing land never before seen by Americans as for thrusting the Great West into the awareness of a nation hungry to expand. He was the classic example of the right man in the right place at the right time.

As Senators Benton and Linn were eager to prove. Even as the report hit the desks of congressmen, Frémont perused his War Department orders for a second and far more ambitious expedition into the West.

Just as, in 1842, plunging into the Wind Rivers, Frémont had gone beyond the letter of his instructions to pull off a flamboyant triumph irrelevant to his exploring mandate, so on his second expedition he would far exceed the orders given to him—which were, quite simply, to survey the Oregon Trail all the way to the Pacific. The expedition, planned for eight months, would last fourteen, radically overspend its budget, and cost the lives of two of its men. Yet upon publication of his second report, Frémont found himself lionized as a hero who could do no wrong.

During those fourteen months, the party's weary explorers covered a total of 3,500 miles—even more than Lewis and Clark had in twenty-eight months from 1804–6. It is not easy, however, to state precisely what the expedition achieved. Few of the long stretches of desert, river valley, and mountain range that the team traversed had not been previously explored by Americans. To a great extent, the outstanding accomplishment of Frémont's second expedition was to lay the groundwork for his third—the grandiose campaign that can and has been called, in both honorific and derisive senses, the Conquest of California.

By May 1843, Frémont was poised at Kaw Landing (the site of today's Kansas City), ready to head west again. "Never had an American exploring expedition, private or governmental," writes Nevins, "been better fitted out than this second body." Frémont's thirty-nine adventurers included the crème de la crème of the voyageurs lingering around Missouri, among them Basil Lajeunesse, the leader's "favorite man" in 1842. As guide, Frémont signed on Thomas "Broken-Hand" Fitzpatrick, one of the most experienced of all the mountain men in the West. But as the party started up the Kansas River, Kit Carson was not among their number.

For that matter, the expedition came perilously close to grinding to a halt before it really got in motion—all thanks to an utterly characteristic piece of overstepping on Frémont's part. The presentation of the expedition was considered a delicate matter by Frémont's superiors in the War Department. Without question, the explorer's mandate was to sniff out the British presence in Oregon, yet at the same time it was vital to avoid antagonizing Great Britain. The party, then, must have the look and feel of a harmless topographic survey.

Frémont knew this; yet, inexplicably, in St. Louis he requisitioned from the government arsenal thirty-three rapid-loading Hall carbines and a brass howitzer that shot 12-pound balls. It is hard to imagine why Frémont did so: his requisitioning letter cites the Indian danger, but he had learned from his first expedition that he didn't need a cannon to keep off hostile Indians. Could he have half-hoped to provoke a battle with British settlers in Oregon, and so turn manifest destiny into a shooting match?

Frémont's boss, Bureau of Topographical Engineers chief J. J. Abert, learned about the howitzer and hit the ceiling. On May 22 he sent a letter to Frémont severely castigating the lieutenant ("Now Sir what authority had you to make any such requisition[?]"), reminding him that "the object of the Department was a peaceable expedition," and ordering him at once to "desist in [the expedition's] further prosecution and report to this office." Unaware, as he watched his teamsters hitch mules to wagons at Kaw Landing, Frémont had come within an inch of being fired.

But the Pathfinder's extraordinary luck was still holding good: this time it came in the form of a timely intervention by Jessie. Abert's letter arrived at the Benton home in St. Louis. Jessie opened it and read it. "I felt the whole situation in a flash," she wrote many years later, "and met it—as I saw right." Rather than forward Abert's dismaying reprimand, she found a messenger and scribbled a two-line note to her husband: "Do not delay in Camp one minute longer. Trust me, and move westward at once." John read the note, wrote back, "Good-bye, I trust, and *go*," and immediately got his team on the road. By setting out at once for the West, Frémont eluded the recall that could have ruined his career.

So the topographic party trundled west, dragging their awkward howitzer across the prairie. So slow was the team's progress that voyageurs grumbled as they watched homesteaders—there would be 900 of them that summer, men, women, and children—outstrip them on the Oregon Trail.

Frémont veered south, looking for an alternative route to Wyoming's South Pass as a way to cross the Rockies. Somewhere near today's town of Pueblo, Colorado, Kit Carson heard the news that Frémont was nearby. "I wished to see him and started for his camp," Carson later dictated in his artless way. "My object was not to seek employment. I only thought that I would ride to his camp, have a talk, and then return." But when Frémont offered his old comrade a job as a guide, Carson accepted on the spot. Without even returning to Taos to say good-bye to the beautiful Josefa, his bride of a mere five months, Kit set out on a harrowing journey that would last more than a year. At thirty-three, Carson had not even begun to tame the itch of his wanderlust.

Frémont's register of disbursements from the expedition indicates that he paid Carson only $885 for the twelve months during which Kit was in his service, or about $70 a month. (Broken-Hand Fitz-patrick was paid twice as much.) If Carson resented the drop in salary from the year before, he never let on.

For all his grousing in his diary the year before, all the avowals of "never again," the still trail-soft cartographer Charles Preuss was along. Once more, the landscape bored him to distraction: "This is the most miserable country I have ever seen. Lüneberger Heide [a desolate heath in Germany] must be a paradise compared to this." And once more, he had no use for his commander: "Frémont be-came angry when my horse urinated. He whipped its tail when it had only half relieved nature."

By September, circling north of the Wasatch Range, the expedi-tion had reached the Great Salt Lake, first seen among white men by Jim Bridger in 1824. In Frémont's arsenal of gadgets was another inflatable rubber boat. Undaunted by his near disaster on the Platte the year before, the lieutenant launched this leaky craft on the lake and had his men row it to an island, where they camped overnight. On the way back, a late-summer storm came out of nowhere. Car-son dryly relates the close call: "Frémont directed us to pull for our lives, if we do not arrive on shore before the storm commenced we will surely all perish. We done our best and arrived in time to save ourselves."

Relatively uneventfully, the expedition made its way to Oregon. The Hudson's Bay Company agents whom Frémont met with were surprisingly cordial, given that they clearly foresaw a coming inter-national struggle over the territory. At Fort Vancouver on the Columbia River, to make a good impression at the company's headquarters, Frémont made a demand that incensed Preuss.

Mr. Frémont thinks I shall have to cut off my beard in order to make myself presentable. Nothing doing! That would be the last straw, to have the disagreeable feeling of a growing beard for two weeks just for the privilege of a few dinner invitations. No! No! I'd rather stay with the Indians in the tent, especially since we have good bread, butter, milk, and potatoes.

Although Preuss does not comment, it seems unlikely that Frémont cut off his own scraggly beard to please the British.

By this point, less than six months into the journey, Frémont had accomplished all that his orders bade. But now, rather than trudge homeward by the same path on which he had come out, Frémont began a long, meandering foray to the south. His ultimate motives can only be guessed at, but it does not seem far-fetched that the lieutenant had cooked up his plan in private sessions back in St. Louis with Senators Benton and Linn.

Frémont's party traversed Oregon from north to south, entered the corner of today's Nevada, and crossed the Great Basin (which the explorer named). By mid-January, beaten down by the rough journey of the past eight months, they camped in the relatively mild flats near what is now the town of Reno. Thirty-seven of the team's 104 horses and mules had died on the jaunt south from Fort Vancouver.

The obvious course would have been to head home toward Missouri. None of his superiors in the War Department—not even J. J. Abert, who seemed to have forgiven Frémont his howitzer—could have found much to fault in the ambitious reconnaissance the lieutenant had already performed. But at this juncture, with his incurable obstinacy, Frémont turned his tattered team to a task that nearly ended in disaster. Nor would the explorer learn anything from his near escape—except to repeat his folly five years later, this time with genuinely tragic consequences.

The decision was to cross the Sierra Nevada in midwinter and enter California. From the broad valley beneath the mountains, the party stared at the inaccessible crest of the jagged range, its highest summits looming fully 10,000 feet above them. The peaks were buried in heavy snows, which Indian informants told them were forty feet deep. Yet, unbelievably, Frémont argued that the very dilapidation of the animals—horseshoes falling off their hooves, which had been lacerated by the rocks; the mules and horses grown skeletal in their hunger—not only precluded an arduous push east, but made California logical. Kit Carson, who had trapped its inland valleys way back in 1830 with Ewing Young, painted a paradisiacal picture of the refuge to the west. Showing off his cartographic acumen, Frémont proved to his men that Sutter's Fort, the stronghold that the Swiss entrepreneur had built in 1839, lay only seventy miles away. He anticipated crossing those seventy miles in six or seven days. It would take five weeks.

Thus, in the sardonic words of Rolle, Frémont once again demonstrated "the capacity to rationalize even the worst of decisions and then to believe his own deceptions." Nor would he brook demurral. In his report, the explorer blandly claims, "My decision was heard with joy by the people, and diffused new life through the camp."

For a party in the condition of Frémont's, the wisest course would have been to winter over in the relatively benign basin east of the Sierra, nurse the mounts back to health, trade with the Indians, then head east in the spring. Carson, who had wintered over many a time in his trapping days, knew this in his bones; so did Fitzpatrick. Oddly (perhaps out of loyalty to the commander he would never discredit), in his memoir Kit deals with this foolhardy decision in one unjudgmental sentence: "We were nearly out of provisions and cross the mountain we must, let the consequences be what they may." Even the grumbler Preuss records the fateful decision without a word of criticism.

Had Frémont simply underestimated the Sierra Nevada, his folly would have been more understandable, but he was given unambiguous advice by the leading experts on the range—the local Indians. In sign language, these people (probably Washos) endeavored to convey to the lieutenant that the range was uncrossable in winter; again and again, they repeated the word *tahve*, or snow. When Frémont tried to hire an Indian guide, "They looked at the reward we offered, and conferred with each other, but pointed to the snow on the mountain, and drew their hands across their necks, and raised them above their heads, to show the depth; and signified that it was impossible for us to get through." The Indians even tried to sketch for Frémont a safer, more southerly route, but the explorer dismissed their wisdom: "They seem to have a confused idea, from report, of whites who lived on the other side of the mountain. . . ."

In 1843, no party of Anglos had crossed the Sierra Nevada in midwinter. (Three years later the Donner party of emigrants would come to grief making much the same crossing that Frémont intended.) As if this were not reason enough to dissuade the commander, the journey he was about to attempt was illegal, for Mexican authorities had forbidden entry to California to all Americans. On top of a survival ordeal, the lieutenant was inviting an international incident: in charge of a government-authorized surveying expedition, he was about to invade a foreign country.

This was, of course, the appeal of California to the ambitious topographer. Those private discussions with his father-in-law had no doubt touched time and again on California, for manifest destiny eyed not only the British holdings in Oregon, but the vast and fruitful northern frontier of Mexico. It may be hard to remember today, but in 1843 not only California, but all of Utah, Arizona, Nevada, and New Mexico, as well as half of Colorado and the southwest corner of Wyoming, belonged to Mexico.

Already the glimmerings of conquest that would burst out in the Mexican War in Texas three years hence could be seen on the horizon. As yet, Americans had little knowledge of California, but Senator Benton had no doubt that Mexico's hold on that promised land was weak. Indeed, in 1843 only some 10,000 Mexican citizens lived in the territory, nearly all of them near coastal missions in such towns as Los Angeles and Monterey. As Nevins writes, California "was like a great ripe fruit, ready to fall into the first hand that touched it." One of those grasping hands, the expansionists feared, might be British.

On February 2, the team set out to cross the Sierra. The first day they covered an encouraging sixteen miles; the second, seven. By the fourth day, they were in deep snow, and the trail breaking had become horrendous. Floundering in the drifts, the exhausted horses and mules gave up; only by jettisoning their packs could the men force them onward. Carson reported that the horses began to eat not only the pack saddles but each other's tails.

Three days before setting out to cross the range, with great reluctance Frémont had abandoned his precious howitzer. The team had dragged it almost 2,000 miles without firing it once in action.

Near the crest of the range, the men began to play out like the animals, which were dying daily. One man, Baptiste Derosier, became deranged, wandered off, and was never seen again. (So Frémont maintained in his official report; but scholars Donald Jackson and Mary Lee Spence discovered that the canny voyageur survived his solitary ordeal, returning, after what must have been extraordinary tribulations, to Missouri more than a year after the expedition.) Preuss managed to get separated from the main party; he spent three days lost, surviving only by eating acorns and live ants. "This is beginning to get serious," he wrote in his journal. "I couldn't find the others again. . . ." Though dogged about trying to live off the land, in his despair he addressed his absent Trautchen: "Oh, my old sweetheart! If you knew how badly off I am at the moment!"

Finally, on February 20, the party reached the crest of the range at 9,300 feet. Gazing west through a telescope, Carson recognized landmarks from his journey fourteen years before. The expedition stumbled on, reaching Sutter's Fort two weeks later. They had lost half the sixty-seven horses and mules they had started across the range with. Given one more blizzard, the whole party might have perished. Even Carson, no stranger to privation, admitted, "When we arrived at the fort we were naked and in as poor a condition as men possibly could be."

In his official report, Frémont could not come to grips with how close a call he had inflicted upon his party. The narrative unfolds as a facile adventure story, alternating triumphs and hardships: "We now considered ourselves victorious over the mountain. . . . We had hard and doubtful labor yet before us. . . . We continued to enjoy the same delightful weather. . . . We grew very anxious as the day advanced and no grass appeared. . . ." On the eve of reaching Sutter's Fort, Frémont is in a self-congratulatory mood, noting "a repast of good beef, excellent bread, and delicious salmon, which I had brought along" as his team's "first introduction to the luxuries of the Sacramento."

To his credit, no one ever questioned Frémont's own physical hardiness. One of his men on the second expedition later vouched, "I thought I could endure as much hardship as most men, especially a small, slender man like . . . Frémont, but I was wholly mistaken."

For the next two weeks, as his men recuperated at Sutter's Fort, Frémont discussed at great length with the Swiss emigré the Mexican future in California. From the governor in Monterey, Sutter had won the remarkable permission to build his stockade at the junction of the American and Sacramento Rivers, on the site of today's city of Sacramento. Implicit in the deal was an understanding that the fort would form a buttress between the tamed mission Indians along the coast and the "wild" Indians of the interior. Though swearing his allegiance to Mexico, Sutter felt a strong affinity for the Anglos. Now he spoke freely with the young lieutenant.

Meanwhile, into the valleys of northern California, all but bereft of Mexicans, a slow trickle of illegal American and British home-steaders had begun to flow. By the time of Frémont's visit, perhaps 1,200 such settlers had infiltrated the territory. Already thinking of conquest, Frémont saw these rough-hewn pioneers as potential re-cruits in an action against Monterey. In the meantime, however, he was at pains to keep his government-sponsored invasion as low-profile as possible. Leaving Sutter's Fort, the expedition moved south into the blooming spring all the way to the Spanish Trail, staying inland to avoid contact with Mexican officials.

It would take the party four more months, starred with all kinds of misadventures, to regain St. Louis. One of Frémont's men was killed by Indians; another shot himself in the head, either by acci-dent or as a suicide. Among all the episodes in that long journey home, one stands out as curious and ambiguous: no matter how we read it, it casts a suggestive light on Kit Carson.

In the San Gabriel Mountains east of Los Angeles, in late April the team ran across a pair of addled and desperate Mexicans, an old man and a boy of eleven. On foot, they were the sole survivors, they said, of a Mexican party that had been ambushed by a hundred Paiutes, who had also stolen the team's thirty horses. Frémont of-fered them food and an escort, but was reluctant to delay his home-ward excursion with any retributive raid against the Indians. Within another year, these very Mexicans would become the lieutenant's chosen adversaries.

But when the party came upon the trail of the Paiutes, Carson and another mountain man, Alexis Godey, volunteered to pursue the Indians. It must have seemed unlikely odds, two white men against a hundred Paiutes, but Carson was in the prime of his self-confident life.

As Kit later recollected, "Godey and myself volunteered with the expectation that some men of our party would join us. They did not." No matter. The two ex-trappers trailed the Indians all day and into the night. At dawn they crept unobserved to the edge of the Paiute camp, but a skittish horse gave them away. Guessing the number of the foe at thirty, Carson and Godey charged on foot. These fearless hellions must have struck terror into the Indians, for despite their superior numbers, they fled. Carson and Godey killed two Paiutes; having taken an arrow through the shirt collar for his pains, Godey scalped the victims.

Frémont adds some detail. On the second afternoon, his party heard what sounded like an Indian war whoop, only to see Carson and Godey galloping up from a distance, driving the recaptured Mexican horses ahead of them, Godey swinging a pair of bloody scalps from his rifle.

Frémont's account of the killing is far more dramatic than Carson's. One of the Paiute victims, he recounted at second hand, sprang to his feet, mortally wounded, and let out "a hideous howl." Among the fleeing horde, an "old squaw, possibly his mother, stopped and looked back, . . . threatening and lamenting. The frightful spectacle appalled the stout hearts of our men; but they did what humanity required, and quickly terminated the agonies of the gory savage."

Charles Preuss was appalled by the scalping, which he also credited to Godey. "Are these whites not much worse than the Indians?" he asked his diary. An Indian, Preuss insisted, honorably lets out a war whoop before confronting the man he hopes to kill. Carson, however, had shot a fleeing Paiute in the back. "Godey rode into camp with a yelling war cry, both scalps on a rod before him." Tellingly, Preuss added, "To me such butchery is disgusting, but Frémont is in high spirits. I believe he would exchange all observations for a scalp taken by his own hand."

Frémont, indeed, felt nothing but admiration for Godey's rough brand of justice. In his report, he paused to offer this encomium: "In courage and professional skill he was a formidable rival to Carson, and constantly afterwards was among the best and most efficient of the party, and in difficult situations was of incalculable value."

Carson's frank recollection in 1856 of the vengeance he and

Godey had meted out a dozen years before proves at the very least
that by 1844 he had not revised the code first taught him by Ewing
Young. There were good and bad Indians, and it was an honorable
thing to exact retribution on the nearest band of Paiutes for whatever deed other Paiutes might have perpetrated. (In this case, the
recovery of the horses argues that Carson and Godey had trailed the
right band.)

On the other hand, Carson himself refrained from the scalping
that, according to Frederick Ruxton and others, had been de rigueur
only a few years before. Did this restraint spring from any new
squeamishness about the act, or did Godey simply beat him to the
prize? Certainly in this instance, Carson showed as much alacrity to
chase and punish Indians as he had eleven years before, when, with
the other mountain men who had recaptured their horses from the
Crows, Kit was in the vanguard of the contingent that demanded a
bloody battle to cap off the revenge.

Within the coming year, Carson would begin to rethink those ba-
sic mountain-man axioms about Indians, rules of conduct in which
he had been steeped since he had killed his first Apache at age nineteen.

Once more, Jessie had waited patiently for her husband's return, this
time in the Benton mansion in St. Louis. Each night during his long
absence, she not only set a place for him at dinner, but made up his
bed and left a lamp burning in the window. As Frémont's journey
lengthened to six months beyond its allotted span, she grew fretful
and anxious. In the spring of 1844, a rumor filtered back to St. Louis
that the whole party had disappeared making a winter crossing of
the Sierra Nevada; Jessie's friends kept this alarming intimation
from her ears.

Frémont arrived in St. Louis in the early morning hours of August 5. Rather than wake Jessie from her sleep, he sat till dawn on a
bench in front of a nearby hotel. Decades later, she remembered her
first sight of her prodigal husband: "awfully worn . . . , thin, brown,
and as hungry as I had foreseen." According to family legend, John
"scarcely stopped to greet his well-wishers before gathering his
young wife in his arms and carrying her off to bed."

Two weeks later, back in Washington, John and Jessie began to compose the second report. Nevins insists, "They made a delightful partnership of the undertaking"; Jessie later looked back on these months as "the happy winter." But it is hard not to view the resumption of their peculiar, neurotic collaboration as an ordeal, at least for John. His psychosomatic nosebleeds took up where they had left off two years before, the last time he had had to write; added to them were debilitating headaches. He ground on, however, through the winter, doggedly putting in his four hours of dictation a day, and Jessie turned the scattered details into prose. On March 1, Frémont presented to the War Department a narrative three times as long as his first.

The success of the first report paved the way for the *grand éclat* that greeted the second. This time, Congress authorized a printing of 10,000 copies for sale to the public. The newspapers scrambled to publish excerpts. The debacle over the unauthorized howitzer long forgotten, President Tyler cited the explorer "for gallant and highly meritorious service" and promoted him to brevet captain. Writes Nevins, "Frémont found himself one of the heroes of the hour, holding such a place in the popular imagination as . . . Admiral Byrd and Colonel Lindbergh later gained."

In 1845, the two reports were published in a single volume, which went through six American and two British editions. The impact of these narratives was enormous. Perhaps the most consequential effect they had on history came as Brigham Young, dreaming of a new Zion for his latter-day saints, fixed on Frémont's rhapsodic description of the Great Salt Lake as a destination for the pilgrims he would lead west in 1847.

How often does celebrity thus taunt her subjects with fickle hints of everlasting glory! That spring of 1845, Frémont must have sensed that the world lay all before him. He was only thirty-two years old, and all his grandest campaigns lay still inside his head. But from the hindsight of a century and a half, we can see that this was the moment of zenith in the explorer's life. Wreathed with laurels, his name on everybody's lips, the derogations that would harry him to his grave as yet inchoate, Frémont strode along the avenues of the nation's capital like a Greek warrior charmed by the gods.

In terms of manifest destiny, the United States stood poised on a pivot. Tyler had been cautious about expansion, wary of offending Great Britain and Mexico. But in the November election, James K. Polk had defeated Henry Clay. No more land-hungry president would ever occupy the White House. In his inaugural address, Polk announced the country's "clear and unquestionable" title to Oregon, and he spoke of the "acquisition of California"—by purchase or treaty, he implied, rather than by war. Even before Polk took office, he met privately with Senator Benton and his son-in-law, the newly famous explorer.

In early 1845, Congress authorized $50,000 to finance Frémont's third expedition. By June, the newly minted captain was in St. Louis recruiting personnel. The scene, in an enclosure near the Planter's Warehouse, turned chaotic, as a crowd of several hundred fervent would-be volunteers drowned out Frémont's remarks.

So was launched a journey that, in Nevins's words, "was destined to play a more dramatic and controversial role than any other expedition of the kind in American annals; a role which seemed at the time to change history, and which is even yet wrapped in partial mystery, and the subject of vigorous dispute."

By late June, the expedition, traveling much faster and lighter than the howitzer- and wagon-hindered 1843 entourage, was headed west. Frémont had hired seventy-four men, including twelve Delaware Indians. Among them was, once again, his favorite voyageur, Basil Lajeunesse, who had less than a year to live, and Alexis Godey. For the first time, however, Charles Preuss remained in Washington, deferring to Trautchen's wishes and fears. There would be no iconoclast penning a secret diary on this expedition.

On August 3, the party paused at Bent's Fort on the Arkansas, while its leader sent a messenger south into New Mexico. Kit Carson had finally settled down, starting a cattle ranch with his good friend Dick Owens in the lush Cimarron Valley east of Taos. It was time to start a new way of life, to invest in a solid business. As Carson would later recall, apparently without irony, "Dick Owens and I concluded that, as we had rambled enough, it would be advisable for us to go and settle on some good stream and make us a farm."

Kit had brought Josefa to the Cimarron, perhaps hoping to start a family. It would be seven more years, however, before they had their first child.

As Frémont's messenger arrived on the Cimarron, Carson and Owens were busy planting grain, clearing timber, and building "little huts." The resolves of the homebound year vanished in an instant. Carson and Owens immediately sold their ranch ("for about half it was worth," Carson sourly noted), and rode north to join the expedition. "This was like Carson, prompt, self-sacrificing, and true," Frémont later tipped his hat.

Kit Carson would not return home for another thirteen months, and when he did, it would be to spend a single night with Josefa before heading out again. The settled life would have to wait.

6

PERFECT BUTCHERY

THE essential mystery haunting Frémont's third expedition has to do with the colossal gulf between his official orders and what the explorer actually set out to do. For a century and a half, historians have tried to prove whether or not Frémont acted under covert orders known only to a handful of government officials. Was the third expedition in effect a secret war mission under the cover of an innocuous scientific foray? Or, as he had done so often in the past, did Frémont play the supreme opportunist, ignoring his orders so as to position himself to seize the glory he could see wafting on the wind?

No written document has yet been found to bulwark the theory of an expedition guided by secret orders. Frémont himself never came clean on the question. If there was a covert mandate, we can be sure that the captain never shared it with any of his underlings. From start to finish, the mountain men and Delaware Indians who rode with Frémont believed they were along on a surveying mission that happened to collide head-on with international politics.

What makes the matter all the more odd is that, in the wake of the explorer's bold 3,500-mile journey of 1843–44, the mandate given him in 1845 should have been so timid. J. J. Abert, head of the Topographical Corps, charged Frémont only with surveying "the geography of localities within reasonable distance of Bent's Fort." More specifically, he was to ascertain the navigability of the Red and Arkansas Rivers, and to explore only "the streams which run east from the Rocky Mountains." He was also ordered to "come in during the present year"—i.e., by the end of December 1845.

Had Frémont obeyed the letter of his mandate, he would have journeyed no farther west than the headwaters of the Arkansas, near today's high town of Leadville, Colorado. In the event, Frémont stretched his expedition to the Pacific Ocean, and from his allotted six months in the field to a spectacularly turbulent campaign that lasted more than two years, ending with the erstwhile hero under arrest.

Having picked up Kit Carson at Bent's Fort, Frémont headed west without hesitation. The long trek across Colorado, Utah, and Nevada proceeded like clockwork. The only tricky passage came west of the Great Salt Lake, as the party paused on the edge of a vast, waterless desert. Carson knew nothing about this wasteland; among Anglos, only the redoubtable Jedediah Smith was supposed ever to have crossed it; the local Indians, however, insisted that no man, white or Indian, had traversed the desert. Sixty miles away, beyond this forbidding malpais, Frémont spotted a mountain that he named Pilot Peak. He sent Carson and three other scouts off at night, with a mule loaded with water, to see if they could make the crossing in a single forced march. The next day, he led the rest of the expedition only halfway across, to await a prearranged smoke signal from Carson that would indicate it was safe to move ahead.

Frémont had bribed a local Indian to serve as guide for the party, but as they approached the midway point, the man's knees gave way and "he wabbled about like a drunken man." "He was not a true Utah," Frémont jauntily recalled many years later, "but rather of the Pi-utes, a Digger of the upper class, and he was becoming demoralized at being taken so far from his *gite* [inn]. Seeing that he could be of no possible use I gave him his promised reward and let him go."

The smoke signals were exchanged that night, and in the morning the large team pushed ahead. On the skirts of Pilot Peak, they found plenty of grass, water, and firewood.

Unlike the captain's rash plunge into the Sierra Nevada the previous February, this was a soundly conceived exploratory gambit. Thanks to the plucky effort of Carson and the other scouts, the party tamed a badlands that even the Indians declared fatal. But like the Sierra crossing, this desert dash would help convince Frémont that he could pull off almost anything he tried. The seeds of the disaster that would bloom in 1848 were planted in such bold plunges into the unknown.

Those plunges also counted much, in Frémont's mind, toward establishing his standing as a discoverer of new lands. From California, only three months after his desert crossing, he would write Jessie, urging her to "[t]ell your father" that he had single-handedly overturned the notion of the Great Basin as an arid, barren country; it was instead, he wrote (exaggerating like some desert chamber of commerce), "covered with grasses of the best quality, wooded with several varieties of trees, and containing more deer and mountain sheep than we had seen in any previous part of our voyage." Raising his voice to catch Benton's ear, he boasted, "[I]t is fair to consider this country as hitherto wholly unexplored, and never before visited by a white man." (Long dead, Jedediah Smith could not wave his hand in protest.)

As the expedition wound on, Frémont began to put his firmest trust in three men: Carson, Godey, and Dick Owens. In his *Memoirs* in 1887, the explorer paused to pen an encomium of the trio:

> The three, under Napoleon, might have become Marshals, chosen as he chose men. Carson, of great courage; quick and complete perception, taking in at a glance the advantages as well as the chances for defeat; Godey, insensible to danger, of perfect coolness and stubborn resolution; Owens, equal in courage to the others, and in coolness equal to Godey, had the *coup-d'oeil* of a chess-player, covering the whole field with a glance that sees the best move.

The expedition reached the foot of the Sierra Nevada in early December. That two-month jump on winter, compared to the February start two years before, made all the difference. Instead of forty-foot snowdrifts, this year the party had to contend only with a dusting of new snow. The traverse of the great range took little more than a week, and involved only routine hardships.

Writing Jessie from California on January 24, Frémont looked back on that easy crossing: "Now, the Sierra is absolutely impassable, and the place of our passage two years ago is luminous in snow." It is an odd admission, for the conditions in the mountains as he wrote were no worse than they had been in February 1843. Waxing visionary, Frémont bragged that his trek had demonstrated that emigrants might travel from Bent's Fort to Sutter's in only thirty-five days. It would be going too far to lay any real part of the blame for the next year's Donner Party tragedy to Frémont; but he certainly contributed to the climate of blithe optimism about crossing the Sierra in winter that led that party to their doom.

At Sutter's Fort, which its Swiss founder called New Helvetia, Frémont was greeted with open arms. The captain thought he had slipped in and out of California in 1844 unobserved by government officials. Now he learned, to the contrary, that "our previous visit had created some excitement among the Mexican authorities." Sutter had covered for the Americans, baldly insisting that the party, on "a geographical survey of the interior," had been forced through the mountain snows "simply to obtain a refuge and food" where Frémont knew he could find help.

Like Bent's Fort on the Arkansas, Sutter's Fort has been expertly reconstructed in situ. The prairie and river bottom surrounding the replica of Bent's Fort seem almost as lonely as they did in the 1840s. The rebuilt California stockade, on the other hand, stares bizarrely out not at the grasslands where hostile Indians once crept, but at the offices and apartment buildings of downtown Sacramento. It takes an effort of imagination to conjure up what a blissful refuge New Helvetia must have seemed to Frémont's men in December 1845. Like Bent's Fort, Sutter's was chockablock with useful rooms and shops, including a surgeon's office, a barrel maker's store, a blanket factory, a bakery, and comfortable low-ceilinged bedrooms. In the courtyard, Sutter supervised Indian soldiers drilled by German mercenaries. In the midst of the wilderness, the sturdy stockade defined a frontier ideal of civilized sophistication (Sutter shared with Frémont bottles of his favorite Rhône wines from his well-stocked cellar). On Charles Wilkes's 1841 map of the Pacific coast, New Helvetia is the only settlement shown between Fort Vancouver and San Francisco.

Frémont's plan, now that he found himself in California, was to explore up the Sacramento River north into the Klamath country and the Willamette Valley, which homesteaders already had their eyes on. Thus he hoped to blaze a shorter, easier route to the Oregon Territory than the Oregon Trail itself.

Before he could set out on that mission, however, he took eight men on a side trip to Monterey, where he hoped to meet not only the Mexican authorities, but the American consul, Thomas Larkin. He traveled under a passport issued by John Sutter, who had been granted such powers by the government. The pretext for this journey was to buy provisions and gear for his seriously depleted expedition. Frémont assumed his most deferential mien, reassuring the Mexican officials that he was a topographer, not a soldier, that he "came in the interests of trade and science," that all he asked was "what the scientific workers of one nation might justly request of the courtesy of another." In reality, Frémont's goal was both simpler and cagier. In Nevins's succinct formula, "He was killing time."

For at the moment, Zachary Taylor's troops were marching toward the Rio Grande. The Mexican War was within weeks of commencing. Stretched far too thin over too large a territory, torn by upheavals in the capital, Mexico was losing its grip on the empire founded three centuries before by Cortés. In California, the authority was divided between Los Angeles, where Pío Pico served as civilian governor, and Monterey, where José Castro was military commandant. That spring of 1846, a civil war among Mexicans in California seemed as likely an outcome as any other.

California, then, in Nevins's pithy phrase, had become "a derelict craft, ready to be picked up by any captain who would take it into the port of a strong and stable government." Though nothing would come of the threat, all interested Americans in 1846 genuinely feared a British takeover of the territory.

The campaign that Frémont waged in and around Monterey that March plays not as the heroic drama the captain aimed at, but as opéra bouffe. Frémont met with Thomas Larkin (who would have been privy to any secret orders), then with José Castro, who grudgingly granted the explorer the right to buy supplies. Then, rather than head back to Sutter's Fort, Frémont made himself comfortable in the Santa Clara Valley, at the hacienda of one of the several American settlers uneasily tolerated by the Mexican government. There he was reinforced by the remainder of his large entourage. In

his *Memoirs*, Frémont speciously insists that this interlude was moti-
vated by a search for "the home I wished to make in the country" in
later years.

For Castro, this was the last straw. On March 5, he sent Frémont
a letter unequivocally demanding that "on receipt of this you will
immediately retire beyond the limits" of California. Still Frémont
lingered. Even Larkin seemed perplexed. The consul wrote the captain, explaining as if to a child that Castro was perfectly within his
rights to order Frémont out of the territory: "You are officially ordered to leave the Country; I am shure [*sic*] you will use your own
discretion on the subject." Frémont's disobedience, Larkin went on,
"may cause trouble hereafter to Resident Americans."

Frémont's impetuous response might have turned into a tragedy,
had it not devolved into farce. President Polk was still hopeful of
winning California through peaceful negotiations. Frémont's very
presence in California, with a well-armed army of what were unmistakably American soldiers, could constitute an act of war.

On March 6, Frémont ordered his men to the top of a flat
promontory called Hawk's Peak in the Gabilan Mountains (Fremont State Park today commemorates this takeover). There they
cobbled together a makeshift fort and raised the American flag. On
March 8, Castro issued a proclamation condemning the "band of
robbers" who had infiltrated the country, and pleading for volunteers to help him "lance the ulcer" of the invasion.

This blustering threat brought out the melodramatic streak in
Frémont. From Hawk's Peak, he wrote Larkin to explain that "I am
making myself as strong as possible in the intention that if we are
unjustly attacked we will fight to extremity and refuse quarter, trust-
ing to our country to avenge our death." In the captain's fantasy,
perhaps he hoped to concoct a California Alamo out of his flimsy
fort. But, as Bernard De Voto mordantly put it, "Nobody was ready
to confer martyrdom on him. . . ."

A motley gang of Mexican soldiers and volunteers marched toward the peak, thought better of opening fire, and retreated. On the
third day, the flagpole fell down. Frémont told his men they had
done enough to salvage American honor, and began his march back
to Sutter's Fort.

If Kit Carson found this whole misadventure absurd, he kept his feelings to himself. In his memoir, he saves his scorn for José Castro: "We remained in our position on the mountain for three days, had become tired of waiting for the attack of the valiant Mexican General." Another seasoned mountain man whom Frémont had hired, however, was less reticent. Joseph Reddeford Walker was so disgusted with the failure to have it out with the Mexicans on Hawk's Peak that he quit the expedition. Years later, he told an interviewer, "Frémont, morally and physically, was the most complete coward I ever knew. . . . I would say he was timid as a woman if it were not casting an unmerited reproach on that sex."

Whatever game Frémont thought he was playing in California, it was a dangerous one. Had fighting broken out between Castro's forces and the sharpshooters on Hawk's Peak, it is doubtful that President Polk would have stood behind the explorer's gratuitous provocations. Thomas Larkin's dismay suggests that if Frémont indeed was acting under secret orders, they did not extend to taunting the Mexicans into an armed battle.

Frémont's own publications cast very little light on this murky matter. Thanks to the turmoil of its denouement, there would be no official report from the third expedition. When Frémont at last composed his *Memoirs* more than four decades later, he was at pains to obfuscate his motives in California. Having quit Hawk's Peak on March 9, in that narrative he takes up the return to Sutter's Fort and subsequent foray northwards as if it were the most natural continuation of the expedition imaginable, implying that the standoff with Castro was a mere distraction in the otherwise smooth course of his exploratory jaunt.

In a letter to Jessie written on April 1, Frémont waxed indignant about the impasse with the Mexicans:

> Without a shadow of a cause, the governor suddenly raised the whole country against me, issuing a false and scandalous proclamation. Of course I did not dare to compromise the United States. . . . I refrained from committing a solitary act of hostility or impropriety. For my own part, I have become disgusted with everything belonging to the Mexicans.

Unless he deliberately misled his wife in this letter, Frémont was planning to leave California soon: "[A]bout the middle of next month, at latest, I will start for home. . . . Glad will I be when we finally turn our faces homeward." He had already overstayed his official leave for the expedition by three months.

A few days before, the party had reached Lassen's Ranch, some two hundred miles north of Sutter's Fort. Peter Lassen, a Dane, had worked for Sutter as a blacksmith, then struck out on his own in 1844 to homestead here, spreading his livestock along the fertile banks of Deer Creek, a small eastern tributary of the Sacramento River. (The handsome, isolated volcano of Mount Lassen, in plain sight to the northeast, would be named for him.) The Dane greeted Frémont's party with all the hospitality his Swiss colleague had, so the explorer decided to lay over for a few days.

Those days stretched into a month. It was clear that Frémont was still marking time, carrying on the pretense of his topographic survey while keeping his ear cocked for the sounds of gunfire emanating from Monterey.

During the four months his party had already spent in California, Frémont had fought the occasional skirmish with raiding bands of Indians along the trail. He had quickly adopted the Mexican taxonomy for the genus *Indio,* distinguishing between the "good" Mission Indians who labored faithfully for their Hispanic betters, and the "bad" Horse-thief Indians, many of them rebels who had broken out from the missions to return to their aboriginal ways.

James Clyman, a percipient American settler from Virginia, saw as Frémont could not the demoralized fiefdom to which the "good" Indians had been reduced. Visiting Sutter's Fort in July 1845, he jotted a memorable vignette in his notebook:

> The Captain [Sutter] keeps from 600 to 800 Indians in a perfect state of slavery. I had the mortification of seeing them dine. A lot of troughs, three or four feet long, were brought out of the cook room and set out in the broiling sun. All the laborers, great and small, ran to the troughs like so many pigs and fed themselves with their hands as long as the troughs contained the least bit of moisture. There was no need of cleaning up after them.

To Frémont's men, on the other hand, the "wild" Horse-thief Indians were fair pickings. After one confrontation on the Merced River that cost several Indians their lives, Frémont wrote Jessie, "Tell your father that I have something handsome to tell him of some exploits of Carson and Dick Owens, and others."

On this glancing battle, Frémont lavished four full pages of his *Memoirs*. He even essayed a rudimentary ethnography of his foe: "The Horse-thief tribes have been 'Christian Indians' of the Missions, and when these were broken up by Mexico the Indians took to the mountains. . . . Familiarity with the whites and the success of their predatory excursions made the Horse-thief Indians far more daring and braver than those who remained in fixed villages. . . ."

It is all the more astonishing, then, that in his *Memoirs* Frémont expends not a single word on an episode that occurred during his long stay at Lassen's Ranch. Among all the battles fought against Indians by the men on all five of Frémont's expeditions, this inexcusable and ignoble attack deserves a special place of infamy in the annals of the West. Instead, it has all but escaped the record. Carson sketches its onset:

> During our stay at Lawson's [*sic*], some Americans that were settled in the neighborhood came in stating that there were about 1000 Indians in the vicinity making preparations to attack the settlements; requested assistance of Fremont to drive them back. He and party and some few Americans that lived near started for the Indian encampment. Found them to be in great force, as was stated. They were attacked.

In Carson's telling, then, Frémont rode at the head of this punitive army. Thanks, however, to a memoir dictated by one of the participants, Thomas S. Martin, in 1878, we have the only full account of the debacle that is ever likely to surface. It is worth quoting in full:

> When we got back to Deer Creek the settlers of that section were very much alarmed, the indians having threatened to massacre them all, and it was reported that they were already gathering for that purpose. They asked Fremont to protect them. He refused as

he had no right to fight the inds. but he told us that those who
wished [to] take part in an expedition against these indians he
would discharge, and take us again afterwards. Four of our men
were hired by the rest to stay and take care of our camp while all
of the remainder were gone in the expedition. At the foot of the
low hills where the Sac. riv. comes out of the mts., on the left
hand side of the river going up we found the indians to the number of 4000 to 5000 on a tongue of land between the bends of the
river, having a war-dance preparatory to attacking the settlers.
Our advance guard of 36 first came in sight of them and immediately charged and poured a volley into them killing 24. Then
they rushed in with their sabres. The rest of the party coming up
they charged in among them and in less than 3 hours we had
killed over 175 of them. Most of the inds. escaped to the neighboring mts.

Martin's estimate of 4,000 to 5,000 Indians is wildly exaggerated;
even Carson's guess of 1,000 is surely too high. But there is no reason to doubt Martin's body count of "over 175." One other patchy
mention of the "battle" has survived, in the form of a manuscript in
the University of Missouri archives; in it another participant,
Thomas E. Breckenridge, put the number of Indians more realisti-
cally as "150 bucks and 250 squaws and children." Breckenridge
goes on to say, "There was some 120 to 150 Indians killed that day."

One must read between the lines of these dry recitals to plumb
the full horror of the massacre: three steady hours of killing, women
and children cut down beside the men. If there were no other reason to doubt that the victims were engaged in a war dance, the apparent fact that Frémont's men suffered not a single casualty would
argue that they had attacked an unprepared and peaceful assemblage.

In the Sand Creek Massacre in eastern Colorado in 1864,
Colonel John M. Chivington laid waste a village of Cheyenne and
Arapaho Indians who were suing for peace, slaughtering some 200
men, women, and children. On Aravaipa Creek in 1871, in what
has been called the blackest day in Arizona history, a gang of Tucson
vigilantes attacked an Apache camp, killing between 125 and 144.
The last of the notorious Indian massacres came in 1890, when the

Seventh Cavalry murdered about 150 Sioux at Wounded Knee, South Dakota.

All three of these massacres provoked a nationwide outcry, and their perpetrators were brought to account—though in all three cases, the punishments were minimal (a Tucson jury acquitted the vigilante leaders of the Apache massacre after deliberating for nineteen minutes). A century later, the names Sand Creek, Aravaipa, and Wounded Knee have become touchstones for Anglo persecution of Native Americans at its most diabolical.

Yet here, on a tongue of Sacramento River bottomland in 1846, Frémont gave his government soldiers carte blanche to perpetrate an unprovoked massacre in every respect the equal of Wounded Knee or Aravaipa, and Carson and the others carried it out with grim efficiency. Not only were Frémont and his men never called to a reckoning for this slaughter; the massacre itself has slipped between the cracks of history. The reasons for this are various.

At the time, neither Frémont nor his soldiers had any qualms about the justice of their attack near Lassen's Ranch. Martin tells us that to celebrate their victory, the veterans lingered for a two-day dance with the jubilant settlers. Of the party's subsequent march north, he goes on blandly to recount, "We followed up the Sac. river killing plenty of game, and an occasional indian. Of the latter we made it a rule to spare none of the bucks."

Carson himself concluded that the attack had taught the Indians a proper lesson: "[We] had accomplished what we went for and given the Indians such a chastisement that [it] would be long before they ever again would feel like attacking the settlements."

Yet the slaughter must have disturbed the seasoned mountain man, for Carson adds, "The number killed I cannot say. It was a perfect butchery."

Here is the first note in Carson's autobiographical narrative of doubt over an Indian killing. That hint of regret, piercing the confident code of wilderness conduct by which he had lived for the past fifteen years, marks the onset of a slow and thoughtful evolution in Carson's heart, the dawning glimmer of a humanitarianism all but unknown among the unlettered veterans of the fur trade. Carson would never become a true pacifist, but he would emerge as a champion rather than an antagonist of the Indian. In the terrible persecution of the Navajos in the 1860s that led to the Long Walk, Carson's ambivalence would burst to the surface, vexing his soul, but in the end mollifying what might otherwise have been a campaign of relentless genocide.

Who were the victims of the massacre on the Sacramento River? One measure of how thoroughly this catastrophe has disappeared into a trackless vortex of the past is that we cannot ascertain with any certainty what tribe suffered the annihilation. The natives whom Frémont's men attacked were not what he called Horse-thief Indians; they had never known the paternalism of the missions. They were indigenes who had lived in the Sacramento Valley for at least centuries, maybe millennia.

Today the region surrounding the tongue of land where the massacre took place is more sparsely inhabited than it was in 1846. The only town is Vina, a forlorn collection of two or three stores, a gas station, and a handful of tumbledown houses. The surrounding fields are given over to walnut, almond, and olive groves. No Indians now live in this vicinity. None of the locals has ever heard of Frémont's long-ago massacre, and only a few can point out the brush-choked river shelf where Lassen's Ranch once flourished.

In 1846, however, the site of the massacre stood exactly at the common corner of the homelands of three distinct peoples—the Maidus, the Wintus, and the Yanas. We can be sure that one of these three tribes suffered the devastating massacre; but even to make an educated guess as to which requires a certain amount of anthropological sleuthing.

At the time of first contact, California possessed a greater ethnic complexity than any other part of what would become the contiguous United States. Fully a hundred different tribes lived along its fertile valleys and mild seacoast. These peoples belonged to six different major language groups. The Wintus, whose homeland ranged along the west side of the Sacramento River, and the Maidus, who occupied the quadrant southeast of the Deer Creek–Sacramento confluence, were Penutian speakers, linked thus to such other peoples as the Miwoks and the Modocs. North of the Maidus, the Yanas, who were subdivided into four distinct dialect groups, spoke a Hokan tongue.

What the three tribes shared in common was a lifeway based principally on acorn gathering and salmon fishing. They ranged with the seasons to hunt game—deer, elk, antelope, and rabbits—and to gather other edible plants. Yet compared to all the mountain and Plains tribes Kit Carson had dealt with during his trapping days—Arapahos, Blackfeet, Utes, Sioux, Shoshones, and the like—these California Indians were relatively sedentary. They built sturdy round houses out of earth, thatch, and wood, and they made beautiful decorated baskets woven tight enough to cook with.

Thanks not only to warfare but to the ineluctable spread of diseases, the Indians of California were literally decimated by the encroachment of first Spanish, then Mexican, then American civilization. S. F. Cook, the leading expert on the nineteenth-century demography of Native Americans in California, estimates their total population in 1831 as 111,900. By 1880, they would number only 12,500.

The first great plague to hit the California interior was an epidemic that lasted three years, from 1830 to 1833. As Kit Carson pushed into the Sacramento Valley with Ewing Young on his first long trapping expedition in 1830, he may have witnessed the early ravages of this disease. In a brilliant piece of historical detective work, Cook traces the epidemic's origins to Fort Vancouver on the Columbia River, in July 1830. From there, the plague spread south into California's Central Valley. Usually referred to as "ague" or "intermittent fever" in the contemporary accounts, the disease's identity remains uncertain: Cook rejects smallpox, typhus, and cholera, concluding that malaria was the most likely agent.

By 1833, when the plague peaked, according to Cook's estimates, some 75 percent of the Indians of the Central Valley had died (more than 20,000 people in 1833 alone). This means "that three-quarters of the Indians who had resisted seventy years of Spanish and Mexican domination were wiped out in one summer."

The accounts of early travelers abound in gothic evocations of the plague's toll. At the mouth of the Feather River in 1844, Charles Wilkes came across a chilling sight: "[T]he ground was strewed with the skulls and the bones of an Indian tribe, all of whom are said to have died, within a few years, of the tertian fever, and to have become nearly extinct in consequence. . . ." William D. Breckenridge in 1841 came across another abandoned village where 1,500 Indians were supposed to have perished: "[T]he bones lay strewed about on the hills in all directions, there not being enough of the Tribe spared—as we were told—to bury the dead."

Despite the depredations of the mission system, by which the Spanish had virtually enslaved huge numbers of Native Americans, the Hispanic impact on California's Indians was relatively benign compared to the American, as launched by explorers such as Frémont and settlers such as Pierson B. Reading (for whom the town of Redding is named), to be culminated after 1849 in the onslaught of prospectors who sometimes hunted "redskins" for sport.

Cook distinguishes between the Hispanic and American attitudes toward Indians. The Spanish encouraged interbreeding; "The American civilization, on the contrary, viewed miscegenation with the greatest antipathy. . . . All Indians were vermin, to be treated as such. . . . The native's life was worthless, for no American could even be brought to trial for killing an Indian." From 1847 to 1880, Cook concludes, some 4,000 California Indians were killed by American soldiers and settlers. Frémont's massacre thus set in motion a campaign of wholesale extermination the likes of which the nation has seldom seen before or since. That campaign is all the more inexplicable in view of the fact that, unlike the Blackfeet or the Chiricahua Apaches, such tribes as the Maidus and Wintus had no reputation as warriors.

What, then, was the threat that led the settlers near Lassen's Ranch to plead with Frémont to wipe out the Indians gathered on the banks of the Sacramento? To be sure, the indigenes resented the whites who without asking permission had begun to settle in their homeland. They conducted the occasional raid, even took the occasional settler's life. But the large gathering that spring was almost certainly not a party gearing up for war.

Says Jim Johnston, archaeologist for the Lassen National Forest, "Those people could have been Wintu, Maidu, or Yana. It's hard now to tell which group it was. What the settlers saw was no doubt *not* a war dance. In March and April the salmon run up the Sacramento River—that could explain the gathering. It was a big social occasion. There would have been dances. And the Maidu used to have a spring ritual they called the Bear Dance."

That April of 1846, then, the Indians whom Frémont's men so casually slaughtered had most likely gathered to celebrate some seasonal round in their economic and social lives. Further evidence comes from the ethnographies of each of the three peoples whose misfortune it was that spring to have Frémont's army blunder through their homelands.

In the 1840s, the Wintus were a prosperous, powerful tribe. Cook estimates their 1831 numbers as 14,250 men, women, and children. According to Cora Du Bois, in *Wintu Ethnography*, there were many reasons for large numbers of the people to gather in a given place: for the salmon run, to distribute an abundance of food, to burn the grasslands and rid them of grasshoppers, for deer and bear hunts, or for a girl's puberty rite. One subgroup, the Dau-nom, or Bald Hills, tribelet, came each spring and fall to the Sacramento River near Deer Creek to fish the swarming salmon.

The Wintus had a war dance, for which they painted faces, upper bodies, and legs black, but it was held after a battle, not before. The dance centered around an enemy scalp hung from a pole; in battle, the Wintu scrupulously took only a single scalp for that purpose. Du Bois goes on to point out, "The Wintu were a nonbelligerent people. Their warfare was usually nothing more pretentious than a neighborhood feud originating in quarrels between individuals. . . . War was not waged by large numbers, nor were more than a few individuals killed."

The Maidus counted the Yanas among their traditional enemies. Numbering about 8,000 people in 1831, the Maidus were virtuosi of acorn processing and basket weaving. They were also famous as distance runners. Aside from an occasional skirmish with the Yanas, the Maidus were a predominantly peaceful tribe. "[T]here was no open warfare with the [Yanas]," writes Marie Potts in *The Northern Maidu*, although "they would sneak into our camps when the men were gone and kill or carry off the helpless ones."

The Maidu bear dance was held every spring "when the first edible shoots came through the ground." A rite of thanksgiving for having survived the winter, the dance aimed to appease the bear spirits. One man wearing a bearskin imitated the great beast, while the people feasted, prayed, and played games. Though it seems farfetched, it is just possible that such a ritual was the one the settlers mistook for a tribe making preparations to massacre the settlers.

Both the Wintus and the Maidus were threatened with extinction by the end of the nineteenth century. Cook found only 940 Wintus still alive in 1918, and 900 Maidus in 1910. But both peoples rebounded from this low ebb. Though much dispersed geographically and ethnically assimilated, there are many Indians alive today who are at least part Maidu or Wintu.

A massacre such as the one Frémont's men performed in March 1846 may all but escape the Anglo record, but it is not likely to fade from tribal memory. The most compelling argument that the Indians wiped out on the banks of the Sacramento that spring were neither Wintu nor Maidu lies in the fact that neither people preserves any oral tradition of such a catastrophe.

This leaves the Yanas. Much less populous than their neighbors to the south and west, these mountain dwellers numbered only about 1,900 in 1831. Hostilities between whites and these natives were not recorded before 1851. The homeland of the southernmost of the four dialectically distinct subtribes—the Yahi-Yanas—ranged down Deer Creek almost to the Sacramento.

By 1880, according to Cook, the Yanas numbered only 12. Unlike the Wintus and Maidus, they had no chance to recover. But in the act of disappearing from the earth, the Yanas left the most poignant memorial in all American Indian annals to what it meant to live on the edge of extinction. After a disastrous massacre in 1865, when 40 to 45 of the people were killed on Mill Creek by white settlers, the remaining Yanas hid in the mountains. During the following decades, only the occasional theft from a cabin or furtive sighting in the woods testified to their survival.

By the turn of the century, it was supposed that the Yanas had vanished. Then, one day in 1908, surveyors for a power company accidentally stumbled upon the last Yana village (known to the people as Wowunupo'mo tetna, or "Bear's Hiding Place"); the startled denizens fled in terror. Three years later, on August 9, 1911, a man who had reached the absolute limits of fear and exhaustion appeared without warning in the corral of a slaughterhouse near Oroville.

He would become famous as Ishi, "the last of his tribe." A Yahi-Yana, he would survive for another five years, installed as a kind of living exhibit in the University of California Museum of Anthropology in Berkeley. During those years, thanks to an extraordinary collaboration with his scientist "keepers," Talbot Waterman and A. L. Kroeber, Ishi delivered an ethnographic portrait of his dwindling people unique in the anthropological record. The story is superbly told in Theodora Kroeber's *Ishi in Two Worlds*.

During those decades in hiding, Ishi's handful of fellow Yanas had hung on in a remote lava canyon on Deer Creek, only ten miles above its junction with the Sacramento. The sanctum, in Waterman's words, was "wild and comparatively impenetrable, a wilderness of rocks and undergrowth, masked by clumps of pepperwood, and encircled by the towering cliffs." The Yanas supplemented hunting and gathering in their circumscribed fastness with the occasional raid on an empty cabin or poaching of a stray sheep.

Though Kroeber and Waterman were able to learn in exquisite detail the tragic particulars of his people's last years, by 1911 the memory of Frémont's massacre had so faded among Californians that no one thought to ask Ishi about the 1846 debacle. Was that slaughter on the Sacramento, which would have cost the Yanas the lives of a sizable portion of their total population, the disaster that set them on the slow road to extinction? We have no way now of knowing for sure, but the possibility lingers among the dismal annals of Indian affairs in California like a wraith of doom.

On April 24, Frémont's party headed north from Lassen's Ranch. During the next two weeks, they followed the Sacramento River to its headwaters, skirting lordly Mount Shasta on the west, then crossed a low pass and followed the Klamath River into Oregon Territory. In his *Memoirs*, Frémont vaguely indicates his goal: "to connect my present survey of the intervening country" with the route his expedition had made coming south two years before. In addition, "I wished to penetrate among the mountains of the Cascade ranges." In the end, Frémont would get nowhere near the Cascades.

As he traveled, the explorer botanized away, collecting flowers and plants, took temperature readings, and figured his latitude and longitude. Insisting that he passed through country "never explored or mapped," Frémont named lakes and rivers right and left after childhood friends from South Carolina (fortunately these names failed to stick). As they entered the homeland of the Klamath Indians, the party kept up its guard, for these natives, Frémont averred, "were known to be hostile and treacherous, with a fixed character for daring."

On the outlet of Upper Klamath Lake, at the site of today's town of Klamath Falls, the expedition traded for dried fish and salmon with the first Klamaths they had encountered. "Our arrival took them by surprise," noted Frémont, "and though they received us with apparent friendship, there was no warmth in it, but a shyness which came naturally from their habit of hostility."

On May 9, the party camped in a grove of junipers on a winding creek that flows into Upper Klamath Lake from the west. Frémont spread his blanket on the ground, making a pillow out of his rifle covered with a juniper bough. Three fires crackled in the night. The leader had just fallen asleep, only to be wakened by Carson's call to Basil Lajeunesse: "What is the matter over there?" There was no answer. Then Carson yelled out, "Indians!"

"I heard a noise as of an axe striking," Carson later recalled. As he and Dick Owens ran toward the disturbance, they saw that Lajeunesse's skull had been split open with a sudden blow of an ax. Next to him, a Delaware named Denny had also been killed in his sleep. Another Delaware, known only as Crane, stood in the firelight, trying to hold off the attackers by swinging the butt of his unloaded rifle; five arrows planted in his breast quickly laid him low. A fearless warrior whom Frémont called "the Tlamath chief" single-handedly held the white men at bay for long minutes, while his comrades retreated, until a pair of rifle shots finally felled him. Expecting their attackers to make a second charge, the addled soldiers posted guard, one man to each nearby tree, and stayed up the rest of the night, rifles cocked, peering into the gloom.

In the morning, according to Frémont, Carson approached the body of the slain "chief," seized an English half-ax that dangled from the Indian's wrist, "and knocked his head to pieces with it, and one of the Delawares, Sagundai, scalped him." Carson later recalled, "He was the bravest Indian I ever saw. If his men had been as brave as himself, we surely would all have been killed."

Shocked by their reversal, Frémont's men moved warily on in the morning, carrying the bodies of their dead companions. "Of the three men killed," Carson would testify, "Lajeunesse was particularly regretted. He had been with us in every trip that had been made. All of them were brave, good men." In dense forest, the party found it impossible to carry their dead, for "the bodies knocked against the trees, and becoming much bruised, we concluded to bury them when we did." Half a mile off the trail, the three were laid in shallow graves scraped out of the hard ground and covered with logs and brush.

The surviving Delawares were particularly distraught at the loss of their two men. They went into formal mourning, blackening their faces. "Very sick here," said one of them, Swonok, striking his chest, as Frémont tried to console him. Scouting in the forest, the Delawares found signs of Indians nearby. They asked the main party to move on while they laid an ambush. When they caught up a few hours later, they were carrying two scalps. "Better now," said Swonok. "Very sick before, better now."

Yet that killing by the Delawares was not sufficient retribution for either Frémont or Carson. Two days after the attack in the night, the party circled Klamath Lake on the north and west and approached the main Klamath village, which was scattered along both shores of the Williamson River. Frémont sent Carson and Owens ahead to reconnoiter, but before he could bring the main body of the party up, firing erupted. In his usual laconic way, Carson indicates that, as he approached the Klamath village, a commotion broke out: "I knew that they had seen us and, considering it useless to send for reinforcements, I determined to attack them, charged on them, fought for some time, killed a number, and the balance fled."

More than twenty Klamaths died in this action. After the natives had abandoned their village, Frémont ordered his men to burn it to the ground and to smash or burn all the Klamath canoes.

In his *Memoirs,* Frémont would maintain that, as he had approached the scene of carnage, he saw "a dead Indian sitting in the stern of a canoe, which the current had driven against the bank. His hand was still grasping the paddle. On his feet were the shoes which I thought Basil wore when he was killed." Scholars doubt this facile confirmation of Klamath guilt. The village which Frémont's men destroyed—called Dokdokwas, in reference to the osprey, or fish hawk, once ubiquitous on the lake—was that of the

Eukskni subtribe of the Klamaths. They were almost certainly not the Klamaths who had attacked Frémont's camp in the night—if indeed those stealthy warriors were Klamaths at all. One of the region's first settlers, the Klamath reservation's first agent, Lindsay Applegate, would insist that he learned from informants that Frémont's attackers were Modoc Indians, traditional enemies of the Klamaths.

Over the course of three expeditions, Kit Carson had saved John C. Frémont's life a number of times. Only hours after the attack on the village, Frémont would save Carson's life. Mopping up after the "battle," Carson, Frémont, and four others pushed into the forest after fleeing Klamaths. Suddenly, they stumbled on a Klamath scout drawing an arrow. Carson tried to shoot, but his rifle misfired. With the arrow aimed point-blank at Carson's chest, Frémont fired at the scout and missed, then instinctively charged his horse, Sacramento. The sleek animal "was not afraid of anything, and I jumped him directly upon the Indian and threw him to the ground. His arrow went wild." Running up, Sagundai, a Delaware, clubbed the scout to death. "It was the work of a moment," Frémont reflected, "but it was a narrow chance for Carson."

This close call in the forest sounds like another of Frémont's chivalric inventions, but it is corroborated by Carson, who gives a similar account. In a characteristically homely sentence in his memoir, Carson voiced his lasting gratitude: "I considered that Frémont saved my life for, in all probability, if he had not run over the Indian as he did, I would have been shot."

Up Denny Creek, named by Frémont for his fallen Delaware, a rutted dirt road leads today. Tall ponderosa pines stand over the grove where, a century and a half ago, Frémont made his camp among the junipers. An old powerhouse, built in the 1920s, stands derelict beside the creek. From this quiet glade, the distant shore of Upper Klamath Lake can just be glimpsed.

The spot is almost never visited by tourists, although the Daughters of the American Revolution built a small monument some years ago. The plaque reads:

Denny Creek
Here
John C. Fremont
Camped on His Second
Journey of Exploration
In May of 1846, Was Attacked
By Indians and Lost Three Men
For One of Whom He Named
The Stream

Despite the numbering error (it was Frémont's third journey in the West), the plainspoken legend eschews the jingoistic tone so common to monuments to slain American heroes. It states a historic fact, avoiding questions of motivation or blame.

No plaque or monument stands at the site of Dokdokwas. On either bank of the crystalline Williamson River, tall grasses billow in the wind. There is no sign that anyone ever lived here.

The Klamath people, however, flourish today around the town of Chiloquin, east of the lake. Here in 1864, the Klamath reservation was established. After Washington bureaucrats forced the outnumbered Modocs to live cheek-by-jowl with their hated enemies, in 1872 a group of 160 men, women, and children under the charismatic leader Kientpoos, or Captain Jack, fled the reservation and occupied the lava beds south of Tule Lake, at the heart of their own homeland. When the U.S. Army marched on these fugitives, the Modoc War began; it would prove to be one of the bitterest of all the Indian campaigns, the only one in which a full-fledged general (E. R. S. Canby) was killed.

The reservation was officially terminated in the early 1950s. Today, as the Klamath Tribes, the Modocs, Klamaths, and their erstwhile neighbors the Yahooskins live in multiethnic harmony on land they themselves own, where once the reservation hemmed them in. Among Native Americans, these people are relatively well off, sharing the profits of a major timber industry and their jointly run Kla-Mo-Ya Casino. The Klamaths alone number some 3,200 souls today. In towns such as Klamath Falls, unfortunately, a wide streak of anti-Indian prejudice still poisons Anglo hearts. (Hanging in the Favell Museum, which boasts of its collection of 60,000

Indian arrowheads, is a painting called "The Death of General Canby," in which the Modoc warriors are portrayed as wild, slack-jawed, apelike monsters.)

But Frémont's attack on Dokdokwas has not been forgotten. As if recalling an event that happened a few years ago, Gordon Bettles, culture and heritage director for the Klamath Tribes, conjures up the fatal day: "The men were out hunting. Old men, women, and children were all that was left at camp. Without warning, the soldiers went in and started the slaughter. Some boys got away, swimming in the river, using reeds to breathe under water.

"In school, we Klamaths were told this should all be forgotten. But the event is very vivid in oral memory. We wonder how they can honor that man. Frémont set the pattern as to how we would be treated for the next fifty years.

"Some members of our tribe have been over there at the right time of year, and they can hear horses whinnying, rifle shots, and the ghosts of women and children screaming."

7

NEMESIS

THROUGHOUT the rest of his life, Frémont would agonize over the fact that on the night of May 9, 1846, for only the second time on his expedition, he had failed to post sentries around his camp. The reason was that he was distracted, by the advent of a most unlikely messenger.

Archibald Gillespie, a young lieutenant in the navy, had left New York the previous November, crossed Mexico, and sailed to Monterey via Hawaii, carrying a confidential message from Secretary of State James Buchanan. In Mexico, to avoid detection, he had memorized the letter and destroyed it. On arriving in Monterey, he wrote it down once more and delivered it to the consul, Thomas Larkin. The text of this missive has survived: in essence, it commanded Larkin to attempt to foment a peaceable annexation of California by the United States. The territory's Hispanic citizens were to be wooed, not conquered. And Larkin was to "exert the greatest vigilance in discovering and defeating" any British attempt to take over California.

Yet having delivered this dispatch to Larkin, Gillespie set out on horseback to find Frémont. After a dangerous six-hundred-mile ride through Indian country, he had sent a pair of messengers ahead to give Frémont notice. The captain had immediately backtracked. The meeting with Gillespie had taken place in the grove of junipers at sunset on May 9.

"[H]ere we are confronted," writes Allan Nevins, "by the most baffling problem of Frémont's career." What message did Gillespie deliver to the explorer? In his *Memoirs*, Frémont lavishes three long pages on the excitement of Gillespie's arrival, while managing to circumlocute the question of exactly what he was told. The essence of the message, he writes, "absolved me from my duty as an explorer, and I was left to my duty as an officer of the American Army." What Frémont realized, during those animated hours of private conversation in the juniper grove, was that "[t]he time has come. England must not get a foothold. We must be first. Act; discreetly, but positively."

It was the turn of events the explorer had spent his five months in California waiting for. It might, he sensed, be the greatest stroke of fortune in his life. Still without saying precisely what Gillespie told him, Frémont acknowledges that fortune in his *Memoirs*: "I saw the way opening clear before me. War with Mexico was inevitable; and a grand opportunity now presented itself to realize in their fullest extent the far-sighted views of Senator Benton, and make the Pacific Ocean the western boundary of the United States." At the moment, the captain headed the only detachment of the U.S. Army that was anywhere near California. He decided at once to return to the Sacramento Valley "to bring to bear all the influences I could command."

Frémont scholars Mary Lee Spence and Donald Jackson conclude that the captain told his men, as one of them wrote in his journal, that Gillespie had carried "orders directly from the United States for us to return to California," but that in fact he acted on his own initiative. Frémont himself says vaguely that "I resolved to move forward on the opportunity," but in his next breath adds, "This decision was the first step in the conquest of California."

Thirty-eight years after that meeting with Gillespie, the young Harvard philosopher Josiah Royce, who had been born in California during the Gold Rush, interviewed Frémont in his old age as background for his brilliant, angry book, *California, from the Conquest in 1846 to the Second Vigilance Committee in San Francisco*. By then, Gillespie's errand had become enshrined as a pivotal turn in the glorious legend of the Pathfinder. Wrote Royce, "The meeting was a romantic one, but its romance sounds very hackneyed now, since the tale has been repeated in so many books of Western adventure."

Throughout his long interview with the young professor, Frémont equivocated in much the same way he would three years later when he dictated his *Memoirs*, dancing all around Royce's central question. He did admit that the thrust of Gillespie's message was that there was no doubt the American government intended to take California, "by force if necessary." Hovering near the interview, Jessie put in her two cents' worth: she had been privy to the frequent discussions between her father and Secretary of State Buchanan, whose purport she summed up in a single sentence: "Since England intends to take California, we must see that she does not."

This, however, was still a far cry from a direct order to intervene militarily. Royce, who wore his hostility to Frémont on his sleeve, was at pains to prove that the captain took upon himself his subsequent actions in the "conquest." From the distance of a century and a half, one is inclined to agree. Probably the message Gillespie conveyed was itself ambiguous, falling short of an order to wage war. In his old age, Frémont could have his cake and eat it too. To Royce and in his *Memoirs*, he would not lie about Polk's or Buchanan's instructions, claiming a direct order that would have flouted international law. Meanwhile the legend that had fossilized around the conquest painted him as a hero carrying out his government's secret orders. He would neither confirm nor contradict such a flattering myth.

As Royce sardonically put it, "a violation of the laws of nations, under circumstances of peculiar atrocity," was transmogrified in the popular mind into the deeds of "a gallant, energetic, and able young officer, who thenceforth gets general credit as faithful secret agent of his government and heroic defender of his countrymen, as well as savior to us of the territory of California."

So Frémont led his men back south. They set up camp near Sutter Buttes in the Sacramento Valley. Settlers pleaded with him to lead them into battle against the hated Californians, but Frémont bided his time. On May 13, the U.S. government declared war against Mexico, several days after Zachary Taylor had fought the first battles of that war in Texas. It would be some time, however, before the news reached California. Meanwhile, in Monterey, José

Castro had ordered all noncitizens to prepare to leave the territory.

The powder keg was ready; all it would take was a match to light the fuse.

The sortie that would go down in history as the Bear Flag Revolt may or may not have originated in Frémont's brain. Anticipating military action, the captain had set his sights on Sonoma, a small town forty miles north of San Francisco. There, in 1823, Franciscans had founded the Mission San Francisco de Solano, the northernmost of the string of missions that formed California's backbone and the only one founded by Mexico after its independence from Spain. Eleven years later, General Mariano Vallejo was ordered to build a town around the mission; the reason was to forestall not the British, but Russians who, from their stronghold in Alaska, might reach south with their colonizing tentacles.

By 1846, there were cannons, rifles, ammunition, and horses in Sonoma, but no soldiers to defend the sleepy outpost. In his *Memoirs*, Frémont says that he sent a settler named Ezekiel Merritt to Sonoma with "instructions to surprise" the town—this although Merritt was not a member of his expedition, and the captain had no authority to tell him to do anything. Whether or not Frémont appointed Merritt—a rabble-rousing zealot bent on seizing California from the Mexicans—his "field lieutenant," as he claimed, he certainly nudged the man toward Sonoma.

On June 14, at the head of a ragtag band of 33 armed settlers, Merritt surprised General Vallejo as he lay sleeping in his bed. The mob arrested the general and his two junior officers and marched them off to Frémont's camp. On the spot, the conquerors improvised a crude flag that juxtaposed a red star and a bear walking awkwardly on its hind legs, raised it over the barracks, and proclaimed the Republic of California. (The flag was patched together out of a chemise belonging to the wife of one of the "revolutionists" and a petticoat belonging to another.) The Republic of California would last a grand total of twenty-five days.

For the patriots of the era, there was nothing ludicrous about this takeover. Like the Boston Tea Party, it was seen as a bold stroke by common Americans to overthrow their oppressors. The next year,

in San Francisco, a Fourth of July orator would stir the crowd by declaring that "no tyrant hand is laid upon [the Californians], but the
glorious American eagle spreads her balmy wings over even a conquered people, and affords them protection and freedom."

In Sonoma ever since 1846, the Bear Flag Revolt has been played
in much that same vein. Around the town square today, the historic
buildings (some of them now nestling boutiques and wine-and-
cheese shops) sport plaques evoking the town's role in the conquest.
The Blue Wing Inn boasts that Carson and Frémont slept here. In
1996, the Native Sons of the Golden West planted a time capsule
on the corner of the plaza where the bear flag was first raised. Above
city hall, a replica of the flag flies side by side with the star-spangled
banner (the original is archived by the Society of California Pioneers in San Francisco).

For Josiah Royce, on the other hand, the Bear Flag Revolt was "a
very curious episode of California history—one that seemed to some
of [its perpetrators] afterwards ineffably glorious, and that in fact was
unspeakably ridiculous, as well as a little tragical, and for the country disastrous." And Bernard De Voto penned a satiric vignette of
the arrest that launched the revolt:

> They told Vallejo that he was a prisoner of war. He had some dif-
> ficulty understanding what war he was a prisoner of and set out
> brandy for his captors, so that they could talk it over. Conquerors
> and conquered wrote out a formal statement of terms, and by its
> third paragraph, the product of good native liquor, the California
> Republic was born.

In the perspective of history, the Bear Flag Revolt reads almost as
comedy; but there was nothing comic about the cultural clash that
set it in motion. To the rough-and-ready American squatters in California, the Mexicans were "greasers," indolent, thoughtless, poetic
people, incompetent to govern. The American right to the territory
inhered in the moral superiority of the Americans' culture.

As late as 1928, a historian as otherwise perspicacious as Allan
Nevins could slip into Hispanic stereotypes: the clash, he wrote,
pitted "Anglo-Saxon against Latin, Protestant against Catholic,
strenuous pioneer against loiterer." (Even more egregiously, Nevins

would sum up all the Indians in the California interior in one dismissive formula: "Both physically and mentally, this lazy, treacherous, and thievish race were greatly inferior to the best plains Indians, like the Sioux or Cheyenne.")

Indeed, the legacy of racial conflict between Anglos and Hispanics that stretches into the present day may be the central sociological fact about California. The melting pot has not begun to dissolve those old prejudices about the gay, indolent "greasers."

Writing four decades before Nevins, having grown up in the state, Josiah Royce saw racial antagonism lying at the heart of the tragedy of the conquest of California:

> From the Bear Flag affair we can date the beginning of the degradation, the ruin, and the oppression of the Californian people by our own. In all subsequent time the two peoples, as peoples, have misunderstood and hated each other, with disastrous effects for both, and especially for the weaker. . . . Yet much of this hatred might have been saved, had we come peaceably and openheartedly. We came, as it seemed to them, by stealth, and we used unprovoked violence.

For Royce, the culture of California before the American invasion was a sophisticated one, marked by hospitality, generosity, and a modest agrarian life centered on the ranchero. In contrast, he was not impressed with the caliber of mountain men such as the ones that made up Frémont's army: "However worthy our American merchants and immigrant families often were in those days, our trappers and other like homeless wanderers in California in the years before 1846 were commonly a very far worse set than the Californians." The conquerors, in Royce's view, were not the self-styled paragons of the Bear Flag Revolt, but rather "the carelessly brutal American settler or miner."

Frémont received General Vallejo and his two fellow captives and sent them on to be imprisoned at Sutter's Fort. Unfortunately, he had not consulted with its owner. Having flourished in California since 1839 thanks to the good graces of Mexican officials, John

Sutter was outraged by the arrest of Vallejo, and he let Frémont know it. The short-tempered captain, however, flung the outrage back into Sutter's face, telling him, according to a witness, "that if he did not like what [Frémont] was doing, . . . he could go and join the Mexicans." All the hospitality over the years that Sutter had lavished on the explorer was now repaid by Frémont's telling the Swiss that he would be severely punished if the prisoners escaped, then by summarily putting his own man Edward Kern in charge of the fort.

About this time Frémont began signing his dispatches "Military Commander of U.S. Forces in California." He had already overstayed his expedition leave, as specified in J. J. Abert's original instructions, by almost six months, but his good angel still perched on his shoulder. Far from being recalled, Frémont was promoted to lieutenant colonel on June 26 by President Polk, who in his commissioning letter praised the explorer for his "patriotism, valor, fidelity and abilities."

Meanwhile, Frémont learned that General Castro was sending troops under Captain Joaquín de la Torre to dislodge the Bear Flag revolutionists in Sonoma. At last he acted decisively, reaching the outpost on June 25 at the head of an army of soldiers and volunteers that had swelled to 160 men. By the time he reached Sonoma, however, the Bear Flaggers had already repulsed the Mexican troops. Frémont set off after the retreating army, which escaped by a clever ruse, when de la Torre gave a false message to an Indian runner whom he expected Frémont to intercept.

On June 28 occurred one of the most inexplicable events of Frémont's whole third expedition. A week earlier, the Bear Flaggers had sent two men out as messengers to seek gunpowder from American settlers. The two had not returned. In a minor skirmish, Frémont captured a Mexican who revealed that the two had been caught and then gruesomely tortured to death. The Bear Flaggers were hot for revenge.

On the twenty-eighth, out scouting for enemy soldiers, Kit Carson and two other Frémont men saw a small boat landing on the west shore of San Pablo Bay. In the boat were a pair of twenty-year-old twins and their elderly uncle. There was no way these innocents could have been mistaken for soldiers, but Carson seized them as they climbed out of their craft, then shot them to death, either on the spot or shortly afterward.

It is hard to understand this gratuitous atrocity. One of the Bear Flaggers, to whom Carson told the story only days later, recorded the deed thus:

> He discovered and reported [the three Mexicans] to Fremont, his superior officer, as prisoners his squad had taken, and asked what he should do with them. Fremont's reply was that "he had no use for prisoners; but do your duty."

Another account, appearing in a Los Angeles newspaper ten years later, seems to square with this recollection. Carson acted, the reporter swore, "unwillingly by Fremont's order. 'Captain, shall I take these men prisoners?' " Carson asked. Frémont waved his hand, saying, " 'I have no room for prisoners.' "

Later, when this cold-blooded murder became an issue in the 1856 presidential election, Frémont disowned all part in it. Yet it is hard to imagine Carson performing this cowardly and ruthless deed on his own authority. From all available evidence, Carson had no racial antipathy toward Mexicans: he lived among them in Taos, and only three years before had married one of them, the young and beautiful Josefa.

A third account, by Thomas Martin, the expeditioner who alone reported the massacre near Lassen's Ranch in full detail, offers an extenuating factor. Martin claimed he was present at the killing. On seizing the old man and his two nephews, "We asked if they had any dispatches for de la Torre and they said no. We shot them then and there, and upon searching their bodies we found dispatches which we took to Fremont."

Frémont's biographers lay the blame for this savage act squarely on Carson; some even regard it as characteristic of the mountain man. Writes Ferol Egan, "No questions were asked. No chance to surrender was offered. Bear Flaggers, fellow Americans, had been butchered in the most savage manner possible, and as far as Carson was concerned, this was all the excuse he needed." Ten or fifteen years earlier, it is true, Carson had subscribed to the eye-for-an-eye code of reprisal against Indians: if Apaches had killed some whites, then other Apaches must die as a consequence. But if in 1846 Carson applied this barbaric ethic to the Mexicans, it remained an act unique in his life. In the memoir he dictated in 1856, he does not mention the killing. Carson's own biographers, understandably, blame Frémont for the deed.

From the end of June on, the conquest of California seemed to proceed as easily as toppling a string of dominoes. On July 7, the U.S. Navy arrived in Monterey, bringing with it the news that, two months before, the country had declared war against Mexico. Commodore John Sloat promptly ran up the American flag, having captured the capital without firing a shot. But when Frémont, as the junior officer, reported to Sloat, the navy man, in a fit of pique, demanded to know by what authority the newly appointed lieutenant colonel had taken up arms against the Mexicans. When Frémont admitted that "I had acted solely on my own responsibility," Sloat "appeared much disturbed."

Only weeks later, however, Sloat abandoned California, debilitated by ill health. His successor, Commodore Robert F. Stockton, took a much more charitable view of Frémont's intrigues and authorized him at once to form what would be called the California Battalion. Around Sonoma and Sutter's Fort, the explorer recruited a force that eventually numbered 428 men—to be paid the modest sum of $25 a month each—plus fifty Walla Walla Indians from Oregon.

During the "capture" of Monterey, a single British ship had hovered outside the port, observing the maneuvers. Frémont convinced himself that but for the presence of his California Battalion, the English admiral would have tried to seize the town and claim California for Britain.

Thus, as he began to grasp the opportunity of a lifetime, Frémont allowed the grandiose self-importance that lay always just beneath his surface to emerge. If the man had a tragic flaw, this was it. Now he rode at the head of his battalion surrounded by a personal bodyguard of five fierce-looking Delaware Indians; sometimes he tied green ribbons around his horse's neck and tail. His dispatches took on an ex cathedra tone, as when he instructed Edward Kern, in charge of Sutter's Fort, to "[i]ron and confine any person who shall disobey your orders—shoot any person who shall endanger the safety of the place."

Mexican California was all but helpless to defend itself against the well-armed Americans. Already, Castro was fleeing southward with the only army the territory could muster. The California navy consisted of a single ship without guns. It was hardly surprising, then, that Frémont's battalion was able to take one small town after another without bloodshed. In the course of his triumphant march south, the colonel paused near San Francisco to name the narrow channel separating bay from ocean the Golden Gate.

Word came that Castro was heading toward Baja California in hopes of bolstering his force with fresh recruits and weapons. Stockton sent Frémont's battalion south to San Diego aboard a warship to cut off the Mexicans. On this sea voyage, Kit Carson got wretchedly seasick. As an explorer, the mountain man had this single weakness: journeys on water terrified him. During a much shorter sea voyage, Carson had told a crony, "Cap, I'd rather ride on the back of a grizzly than on this boat."

To Frémont's surprise, not only did San Diego surrender without a peep of opposition, but its citizens seemed almost to welcome an American takeover. Where was Castro's demoralized army? Rumor had him in Los Angeles. On August 13, a twin-pronged force—Frémont from the south, Stockton from just offshore to the west—converged on the outskirts of the Pueblo de los Angeles. Even now, the Americans could not engage the enemy. They took Los Angeles, once more without firing a shot. Castro disbanded his army and headed for Mexico; Governor Pío Pico also fled.

During these heady days, it seemed to Stockton and Frémont that the conquest of California was complete. To the conquerors, there was nothing absurd about their victory. In his official dispatch to the secretary of the navy, Stockton staunchly claimed that he had "chased the Mexican army more than three hundred miles along the coast, pursued them thirty miles in the interior of their own country, routed and dispersed them and secured the Territory to the United States, ended the war, restored peace and harmony among the people, and put a civil government into successful operation." It would take such later historians as Bernard De Voto to put the lopsided triumph into perspective, as, in assessing Frémont's taking of San Diego: "The Conqueror's record remained untarnished; he had yet to face a hostile force in California. He never did."

In their self-congratulatory jubilation, Frémont and Stockton wrote out long letters summarizing the campaign to the president, the secretary of war, and Senator Benton. Frémont asked Carson to choose a small cohort of the best men and ride with these letters all the way to Washington (farther east than Carson had ever been). The journey, Frémont estimated, should take sixty days.

The colonel, still only thirty-three years old, basked in his victory. Who knew what honors and triumphs would follow in its wake? But here, as Carson headed east, the extraordinary luck that had paved Frémont's path through life turned irreversibly fickle. Time and again, the explorer had overstepped his mandates, only to pull off deeds that silenced the grumblers. More than once he had incurred the wrath of his superiors, only to see his triumphs obscure his transgressions.

Frémont's errors, at this crucial bend in his life, were those of a tragic hero. Both he and Stockton had seriously underestimated the resistance of the apparently abject Californians. That August of 1846, the conquest was far from over.

And so far in life, though he had made enemies, Frémont had managed not to antagonize any superior so badly as to turn him into a personal nemesis. At that moment, riding west across New Mexico, Frémont's nemesis came—a man who would eventually prosecute his grievances so rigorously as to hound the explorer to the brink of personal ruin.

As grandiose as Frémont, Commodore Stockton now began to ponder a wholesale invasion of the country to the south, to be capped by a march on Mexico City. Why stop at California? Why not conquer Mexico itself?

Meanwhile, he had left Lieutenant Archibald Gillespie—the same messenger who had found Frémont in the Klamath territory five months earlier—in charge of Los Angeles, with a force of only fifty soldiers. Gillespie quickly antagonized the settlers with his swaggering ways and arbitrary laws.

On September 23, a posse of California vigilantes surrounded Gillespie's headquarters and laid siege to it. Reinforced by troops under one of Castro's captains, the Mexicans won Gillespie's surren-

der six days later. They might well have executed the arrogant lieutenant, but instead turned him loose at San Pedro, where he sailed
for Monterey.

Alarmed, Frémont and Stockton rushed back into the fray. But
the *reconquista* of Los Angeles would prove far more difficult than
the conquest. For the next three months, Frémont would do little
more than ride up and down California, looking for battles he could
not seem to find.

Meanwhile, Brigadier General Stephen Watts Kearny and his
Army of the West had marched on that other provincial capital,
Santa Fe, and had taken it without a shot. President Polk had sent
Kearny toward California with explicit orders to take over the war
from Stockton and Frémont. With him traveled 300 picked soldiers,
under the guidance of Carson's old confederate, Thomas "Broken-
Hand" Fitzpatrick.

Fifty-two years old, a veteran of the War of 1812, Kearny had a
solid and sometimes brilliant thirty-year record of army service behind him. By temperament he was a cold and grudging man: Nevins
calls him "a grim martinet," and an early historian of the Mexican
War analyzed him as "grasping, jealous, domineering, and harsh."
He had, however, a far better grasp of war than did the twin conquerors strutting in California. In De Voto's consistently sardonic
book *The Year of Decision: 1846*, Kearny stands out as "a gentleman,
a soldier, a commander, a diplomat, a statesman, and a master of his
job, whose only superior was Winfield Scott."

On October 6, a week after Los Angeles had fallen back into
Mexican hands, near Socorro, New Mexico, Kearny bumped into
Kit Carson's band of sixteen messengers. Carson promptly told the
general that the conquest of California had been completed in Au-
gust. The mountain man can hardly be faulted in this; the letters to
Polk and Benton that he carried said as much.

Taking Carson at his word, Kearny sent back all but 110 of his
men. It was a decision that came close to costing the general his life.
Fitzpatrick admitted that the country to the west of Socorro was unknown to him. Logically enough, Kearny next ordered Fitzpatrick to
carry east the important letters, Carson to guide him back to California. Kit heard these words with great dismay. It had been almost
two years since he had seen his beloved Josefa; on the way to Wash-

ington, he planned to spend one night at his Taos home, and now
that he was nine-tenths of the way there, to turn around and head
west once more seemed a cruel fate. In addition, Carson had a res-
olute sense of duty about performing Stockton and Frémont's errand. Though Kearny had overruled those officers, Carson was so
reluctant to abandon his mission that he planned to sneak away in
the night until a comrade talked him out of it.

Marching on to California with his reduced forces, Kearny
learned of the Los Angeles insurrection. At once, he headed toward
the trouble. In early December, while Stockton and Frémont were
still rounding up recruits, Kearny located enemy troops in the San
Pasqual Valley northeast of San Diego. Here, on December 6, he
fought the only serious battle of the Mexican War in California.
Though he would claim victory, in fact he was soundly defeated—
not by superior numbers or weaponry, but by tactics he had never
run up against in his three decades of service.

The Mexican troops were led by General Andrés Pico, brother of
Pío Pico, the governor who had fled Los Angeles in August. This
canny soldier turned feigned retreats into sudden attacks that were
shockingly effective. In the initial charge, Carson suffered yet another of his innumerable close calls, when his horse stumbled and
fell; sprawled on the ground, he came within inches of being tram-
pled by his fellow soldiers galloping by on either side. Picking himself up, Carson found that his rifle was broken. After a while, he was
able to rearm by seizing a dead comrade's rifle and cartridges.

Pico's soldiers would ride off as if in panicked retreat, then wheel
and attack the flanks of the oncoming Americans. At close quarters,
they relied more on their masterly skill with long, sharpened lances
than on firepower. The fighting turned chaotic. By nightfall, the
Americans had suffered 36 dead and wounded, the Mexicans only 1
dead and 12 wounded. Holing up desperately among the rocks,
with, in Carson's words, "barely water enough for the men to drink"
and "nothing to eat but mule meat," Kearny's men settled in for a
bivouac that might well prove fatal. The general himself had been
badly wounded, with deep lance thrusts in the buttocks and one
arm; in the night he nearly died from loss of blood.

The battle lasted into the second day. Once more, the Mexicans
pinned down Kearny's men in open ground. Evidently, Kit Carson's

reputation as a fighter had spread even to the Mexican ranks, for Pico, urging his sentinels to be extracautious, was overheard to say, "Carson is there. The wolf will escape."

The wolf indeed escaped, saving Kearny's army a far worse rout. In the middle of the night, Kit and a navy lieutenant volunteered to try to slip through the enemy lines, contact Stockton's forces in San Diego, and bring back reinforcements. Taking off their shoes and tucking them under their belts, this pair crawled for two miles, passing through three rows of unsuspecting sentinels, coming within twenty yards of the closest enemy soldier. "We finally got through," recalled Carson in his sotto voce manner, "but had the misfortune to have lost our shoes—had to travel over a country covered with prickly pear and rocks." Stockton sent 170 men at once to Kearny's relief; the combined force finally drove off the enemy. As it was, however, the Army of the West lost 21 men in this nightmarish battle, to Pico's sole fatality. A number of men, including the fearless Alexis Godey, one of Frémont's three Napoleonic marshals, were captured (Godey was later freed in a prisoner exchange). It took Kearny months to recover from his wounds.

According to Carson, the lieutenant who slipped through the lines with him and ran barefoot to San Diego "became deranged from fatigue" during the ordeal and "did not entirely recover for two years."

General Stephen Watts Kearny was not accustomed to losing battles. He was humiliated by having been rescued by Stockton's troops. And he felt lastingly outraged that Frémont and Stockton had so blithely assumed that the war was over in August.

Weak and hobbled by his injuries, Kearny nonetheless insisted on riding at the head of the combined army formed from his own surviving dragoons and Stockton's men. This force now headed toward Los Angeles from the south at the same time as Frémont, slowed by torrential floods and quagmires of mud, descended on the city from the north.

Kearny attempted to contact Frémont by courier. The tight-lipped tone of these dispatches betrays the general's annoyance: "Join us as soon as you can, or let me know, if you want me to march to your assistance. . . ." "We are in force in this place—sailors and marines—join us as *soon as possible*. We are ignorant of your movements. . . ."

Flushed with impending victory, which brought out his latent arrogance, Frémont responded evasively, and he did not hasten to join his superior officer. The colonel further irritated Kearny by pompously signing his own letters "Military Commandant of the Territory of California." And he gloated to Kearny, in a tone of noblesse oblige, that his troops had recovered from the Mexicans a howitzer Kearny had lost at San Pasqual.

Still without having fought a single battle, Frémont had genuinely begun to think of himself as the conqueror of California. The fall of Los Angeles, which would put a finis to the conquest, was a foregone conclusion in the face of the two-pronged approach of forces far superior to the undermanned garrison that represented the last gasp of Mexican California. A wiser officer would have stepped aside to let Kearny literally salve his wounds by sealing that conquest himself. Frémont could not.

From Kearny's point of view, the last straw came on January 12 and 13, 1847. As the general waited in Los Angeles for the colonel to report to him, Frémont had the good luck to have emissaries from Andrés Pico ride up and tell him that the last Mexican army was ready to surrender. Without consulting Kearny, Frémont received Pico at a ranch on the outskirts of Los Angeles and proceeded to discuss terms. On the twelfth, the Pathfinder issued a proclamation of peace, full of self-congratulation ("it is agreed upon and ordered by me, that an entire cessation of hostilities shall take place"). And the next day, still without consulting the general, Frémont drew up Articles of Capitulation that Pico happily signed, for the terms were far more lenient to the defeated Mexicans than the ones the general of the Army of the West intended.

As Frémont fiddled, Kearny burned.

On January 14, 1847, Frémont rode into Los Angeles at the head of his conquering army "like a Greek hero," in the words of his admiring biographer Ferol Egan, "just in from the plains of Troy." Behind him rode Kit Carson, who had rejoined Frémont's battalion soon af-

ter the battle of San Pasqual. In subsequent years, Carson and Frémont would share many an evening together by the fireplace, hash-
ing over the exploits of their three expeditions. And Carson would
nurse his former commander back to health in 1849, after the most
extreme ordeal of Frémont's life. But never again, after that day of
triumph in Los Angeles, would the two men ride together.

In the first blush of victory, Frémont's star seemed to be fixed in
the empyrean. For fifty days, following his appointment by Stockton, he would serve as governor of California. He had no reason to
doubt the assessment he had read in a long, loving letter from Jessie:
"So your merit has advanced you in eight years from an unknown
second lieutenant, to the most talked of and admired lieutenant
colonel in the army."

The fall from grace that occupied the next full year makes for a
dolorous yet tedious tale. During the early months of 1847, Kearny
repaired to Monterey, while Frémont moved into a mansion in Los
Angeles and began to act as governor. The vitriolic campaign biographers of 1856 later dug up evidence not only that Frémont im-
providently borrowed money during these weeks and padded his
expense accounts, but frequented prostitutes and kept a "harem" of
local Hispanic women. (These rumors, no doubt exaggerated, nev-
ertheless may have had a germ of truth, as Rolle's later biographical
unearthing of Frémont's compulsive womanizing suggests.) Meanwhile Frémont defied Kearny's repeated demands that he ride to
Monterey and report to his senior officer. And Kearny, in his turn,
strung Frémont along in his insubordination by neglecting to in-
form him of the explicit orders from Washington putting Kearny in
charge of California.

Some of Kearny's officers, scandalized by Frémont's effrontery,
wondered why the general hesitated to arrest the colonel. A factor
in that hesitation was the violent opposition of Senator Benton,
who was chairman of the Military Affairs Committee and had Polk's
ear. Later, when Kearny was up for promotion to major general,
Benton did everything he could to defeat the nomination. But Polk
himself, as he admitted to his diary, was appalled by Frémont's behavior in California.

At last, in late March, Frémont rode to Monterey. Kearny
showed him his papers from Washington. The chastened colonel of-

fered to resign his commission, pleading he be allowed to take 60 men south to attempt the conquest of Mexico, but Kearny refused. Instead, when the general headed east in June, he ordered Frémont to ride with him. One can only imagine the weeks of tense, silent hostility between the two men as they moved toward Missouri. On August 22, at Fort Leavenworth, Kearny formally arrested Frémont and presented his charges, which amounted to mutiny, insubordination, and "conduct prejudicial to military discipline."

The court-martial trial, in Washington, began on November 2 and dragged on for eighty-nine days into the new year. Some of Frémont's most loyal supporters, including Archibald Gillespie, testified in his defense; Alexis Godey and Dick Owens were ready to take the stand, but the court declined to call them. Counting on Stockton's unqualified support, Frémont was deeply disappointed when the commodore backed down and stammered out vague equivocations.

Frémont did not help his case by vigorously attacking Kearny in his cross-examination. To the members of the panel—army officers who had worked their way up through the ranks, as the topographical engineer had not—Frémont's counterattack seemed itself insubordinate. And, in the words of biographer Andrew Rolle, "these men had a deep-rooted contempt for the showman in him."

After three days of deliberation, on January 31, 1848, the panel delivered its verdict. They found Frémont guilty and sentenced him to dismissal from the army. In a curious move, President Polk accepted the verdict but remitted the sentence.

Disgraced, Frémont resigned from the army three weeks later. Benton never spoke to Polk again.

When, at the age of seventy-four, the Pathfinder set down his *Memoirs*, he could not bring himself to write beyond this devastating setback in his thirty-sixth year. Though he would later become a millionaire, one of the two first senators from California, and very nearly the first Republican president, he would forever regard his plummeting from glory in Los Angeles to ignominy in Washington as the watershed in his life. Even then, he could not begin to recognize the defects in his own character that had brought about his downfall; it was all the fault of others. Breaking off his *Memoirs* in midstream, he wrote bitterly, "I close the page because my path of life led out from among the grand and lovely features of nature, and its pure and wholesome air, into the poisoned atmosphere and jarring circumstances of conflict among men, made subtle and malignant by clashing interests."

THREE

HORROR
DESOLATION
DESPAIR

8

HARDSCRABBLE

BOTH Indians and whites here report the snow to be deeper in the mountains than has for a long time been known so early in the season, and they predict a severe winter." So wrote Frémont to his father-in-law on November 17, 1848, from Bent's Fort on the Arkansas. "[The mountains] look imposing and somewhat stern; still I am in nowise discouraged, and believe that we shall succeed in forcing our way across."

Even as he had resigned from the army the previous February, the Pathfinder had started planning a fourth expedition. If politics and jealousies within the military had brought him disgrace, then he would turn back to the thing he did best—exploring. At the moment, Frémont was at the peak of his fame. The court-martial, a cause célèbre so spectacular that gossip about it in Washington had actually superseded the news of the final battles of the Mexican War, had won Frémont considerable sympathy among the public. He was seen by many as a classic American underdog, martyr to the sour old despots who ran the War Department. When he would return to California in 1849, he would be greeted as the heroic conqueror he had always thought himself.

The idea for the 1848 expedition was hatched in one of Thomas Hart Benton's pipe dreams. For years, the senator from Missouri had been an avid enthusiast of railroads. Now he envisioned an iron highway stretching clear across the continent, starting in New York and ending in newly acquired California. And in Benton's vision, the railroad ought to follow as closely as possible the 38th parallel—near which his home in St. Louis stood. In many an orotund speech on the floor of the Senate, Benton waxed rhapsodic about his grand scheme, which he saw as fulfilling Columbus's original mission: by linking existing ocean routes with this new iron way across the continent, the "American road to India" would be realized. In Benton's fevered brain, this "great national line," with "San Francisco at one end, St. Louis in the middle, New York at the other," would be "adorned with its crowning honor—the colossal statue of the great Columbus . . . hewn from a granite mass of a peak of the Rocky Mountains, overlooking the road." This, seventy-seven years before the presidents' heads at Mount Rushmore were even on the drawing board!

The person to lead a reconnaissance of this railroad route was, of course, Benton's son-in-law. Frémont was eager to get started: only another triumphant voyage, he believed, could restore his good name. With a certain naiveté, the explorer expected that despite his conviction of mutiny and insubordination, despite the fact that he had resigned from the army, the government would continue to finance his explorations. Benton's clout in the Senate was effective enough to win a $30,000 appropriation by the shaky vote of 18 to 16, but the House overwhelmingly squelched the bill, 128 to 29.

This setback only made Frémont feistier and more determined. With Benton's help, he raised funds for the expedition from a trio of St. Louis businessmen. In early October, he set out with thirty-five men up the Missouri River. But the journey was so financially strapped that the men effectively received no pay, having in many cases to supply their own horses and gear. (These adventurers evidently believed they were undertaking the mission "on spec," to be paid by a grateful government on successful completion of the reconnaissance. Frémont may have made vague promises to that effect. In the end, they would be paid not a dime for the most arduous and risky journey of their lives.)

In the circumstances, the personnel of Frémont's fourth expedition made up a far weaker team than he had ever before led west. There were a few stalwarts among them, including Alexis Godey and Edward Kern, who had served the Pathfinder well in California. Charles Preuss, the grumpy German cartographer, was back on board. But from St. Louis to Bent's Fort, the party traveled without a guide.

Jessie accompanied her husband all the way to Westport, on the Missouri, kissed him good-bye, returned to Washington, and boarded a ship to sail to California via the Horn. On reaching California himself, Frémont planned to reunite with his wife, settle into a home (he had already bought property at Las Mariposas, on the Merced River), pan for gold, and begin a new career in the territory he had won for America.

At Bent's Fort, however, there was already a foot of snow on the ground. Several mountain men told Frémont that it was folly to attempt to cross the Colorado mountains in winter—especially in such a winter as this one boded. They knew—as the Pathfinder, for all his journeying, did not—that in Colorado the 38th parallel ran smack through its roughest mountains, the Sangre de Cristo and San Juan Ranges. No railroad would ever traverse this formidable wilderness.

Characteristically, Frémont ignored these veteran advisors and determined to push ahead. After all, in February 1844, the Indians east of the great Sierra Nevada had warned him against a winter crossing: he had forged on, gained Sutter's Fort, proved the doomsayers wrong, and laid the groundwork for the Conquest.

But now, as he paused for three days at Bent's Fort, Frémont realized that he had to have a guide. At least one mountain man turned him down. Thomas "Broken-Hand" Fitzpatrick may have also declined, for he was in the area, but "unavailable."

In the upcoming months, Frémont would need the best guide he had ever hired. He would need Kit Carson.

Carson had finally reached Santa Fe in April 1847, where he was reunited with Josefa after an absence of twenty months. Instead of a joyous meeting, however, he walked into a shattered circle of family and friends. On January 19, disgruntled Hispanic settlers and Pueblo Indians had tried to throw off the American yoke, perpetrating what came to be known as the Taos Massacre. Breaking into homes, the rebels had slain Charles Bent, governor of the territory and Carson's brother-in-law, as well as Josefa's brother and uncle and a number of Kit's best friends. Most of the victims had been scalped. Josefa herself had survived only by digging through an adobe wall and hiding in an inner room.

By the time Carson arrived, the insurrection had been put down, and its perpetrators were being executed in mass hangings. Oddly enough, in his memoir, Carson fails altogether to mention this devastating event.

Still serving in the army as a dispatch rider, Kit now made two separate journeys all the way to Washington and back. He accomplished these marathon treks as if they were routine errands. In the capital, however, he felt truly ill at ease, worried that his manners and decorum made him laughable. Jessie Frémont took him under her wing, introducing him to her friends and reading great literature aloud to him. (She later remembered that he declared Sir Walter Scott's poem *The Lady of the Lake* "the finest expression of outdoor life that he had ever heard.")

Thanks to Frémont's reports, Carson was famous, and curious bystanders were eager to meet this epitome of the mountain man. On doing so, most were dumbfounded by Kit's appearance. In California, a young army lieutenant named William Tecumseh Sherman recorded his first impression: "I cannot express my surprise at beholding a small, stoop-shouldered man, with reddish hair, freckled face, soft blue eyes, and nothing to indicate extraordinary courage or daring. He spoke but little, and answered questions in monosyllables."

In Washington, Carson found it so vexing to sleep indoors that he was overjoyed when the mother of a California friend offered him the couch on her veranda. In Jessie's tow, Carson was introduced to President Polk, who liked the scout well enough to commission him officially as a lieutenant in the rifle regiment, at a salary of $33.33 a month—one-third the amount he had earned six years earlier as guide for Frémont's first expedition.

On the second of Carson's breakneck dispatch-carrying missions across the country, he was accompanied by a young lieutenant named George Douglas Brewerton. This officer had arrived in California two months after the Mexican surrender, to serve as part of the occupying army. Like many another green recruit, Brewerton had read Frémont's reports and had already formed a heroic image of the laconic mountain man. In California, he heard more stirring tales of Carson's doings. Already Kit's name had become "a familiar household word."

Five years after his cross-country ride with Carson, Brewerton wrote a series of articles for *Harper's New Monthly Magazine*. There he recalled the gap between his idealized image of the man and his first meeting with Kit in Los Angeles:

> The Kit Carson of my *imagination* was over six feet high—a sort of modern Hercules in his build—with an enormous beard, and a voice like a roused lion. . . .
>
> The *real* Kit Carson I found to be a plain, simple, unostentatious man; rather below the medium height, with brown, curling hair, little or no beard, and a voice as soft and gentle as a woman's. In fact, the hero of a hundred desperate encounters, whose life had been mostly spent amid wildernesses, where the white man is almost unknown, was one of Dame Nature's gentlemen. . . .

Brewerton left us the best firsthand account of Carson's habits and behavior on the trail. The lieutenant was impressed by Kit's carefulness each night he made camp:

> A braver man than Kit perhaps never lived, in fact I doubt if he ever knew what fear was, but with all this he exercised great caution. While arranging his bed, his saddle, which he always used as a pillow, was disposed in such a manner as to form a barricade for his head; his pistols half cocked were laid above it, and his trusty rifle reposed beneath the blanket by his side, where it was not only ready for instant use, but perfectly protected from the damp. Except now and then to light his pipe, you never caught Kit exposing himself to full glare of the camp fire. . . . "No, no, boys," Kit would say, "hang round the fire if you will, it may do for you if you like it, but I don't want to have a Digger slip an arrow into me, when I can't see him."

Indeed, on the night of the Indian attack in the Klamath country, when Basil Lajeunesse had his skull split by a tomahawk as he slept, the more reckless Alexis Godey had sprung to his feet directly in front of the campfire, even while arrows whizzed past. In the midst of the pandemonium, Carson had kept his wits, lurking in the shadows; but he was so shocked by Godey's rashness that he uncharacteristically exclaimed, "Look at the fool. Look at him, will you?"

Throughout the western half of Carson's long dispatch ride, his small party passed through hostile Indian territory. By now, Kit had learned other ways of dealing with the natives than simply shooting at them on sight. Brewerton marveled at Carson's ingenuity in traversing a Utah mountain range thick with Paiutes, or Diggers, as the mountain men called them. Carson took a single eighteen-year-old Paiute man hostage and explained to him in his own tongue that he would not be harmed as long as his people refrained from attacking. That night in camp,

> his companions set up a most dismal howling from the adjoining hills. This yelling—sounding more like a chorus of screech-owls, or a troop of hungry wolves, than anything else I can compare it to—was rendered doubly mournful by the gloomy shades of evening, and the otherwise total silence of the hour. This disturbance was finally quieted by Kit's replying in the Paw-Eutaw tongue, aided by the assurances of the young man himself, who yelled back an answer to the effect that he was still in the land of the living.

At the end of their passage through Paiute territory, Carson rewarded his hostage with the gift of a pair of tattered pantaloons, which greatly pleased the Indian. "In fact," wrote Brewerton, "no city dandy, faultlessly arrayed for the fashionable side of Broadway, could have exhibited more perfect satisfaction in his strut and air than our untutored Digger."

At the moment that Frémont arrived at Bent's Fort in November 1848, Carson had been home in Taos only a month, after completing his second journey back from Washington. If the Pathfinder made an attempt to contact and enlist the peerless scout of his three previous expeditions, that effort has escaped history. A single, unreliable secondhand account, published twenty-six years later, insists that Carson advised Frémont against his 38th-parallel beeline, warning him, as did other mountain men, that he "could not get through or over [the mountains] at that period of the year."

That autumn, once more, Carson was trying to settle down. In his 1856 memoir, Kit disposed of this period in a single deadpan sentence: "I remained at Taos during the winter." The next April, he went in with Lucien Maxwell, whom he had met on Frémont's first expedition seven years before, to launch a ranching venture in the Rayado Valley fifty miles east of Taos. Still only thirty-nine years old, he must have felt in his very bones the toll of all his long rides and close escapes, for he struck a valedictory tone: "We had been leading a roving life long enough and now was the time, if ever, to make a home for ourselves and children. We were getting old and could not expect to remain any length of time able to gain a livelihood as we had been [for] such a number of years."

Instead of Kit Carson, who might well have saved his party from the grinding ordeal that loomed along the 38th parallel, Frémont hired another mountain man with whom he had had some experience. It would prove a fateful choice.

No trapper or explorer in the West ever led a more flamboyant life than William Sherley Williams, known by 1848 as Old Bill Williams. Because he wove, like Joe Meek, many a tall tale around his doings, because he was a habitual loner, and because much of what he accomplished violated not only Mexican but American laws, it is particularly hard in Williams's case to separate fact from legend. Immensely talented, a born survivor, he was also deeply flawed and erratic. It is thanks to his biographer, Alpheus H. Favour, who, writing in 1936, had the benefit of firsthand stories from the children of men who had trapped and fought with Old Bill, that we know as much about this outsized character as we do.

As Frémont pushed west from Bent's Fort that November of 1848, he had managed to talk "Uncle Dick" Wootton into guiding his party. But Wootton was evidently leery of the enterprise from the start. In the Wet Mountains, as he gazed thirty miles west at the higher and more rugged Sangre de Cristo Range, he left the expedition, declaring, "There is too much snow ahead for me."

Meanwhile, at Fontaine Qui Bouit (today's Pueblo, Colorado),

Frémont had picked up Old Bill Williams, who had planned to winter over there with friends. Only four months before, in a battle with Utes and Apaches near the Chama River, Williams had suffered a serious injury: in the words of a contemporary newspaper report, he was "shot in the arm, shattering it most horribly." Still recovering from his wound, Williams was dubious about Frémont's project, but he signed on anyway—no doubt hard up for cash, as he was most of his life. A later narrative written by one of Frémont's volunteers, Micajah McGehee, gives the clearest picture of Williams's ambivalence: "[I]t was not without some hesitation that he consented to go, for most of the old trappers at the pueblo declared that it was impossible to cross the mountains at that time. . . . However, Old Bill concluded to go, for he thought we could manage to get through, though not without considerable suffering."

With Wootton's defection, Williams became the party's only guide. The old trapper insisted to Frémont, however, that he knew every inch of the Colorado mountains. As the party headed into the foothills in late November, Williams was sixty-one years old. He looked even older, for years of serious drinking had taken their toll, and he had earned his nickname while still in the prime of life.

Born in North Carolina in 1787, Williams had grown up in a frontier family not unlike Carson's, only twelve miles outside St. Louis. As a young man, fired with religious zeal, he had become an itinerant preacher, traveling a circuit of farmsteads to proselytize anyone who would listen to him. Looking back much later with his habitual self-irony, Old Bill would claim that he became so well known on the Missouri frontier that even the chickens, seeing him approaching, would cackle, "Here comes Parson Williams! One of us must be ready for dinner."

Around 1813, he went as a missionary among the Osage Indians in southern Missouri and Kansas. Rather than converting the savages, however, they converted him. He gave up his preaching, settled among the Osages, and took an Indian wife. Frémont's man Micajah McGehee insisted that by 1848 Williams had also taken two or three Ute wives, perhaps concurrently: "If he was much in need of a horse, or tired of his squaw, he would sell her, or 'swap' her off for one or two horses."

Williams was not the first white man who, in the phrase of the day, "became more Indian than the Indians themselves," but in later years he would shock even veteran mountain men with his zest for certain practices he had learned among the Osages. His culinary predilections were legion: he especially fancied the uncooked legs of a fetal calf, as well as buffalo liver flavored with gall bladder, also uncooked; and when a hog was butchered, he was known, in Alpheus Favour's delicate phrase, for "squeezing out the contents of the intestines, and devouring those choice morsels on the spot, Indian fashion."

Under the influence of Osage beliefs, Williams abandoned his Christianity for the doctrine of transmigration of souls. He was sure that in the next life he was destined to become a bull elk roaming the Bayou Salade (known today as South Park, in central Colorado), and he went so far as to warn fellow hunters not to shoot an elk with certain markings if they ever chanced upon such a beast in that region.

Williams went west to become a mountain man in 1825, at the age of thirty-eight, the year before the teenage Kit Carson ran away from home to head for Santa Fe. He so excelled at trapping that his skill in that arduous craft made him famous. Not one to hide his light under a bushel, at some point he took to signing himself, "Bill Williams, Master Trapper." He had a knack for picking up Indian languages, though not a facility to match Carson's. Despite his time among the Osages, as a mountain man Williams gleefully scalped Indians he had killed, and at least once he waved a pair of scalps in the face of a third Indian who lay mortally wounded. Williams also became an expert marksman, though Micajah McGehee, on Frémont's expedition, would describe his peculiar technique as "a 'double wabble'; he never could hold his gun still, yet his ball went always to the spot on a single shot."

Most mountain men went on sprees when, laden with a season's pelts, they hit an outpost of civilization like Bent's Fort or Taos; but Williams may have outdone them all. McGehee insisted that Old Bill once spent $6,000 on a single bender in Taos. He loved to gamble, often wagering $100 on a one-shot contest with another stalwart marksman. An old newspaper report claimed that Williams once lost $1,000 to Lucien Maxwell in a single game of seven-up.

With the demise of the beaver trade, like many another mountain man Williams was reduced to scrambling for a livelihood. He became a master horse thief, leading expeditions to California to steal whole herds from the Mexicans. Reaching Bent's Fort after one such excursion, with three hundred stolen mules and horses in tow, he reportedly offered its proprietor an even trade: "Bent, take all these horses and roll out that old barrel of whisky that's been in the storeroom so long. I'll kill it, or it shall kill me."

Favour maintains that, as greasy and dirty as a mountain man could get in his long months in the wilderness, Williams's personal slovenliness was in a league of its own. His eccentricity added to the bizarre impression he made. Micajah McGehee recalled Old Bill's costume: "He wore a loose monkey-jacket or a buckskin hunting-shirt, and for his head-covering a blanket-cap, the top two corners drawn up into two wolfish, satyr-like ears, giving him somewhat the appearance of the representations we generally meet with of his Satanic Majesty, at the same time rendering his *tout ensemble* exceedingly ludicrous."

Among Williams's eccentricities, when he hit Taos or Santa Fe loaded with pelts, was to buy a huge bolt of calico, walk out in the street, and, holding one end, throw the bolt as far as he could, then call out to the Mexican women, chortling as they scrambled to seize the precious fabric. His penchant for practical jokes sometimes got him in trouble. In 1845, on the plains near Fontaine Qui Bouit, he spotted a distant patrol of troops under Colonel Philip Cooke. Possibly drunk at the time, Williams pretended he was an Indian, riding toward the soldiers waving his arms in threat, then abruptly retreating until they gave chase. Though the soldiers might well have shot him, he allowed himself to be captured. Unamused, Cooke arrested the mountain man and sent him to Fort Leavenworth.

One crony described Old Bill in the prime of life as "a man about six feet one inch in height, gaunt, red-headed, with a hard, weather-beaten face, marked deeply with the small pox." He was "all muscle and sinew," and "a shrewd, cute, original man, and far from illiterate." McGehee thought him "the most successful trapper in the mountains, and the best acquainted with the ways and habits of the wild tribes. . . . [H]e pursued his lucrative but perilous vocation from an innate love of its excitement and dangers."

Williams had ridden west from Bent's Fort with Frémont on his

John Charles Frémont at thirty-seven, as fortune had begun to turn its back on him.

1

Jessie Benton Frémont, ever-loyal wife, preserver of her husband's legend, and flamboyant stylist who in effect ghost-wrote his best-selling government reports.

2

Kit Carson in middle age, still
trying to settle down, the
cares of his numerous
campaigns etched in
his face.

Josefa Jaramillo, the high-born
Hispanic woman who, at age
fourteen, became Kit Carson's
third wife and the love of his
life. A beauty "of the haughty,
heart-breaking kind—such as
would lead a man with a glance
of the eye, to risk his life for one
smile," wrote an acquaintance.

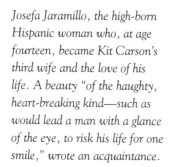

(Opposite) *The summit of Fremont Peak, at 13,745 feet. Though Frémont was
wrong in thinking it the highest summit in the Rocky Mountains, his first ascent in
1842 was the finest mountaineering feat performed to that time by Anglos in
North America.*

5

Alfred Jacob Miller's idyllic painting of the 1837 rendezvous at the junction of Horse Creek and the Green River, with the Wind River Range in the background. Carson, who attended the rendezvous, would guide a party toward the first ascent of Fremont Peak five years later.

6

The San Juan Mountains, 1848. The engraving, probably after a Richard Kern painting, captures the terrible cul-de-sac into which Frémont's party blundered in 1848. Ten of the thirty-three men would die—some to be cannibalized by their comrades—in this forlorn wilderness.

7

An engraving of Camp Dismal, the timberline bivouac that marked the farthest penetration of Frémont's doomed 1848–49 expedition into the La Garita Mountains of Colorado.

8

9

In summer, the same grove at the head of Wannamaker Creek, almost as lost and lonely today as it was in December 1848.

10

In the remote La Garita Mountains of southern Colorado, a stump today bears the furred splinters of the ax blows that felled the tree for fuel during Frémont's survival ordeal in December 1848.

11

Still in place at timberline, the remains of a boot from some hapless member of Frémont's doomed expedition.

This portrait of Kit Carson was taken only four years after the one shown earlier. Here Carson is wracked by the ailment that would take his life at age fifty-eight.

12

(Opposite) *During the siege of Navajo Fortress Rock, an American soldier in an idle moment carved this inscription into the base of the butte.*

13

Canyon del Muerto, the northern branch of Canyon de Chelly, where the Navajos held out against Carson's roundup in 1863–64.

The only route up Navajo Fortress Rock (where the Diné held out against Carson's roundup) takes a perilous line up these chimneys and cliffs.

14

15

16

Halfway up Navajo Fortress Rock stands a breastwork behind which a Navajo warrior fired on Carson's troops in the winter of 1863–64.

17

Inside a wrought-iron fence near the center of Taos, New Mexico, Carson's gravestone marks the place he loved best on earth.

third expedition in 1845 but, with his lifelong distaste for military ventures, had soured on the trip, leaving the party at Salt Lake City to disappear back into the mountains. During his trapping days, he had spent months at a time with Carson, and in 1842, when Kit at last returned to Missouri to deposit his daughter, Adaline, and to see his family, Williams rode with him to visit his own kin. With his characteristic economy, however, Carson mentions Old Bill only once in his dictated memoir, among a list of men with whom he rode to Bent's Fort.

Thus when Frémont engaged Williams at Fontaine Qui Bouit, he had already ridden with the savvy scout for sixty-one days, from Colorado to Utah three years before. On that previous journey, he had paid Old Bill $1 per day. Perhaps he now promised the guide a like recompense, to be paid on completion of a successful journey, if he could shepherd the party safely along the 38th parallel in the dead of what was promising to become a ferocious winter. With all the maledictions from other experienced veterans ringing in his ears, it seems surprising that Williams would have signed up. No doubt he was broke; and as McGehee testified, "He had no other care for the gains of his labors than as a means of affording him a 'big spree.' "

One modern scholar, who has studied Frémont's fourth expedition more assiduously than anyone else, argues that in the back of his mind Williams may have harbored a sinister ulterior motive. Her hypothesis will unwind in these pages as a nagging "what if," while Frémont and his thirty-three men climb to their destiny in the frozen Rocky Mountains.

At Fontaine Qui Bouit, the expedition found a squalid community of trappers and Mexicans living in rude adobe huts. Later they would look back on that settlement as almost a paradise, but at the time, Richard Kern, a brother of Edward, described it in his diary as "a miserable looking place, the inside resembling a menagerie—a compound of Spaniards, Horses mules dogs chickens and bad stench." Pushing on west up the Arkansas, the team came two days later to another "miserable place" called Hardscrabble, a collection of a dozen adobe houses in which some twenty-five mountain men had wintered over each of the last four years. Yet even the dyspeptic Richard Kern could admit that the houses were "very comfortable—they seemed like palaces to us, as we enjoyed the luxuries of a table & stools."

At Hardscrabble the men dined on chicken and baked pumpkin. They spent a whole day shelling corn to use as food for their 120 mounts (nearly all mules, with a few horses), managing to carry away 130 bushels of the precious stuff. And here the party suffered its first desertion, as a man we know only as Yonge left his comrades, darkly predicting that disaster would befall them.

The chief reason that Frémont's fourth expedition remains so little known is that the Pathfinder never published a single word about it. In the Bancroft Library at the University of California, seven pages of notes in Frémont's handwriting give the only direct account of the journey he may have ever penned. They seem to amount to a cursory outline for the chapters that would cover the 1848 voyage in his planned second volume of memoirs—a book he ultimately could not bring himself to write—for the jottings are interspersed with parenthetical reminders of the engravings he hoped to include: "The Sierra mojada (plate here) The Roubidoux Pass (Plate here)—the San Luis Valley—The Del Norte (Plate) The San Juan Mtns. The disaster—"

That we know as much as we do about the expedition depends vitally on the fact that in 1848—contrary to the prohibition he had levied on his first expedition six years before—Frémont allowed his men to keep diaries. Three of them exist today, in addition to three retrospective narratives by party members (possibly based on their diaries), as well as a handful of letters, including two by Frémont, to Jessie and to his father-in-law. Disappointingly, Charles Preuss, who had confided so candidly and at length to his secret diary in 1842 and again in 1843–44, managed on the fourth expedition to jot down only fourteen entries, most of them perfunctory. Perhaps he had wearied of the diary effort, or perhaps the ordeal left him too little energy to record it.

Yet these unvarnished accounts make up a fascinating patchwork, giving us intermittent glimpses into the tragedy that started to unfold that November. And, as Preuss noted, "As far as Hardscrabble, everything went well."

The small town of Florence stands today near where the colony of adobe huts once claimed a creekside clearing. In the early afternoon of November 25, the party left Hardscrabble, some of the men having for the last time in their lives slept under a sheltering roof. And here Frémont made his first important navigational decision. None of the commentaries or diaries dwells on this choice, but it would have profound consequences.

Had the party simply continued up the Arkansas River, they might have marched with relative ease to the headwaters of America's third-longest river. On easy benches they could have skirted the chasm that would come to be called the Royal Gorge; upstream from that, a broad grassy valley would have turned them north between the ranges that would later be named the Mosquito and the Sawatch, past the sites of the future mining towns of Salida, Buena Vista, and Leadville. The expeditions of both Zebulon Pike and Stephen Long had accomplished a good part of this Arkansas peregrination decades before, Pike's men in midwinter. Eventually, the Denver & Rio Grande Railroad would find its way up this natural corridor, crossing Tennessee Pass and descending the Colorado River, to lay the first (and for a long time the only) set of tracks traversing Colorado from east to west. That railway would maintain passenger service until 1997.

But this logical route would have taken Frémont far north of the 38th parallel, and it was not in the Pathfinder's nature to revise an *idée fixe*. So, from Hardscrabble, the party turned abruptly south, climbing Hardscrabble Creek into the pine- and aspen-covered Wet Mountains. Here, for the first time, the going got rough. The men had to proceed on foot, for the mules now were burdened with the sacks of shelled corn that they were consuming at the rate of a quart per day per animal. Moreover, the supply of flour that formed the men's staple food was already exhausted. Frémont had counted on hunting to supplement the diet, but in this winter-struck landscape game was hard to find.

One night the men camped in three feet of snow, but could find no running water for the mules. Their diaries began to record their misgivings. "7 m of hard toilsome travel," wrote Benjamin Kern, a third brother, on November 28; the next day, "bitter cold" and "laborious & weakening"; by December 2, "Boots cut to pieces burst and becoming no protection rapidly." The men paused to make rawhide mittens and moccasins, the latter thought to be superior to boots in deep snow. In trailless woods, the mules often balked at creek crossings and had to be hauled along with ropes tied around their necks. In nearly eight hours of steady work, the men sometimes gained only three to five miles. About this dispiriting passage through the Wet Mountains, Thomas Breckenridge later recalled, "We were continually looking for something better, and the conditions were daily growing worse."

Through these hard days, as November lapsed into December, Frémont kept up his stoic, hearty front, but there is evidence that he, too, was losing his heart for this kind of adventure. From Bent's Fort on November 17, he had written Jessie: "I think I shall never cross the continent again, except at Panama. I do not feel the pleasure that I used to have in these labors. . . ."

One night it snowed five inches while the men struggled to sleep. The cold was unrelenting. Micajah McGehee left the most vivid description of the winter's impact on his struggling comrades:

> The breath would freeze upon their faces and their lips be so stiff from the ice that it was almost impossible to speak, their eyelids in a similar condition from the freezing of the water which the cold wind would force from them, the ice standing on their lashes. Long icicles hung down from the nostrils, and the long beard and the hair stood out white and stiff with the frost, each hair standing to itself.

On November 29, the team at last broke clear of the mountains and emerged in the valley of the Huerfano River. Here the going was much easier, for a few years before, mountain man Antoine Robidoux had built a wagon road along the stream. But the intense cold persisted, and the wild game Frémont had counted on was pitifully scarce. Like a great, white wall ahead of them, the spiky Sangre de Cristo Range seemed to bar all progress.

Uncle Dick Wootton had taken one look at those snow-choked mountains and headed back east. Now another man stared at the range and remarked in earshot of Micajah McGehee, "Friends, I don't want my bones to bleach upon those mountains." But Old Bill Williams insisted he knew a way through the Sangre de Cristo, though he could not resist pointing out to his companions one night in camp that, just the winter before, two trappers had frozen to death at that very spot.

In Colorado, the Sangre de Cristo Mountains form a thin, high, unbroken chain running north and south for eighty miles. Seven of its summits rise above 14,000 feet (one of which would later be named Kit Carson Peak). Yet Old Bill Williams knew his stuff. Under his guidance, the party marched straight for Robidoux Pass (known today as Mosca Pass), one of only two true weaknesses in the long mountain crest.

On the 9,772-foot summit of the pass, fierce winds battered the men and mules. In the hollows and gullies on the west side, the snow was often eight feet deep. To make matters worse, the forest, leveled by winds, lay in a gauntlet of criss-crossed logs. This passage, remembered Micajah McGehee, "was exceedingly difficult, for it was completely filled with the fallen timber prostrated by some previous year's hurricane, amongst which the snow lay deep, and the mules were constantly stumbling and falling over these and down the rocky slants."

Numb with fatigue, on December 3 the men staggered 2,000 feet down the canyon on the west side of the pass. Ahead of them billowed a waste of surreal sand hills (today Great Sand Dunes National Monument), piled over the eons by the incessant west wind hurtling through the gunsight notch of Mosca Pass. The men pitched camp at the south edge of the dunes. McGehee later swore the temperature dropped that night to -17° F.

As grim as the weather was, as debilitated as the men were becoming, Frémont was assailed with even more vexing worry. As soon as his party had headed down to the San Luis Valley from the summit of the pass, he recognized that the canyon was far too steep to build a railroad through it. At the moment, Thomas Hart Benton's grand vision of an iron way spanning the country along the 38th parallel was in tatters.

For a few days, Frémont and Williams poked north along the western fringe of the Sangre de Cristo, hoping to find a more practical gap. They rediscovered Médano Pass, which Pike had traversed in 1807; but this canyon also was too steep for railroad tracks.

Eventually, Alexis Godey led the whole party straight over the sand dunes, which in places lay drifted as deep as six feet in snow. The cold would not quit, with noontime temperatures sometimes below 0° F. Once clear of the dunes, heading northwest, the party entered an equally bizarre landscape. The San Luis Valley is a vast, barren basin more than 7,000 feet above sea level. It is so dry that only six to eight inches of rain fall each year. Yet in the northern heart of the basin, underground aquifers percolate through a thin layer of soil, seeping to the surface to produce a wilderness of marshes and shallow lakes.

It is a difficult and messy flat to traverse in summer. For Frémont's men, in the extreme cold, the marshland turned nightmarish. Frost feathers spangled every leaf of every squat sagebrush; the air danced with what Benjamin Kern called "spiculae of frost," enshrouding the party in a blind and chilling ice fog. And the men's feet and legs got soaked, then froze. In the middle of this "broad, drear plain," the party camped, huddled before a sputtering fire of wet sage. Micajah McGehee remembered "our mules, the poor creatures, which stood shivering in the cold with bowed backs and drooping heads, suffering from their exposed situation and half starved."

At this point in the ill-starred journey, it would have behooved Frémont to call off his mission and retreat southward toward New Mexico. Mosca and Médano Passes had already revealed that no railroad could breach the Sangre de Cristo Range. Men and mules were in poor condition, the cold showed no signs of abating, the worst snows of winter lay ahead, and some thirty miles to the west loomed the first tall peaks of the massive San Juan Range. Already several of Frémont's explorers had frostbitten feet.

But the Pathfinder was too stubborn to quit. The humiliations of the previous year rankled in his breast, and a false confidence born of his lucky traverse of the Sierra Nevada five years before in an equally severe winter kept him from recognizing the gravity of his plight.

Then, on December 8, Frémont and Old Bill Williams had a strenuous disagreement over what route to take into the San Juans. For a century and a half, scholars have struggled to decipher which man counseled which course; for it was this decision that led almost inexorably to the catastrophe that lay only weeks in the party's future.

For the rest of his life, Frémont would blame his guide for that catastrophe. Writing Jessie upon his return to civilization at the end of January, he bitterly inveighed:

> At the Pueblo, I had engaged as a guide an old trapper well known as "Bill Williams," and who had spent some twenty-five years of his life in trapping various parts of the Rocky Mountains. The error of our journey was committed in engaging this man. He proved never to have in the least known, or entirely to have forgotten, the whole region of the country through which we were to pass. We occupied more than half a month in making the journey of a few days, blundering a tortuous way through deep snow which already began to choke up the passes, for which we were obliged to waste time in searching.

As fate would have it, Williams never got a chance to tell his side of the story. But in the recollection of Thomas Breckenridge, who shared a tent with Old Bill (and whose word may thus be the most reliable of all), in the quarrel of December 8, Williams failed to persuade his leader of a course that might have averted the whole disaster:

> In camp there was a disagreement between Colonel Frémont and Williams. Williams was a man that said but little, but he was a long time with Frémont that night, and when he turned in . . . he said that they disagreed in regard to the route we should follow. He said the snow was deeper and the weather more severe than he had ever known it to be before. He said he had advised a route out of our difficulties, to go south around the San Juan Mountains, and then west along what is now the line between Colorado and New Mexico.

The next morning, the party headed not south, but northwest, toward Carnero Creek, which flowed out of the La Garita Mountains, on the eastern fringe of the San Juans. Whether or not Bill Williams knew as much, an almost unbroken massif, crowded with the ruggedest mountains in Colorado, stretched 120 miles dead ahead, across the phantom path of the railroad that would never be.

9

CAMP DISMAL

COMMITTED to an assault on the San Juan Mountains, Frémont's party headed up Carnero Creek on December 8. At once,
the going proved nasty, as men and mules blundered through willow
thickets and stands of cottonwood blanketed in two-and-a-half feet
of snow. To avoid these tangles, for hundreds of yards at a stretch
the party marched on the frozen bed of the creek.

There seems, at this point, to have been a second quarrel between Frémont and Williams over route finding. Eight years later, in
the midst of the Pathfinder's presidential campaign, reacting to
what he considered slanderous criticisms of the 1848 expedition,
Alexis Godey published a lengthy defense of Frémont in a San Francisco newspaper. Like Kit Carson, Godey would remain unswerv-
ingly loyal to his former commander for the rest of his life. In this
broadside, Godey insisted that on December 8, Frémont had argued
strenuously for an alternate valley, that of Cochetopa Creek, which
heads some thirty miles north of Carnero. But Old Bill, according to
Godey, was adamant in his preference for the more southerly route:
he "had, as he said, frequently traveled it." The account of Thomas
Martin seems to corroborate Williams's stubborn insistence on
Carnero Creek, by which valley, wrote Martin, "our guide said he
had crossed for the last 30 years."

If Godey is to be believed, Frémont's misgivings about the

Carnero route persisted into the fifth day, when they exploded in an acerbic confrontation. Frémont rode up to the guide and halted the mule train, then "expressed his fears of trouble ahead." But Williams responded, "If he doubted his capacity to carry the party through, to say so, and he could get another pilot." The mountain man added witheringly "that he knew every inch of the country better than the Colonel knew his own garden." What lends credibility to Godey's account is that he blames himself for siding with the guide and thus persuading a deeply reluctant Frémont to push on up Carnero Creek.

With the 20/20 hindsight of modern maps and roads, one can readily see that the Cochetopa route would have been a far better choice. Debilitated or not, the explorers might have cut off a northeastern corner of the great San Juan range, topped 10,149-foot Cochetopa Pass, and made their way down to the basin of the Gunnison River, pushing on west along the route of what is today U.S. Highway 50, which links Gunnison and Montrose. Patricia Joy Richmond, whose *Trail to Disaster* is the definitive work on the 1848–49 ordeal, is unsparing in her condemnation of Williams's decisions: "[I]t appears now that the old guide selected the worst possible routes to reach the fourth expedition's objectives."

Yet it is conceivable the party would have come to grief on Cochetopa Creek as well, for by December 8 the men were in bad shape and the mules were nearly finished. Two days later, Godey shot a pair of elk to supplement the expedition's meager larder. But the cold and wind ate daily into the men's spirits, and as they gained altitude among the foothills of what are known today as the La Garita Mountains, the snow deepened to an alarming fifteen feet. Micajah McGehee left a disconsolate vignette of the nightly camping routine in the snow. The mules were unpacked, then turned loose to "browse upon whatever shrubs or ends of twigs might chance to remain uncovered." The men dug out fallen timbers to feed their campfire, then slept in blankets laid directly on the snow, "first going through the process of thawing it from our feet where it would gather and become clogged while wading through the deep snow after our mules."

Within a few days, remembered McGehee, one third of the men "were already frost-bitten more or less." The corn to feed the mules

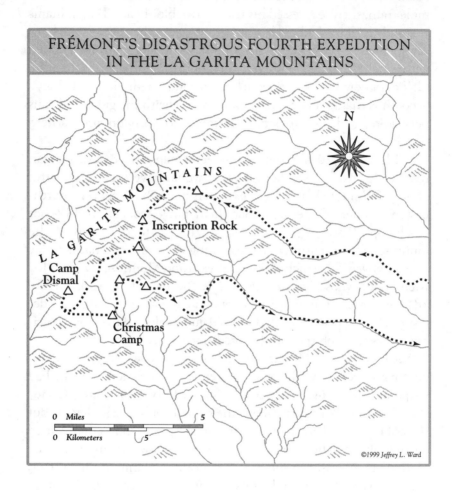

FRÉMONT'S DISASTROUS FOURTH EXPEDITION
IN THE LA GARITA MOUNTAINS

was now gone. As the canyon grew more rugged, the animals took nasty spills, tumbling down hillsides to fetch up among deadfall and talus. "They would fall down every fifty yards under their packs," said McGehee, "and we would have to unpack them and lift them up, and that with fingers frozen and lacerated by the cold." At rocky stream crossings, the mules would balk, forcing the men to haul them along with ropes tied to their noses; sometimes, claimed McGehee, the men had to wade waist-deep in the streams to bully the mules across. On December 13, with the men breaking trail for the animals, the party advanced only a pitiful 300 yards. One afternoon, a scouting party returned with the joyous news that a vast field of grass lay ahead, promising good grazing and a warm camp. On reaching this apparition, however, the team discovered not a grassy meadow but the tops of tall bushes protruding from the snow.

The mules began to die, at least one or two every night. The famished men butchered and ate them on the spot. So intense was the hunger, recalled Thomas Breckenridge, that sometimes the explorers killed a played-out mule just for food. Yet, according to this doughty veteran of Frémont's third expedition, "the men held up well, and although all were more or less frozen, I cannot remember that I heard a word of grumbling." In the privacy of the men's thoughts, however, the landscape was taking its toll: "the cañon a horrid place," wrote Benjamin Kern in his diary.

Today a dirt road leads up Carnero Creek toward the high peaks of the La Garitas. At Hell Gate, a massive notch formed by cliffs of columnar basalt pinches the valley down to a precipitous defile. Even on a genial summer afternoon, there seems something eerie and forbidding about the canyon winding beyond Hell Gate—as its ominous name, bestowed by later settlers, indicates. Yet old pictographs on the rocks reveal that Carnero Creek was a well-traveled Indian route long before the first white men came.

Thanks to the patchwork record—scraps of diary and reminiscence that are maddeningly vague about location—the precise route of Frémont's plunge into the San Juans was lost for 140 years. Allan Nevins in 1928; William Brandon in 1955 (in an otherwise sound book called *The Men and the Mountain: Frémont's Fourth Expedition*); and Leroy and Ann Hafen in 1960, in their superb documentary assemblage, *Frémont's Fourth Expedition*, all tried to recon-

struct the route of the party's December wanderings in the snow-
choked La Garitas, publishing authoritative-looking maps with neat
triangles marking each night's camp. All three were badly off the
mark.

It took a local historian, Patricia Joy Richmond (who lives today
in the tiny hamlet of Crestone, Colorado—past which locale Frémont trudged after traversing the sand dunes), to straighten matters
out. As she writes in the preface to *Trail to Disaster*, as a graduate
student at Adams State College in 1968, she had an assignment to
write a history paper using primary sources. She chose the Frémont
disaster, plumbing the resources of the San Luis Valley Historical
Society. "The night before the paper was due," she writes, "I sat up
in my bed at 2:00 A.M. and announced out loud, 'The mileages are
wrong!'" There followed for Richmond twenty years of research
both in archives and on the ground, as she hiked hundreds of miles
across the lonely plateaus of the La Garitas. By 1990, she had figured out Frémont's actual route to near perfection and relocated all
but one of his camps. The proof came in the discovery of forlorn
relics from the ordeal—most often, the still standing stumps of ax-
cut trees the desperate men had felled for campfires. Some of the
stumps were cut thirty feet off the ground, so deep had the snow lain
that terrible winter!

To the modern traveler, there are many puzzling turns in Frémont's harrowing itinerary. Shortly after passing Hell Gate, the
party veered out of the main Carnero valley to ascend a minor left-
hand tributary, today named Coolbroth Canyon. This rugged gorge
looks unpromising in the extreme, guarded by grotesque volcanic
hoodoos that, in Richmond's phrase, resemble "dwarfs with hats."
Though he misidentified the type of rock, Benjamin Kern had no
doubts about the daunting terrain, writing in his unpunctuated diary: "narrow 200 ft a sharp mountain on one side & perpendicular
friable rocks of sand stone & quartz. . . . very bad mules falling down
the rocks."

The choice of Coolbroth forced the party to traverse two low
ridges before gaining the slightly more ample Cave Creek, another
southern tributary of Carnero. This valley, too, is festooned with
volcanic anomalies: mottled brown cliffs from which dark alcoves
gape south over the canyon. On December 13, the men had their

worst day yet, as they gained those 300 painful yards in the deep snow. That night Benjamin Kern noted, "On going up the mountain the wind commenced from west cold & snowing 1 stocking frozen to my foot & all frozen together so that they must be thawed before being pulled off."

The next day, Kern noted, "mules rapidly giving out." By December 15, fifteen mules had perished. "[H]uge drifts above ones elbows when on mules back," claimed Kern; "prospects becoming somewhat gloomy." Of these grim days in Cave Creek, Thomas Breckenridge later recalled, "At night, all wet to the skin, we would gather around great camp-fires, cook and eat our mule meat, and then wrapping ourselves in wet blankets, would go to sleep."

Surely at this juncture Frémont's men saw the disaster that loomed ineluctably ahead of them. Yet by December 15, not a single diary line—not even a passage in a memoir written years later—toys with the notion of turning back. Why did Frémont insist on forging on? In Coolbroth Canyon and Cave Creek, he could no longer harbor any delusions about a railroad route. What was to be proved by stumbling on upward into deeper snows and fiercer winds? Had the team turned around at this point, Frémont might have suffered an ignominious defeat, but he could have escaped with all of his men and most of his animals still alive.

The Pathfinder's sheer, stubborn pride must be implicated in the folly that was about to unfold. Always in his memory gleamed the comparable ordeal in the Sierra Nevada in February 1844, through which he had persevered to gain Sutter's Fort and, ultimately, California itself. During the election campaign of 1856, the by then embittered Richard Kern published in a Washington newspaper a revised version of his 1848 diary. One passage, dated December 9 but wholly absent from the original diary, may have reflected his thoughts at the time, but more likely breathes a retrospective calumny: "*The deep snow of today should have warned Col. Frémont of his approaching destruction, but, with the wilfully blind eyes of rashness and self-conceit and confidence, he pushed on*" (italics in original).

Another factor, however, no doubt contributed to the decision to push on. At the head of Cave Creek, the men could see an "immense bald hill." They took—as beleaguered mountain travelers have countless times done, out of vain hope—that hill for the divide itself. And, as Charles Preuss wrote on December 15, "Bill kept insisting that we need only cross the mountain range in order to reach a snow-free tableland. We believed him, in spite of the fact that we saw here only snow on mountains and in valleys."

Unfortunately, the "immense bald hill" at the head of Cave Creek is not the main San Juan divide, but 12,422-foot Boot Mountain, a windswept dome on the far side of which yawns yet another cirque, at the head of yet another southeast-flowing creek. Among these ridges, in the heart of the La Garitas, one cirque crowds against the next, in a bewildering maze of slopes and crests. From Frémont's December 15 camp, the true divide still lay almost twenty miles to the west.

On December 14, the men and mules climbed out of Cave Creek, reached timberline for the first time, skirted Boot Mountain on the south, and slid down into the headwaters basin of La Garita Creek. No divide had been crossed: all these drainages ultimately fed the Rio Grande and flowed into the Gulf of Mexico. Yet the need to believe in such a divide persisted in the hearts of the weary men. From a shoulder of Boot Mountain, they stared west four miles to another dome, 500 feet higher, that would come to be called Mesa Mountain. The shock at not having crested the crucial watershed ebbed, as Frémont and Williams convinced their men that that higher peak must stand athwart the divide.

To deal with eight faltering mules, six men were left behind. Though they caught up with the main party and joined their camp an hour and a half after sunset, this first division of the team marked a further inching toward catastrophe. At sunset, long streaks of cirrus portended yet another storm. The snow began to fall at 9 P.M.; by morning, three new inches lay on the already smothered terrain.

In 1973, Richmond rediscovered the La Garita camp, in a grove of pines at 11,800 feet. Nine stumps still stood, cut off between 4 and 8 feet off the ground. In her sleuthing, the historian had come to recognize the signature of Frémont's mountain camps: "a copse of trees detached from the main forest, the west bank of a stream, assuring first light, and tall stumps either hacked or chopped with an upward swing."

The next day, December 15, stretched the men beyond any limits they had previously reached. "Very bad hill at start," wrote Richard Kern in his terse diary. "Snowed all day—3 miles." Aiming toward Mesa Mountain, the party crested a broad ridge above timberline that angled northeast-southwest. The wind screamed across bare talus as the men leaned into it and stumbled forward. And here, the true gravity of the team's predicament began to emerge. By late afternoon, they were still at 12,500 feet, with no prospect of shelter. An hour before sunset, blinded by the falling snow, they had the good fortune to blunder upon an anomalous stand of trees that clung to the east slope of Mesa Mountain, fully 500 feet above "true" timberline. In the gathering dusk, they set up camp once more.

On the ridge, Alexis Godey's mule had collapsed and died. Six others perished that same day. According to Thomas Martin, four of the beasts died when "they stepped out of the narrow track which we had tramped down quite hard, and sank out of sight in the soft snow." The ordeal had driven the mules to extremes that Frémont had never before witnessed, not even in the awful 1844 crossing of the Sierra Nevada. Micajah McGehee left a vivid picture of the derangement to which hunger drove the animals:

> Finally the mules began eating the ropes and rawhide lariats with which they were tied, until there were no more left in camp to tie them with, then they ate the blankets which we tied over them at night, then came in camp and ate the pads and rigging off the pack-saddles, and ate each others tails and manes entirely bare, even into the flesh, and would come to us while sleeping and begin to eat the blankets off us; would tumble into our fires over the cooking utensils, and even stick their noses into the kettles for something to eat.

In the 1970s, as Patricia Joy Richmond hiked the La Garitas, she was aware that early sheepherders had passed down a tradition that one of Frémont's men had left an inscription near the December 15 camp, at the head of West Benino Creek. But over the years, its location had been forgotten. Almost by accident, one day in 1975, high on the diagonal ridge leading toward Mesa Mountain, she paused to examine a small rock outcrop and discovered vestigial traces of the date "1848" carved in its lichen-crusted surface, only some three inches off the ground. Encircling the inscription was a D-shaped ring of stones, just large enough to enclose a recumbent human being. Evidently one of the stragglers on that wretched day in the snowstorm had taken refuge here, or even bivouacked through the night, on a wind-lashed prow at 12,600 feet, and as he lay there, mustered the energy to take out his knife and carve the dreary date. He had survived the ordeal, for the first of Frémont's men to die still had more than three weeks to live. By 1997, the inscription had crumbled beyond recognition, but the D-shaped bivouac wall was still plainly in evidence.

The camp in the high grove at the head of West Benino Creek had been pitched as a stopgap—a poorly sheltered refuge on a steep hillside where the party struggled just to get through the night. But in the event, they would be forced to spend a second night there.

If December 15 had been the men's roughest day so far, the sixteenth would be measurably worse. At dawn, a rosy sky promised fair weather, but shortly thereafter the snow again began to fall, and a bitter wind blew out of the west. The mercury had plunged to twenty degrees below zero—the expedition's coldest day yet. From their makeshift camp, the men struggled into the storm, climbing to 12,600 feet as they shaved the southern shoulder of Mesa Mountain. From downed timbers, they had manufactured mauls—clumsy wooden mallets—with which they laboriously pounded a trail in the soft and drifting snow.

On top of the ridge, however, exposed to the full fury of the gale, the men realized that they could not go on. "[I]t was so cold & windy that none could see ahead & the drifting & falling snow obscured every thing," wrote Benjamin Kern; "in danger of all being frozen we took the back trail." The party's sixty-one-year-old guide came very close to perishing in the storm. "That old fool Bill lay down and wanted to die, just at the summit," wrote the dyspeptic Charles Preuss. Micajah McGehee was more generous in his assessment of the close call: "[B]efore we could beat our way half a mile against the tempest, our guide, Old Bill Williams, had nearly frozen; he dropped down upon his mule in a stupor and was nearly senseless when we got into camp."

The retreat to the previous night's camp was the party's only option. "It was a day that tried the stoutest hearts & the whole party
came very near to total destruction," wrote Benjamin Kern. "Many
had their noses &c frozen & some became stupid from the cold—
My eyelids stuck together from cold & for a time I saw nothing but
red." Kern's brother Richard concurred: "Had the animals gone over
the hill or had we remained there half an hour longer the whole
party might have been lost."

Back in the makeshift camp on the east slope of Mesa Mountain,
the men built a campfire and tried to make a windbreak out of their
blankets. All night, the gale howled, driving snow into the best-
guarded crannies of the men's bivouacs.

Today, in the high grove of trees where Frémont's party spent the
nights of December 15 and 16, some thirty stumps bear testimony to
the ordeal. Some still stand, guarded by surrounding trees that have
sprung up only twenty or thirty years ago; others lie decomposing in
the tundra. The splintered sockets where timber was cut loose from
stump, blurred with lichens and age, look as though each tree had
been hacked at by innumerable feeble blows of a small hatchet.
Deeply imbedded in the grass and soil, two ancient, rusted metal
cans may date from the 1848 ordeal. No modern trail leads anywhere near this lonely stand of spruce and pine.

Through the patchy record of this desperate trek, Frémont himself
moves like a ghost. From Cave Creek to Mesa Mountain, the diaries
and reminiscences scarcely mention him. The commander seems to
have made few decisions, except the all-important one to push onward. One can only speculate what must have been going on in his
mind. For in the defeat of December 16, Frémont was given as clear
a warning as nature can grant that if he did not at once retreat toward the San Luis Valley, his team would come to grief. Can the
38th parallel still have meant so much to the Pathfinder, that with
Benton's vision in his head, he was blind to all else? Perhaps: the
camp on Mesa Mountain, near which no railroad would ever run,
stood at 37°54' N.

Yet if any of the men now contemplated mutiny in hopes of saving his life, no record of that vacillation has come down to us. Read-

ing the laconic diary entries, the mournful reminiscences of the party's survivors, one imagines a column of thirty-three fanatic pilgrims stumbling through the snow, driven by their own dogged fatalism toward some phantom goal in the west, even as the mules collapse and die around them.

In a letter to Jessie, written from Taos six weeks later, of this aborted traverse Frémont writes as if oblivious to the option of retreat: "On our first attempt to cross we encountered a *pouderie*— (dry snow driven thick through the air by violent wind . . .)—and were driven back, having some ten or twelve men variously frozen —face, hands, or feet. . . . The courage of some of the men began to fail."

Was courage all that mattered? Even *in extremis*, was the Pathfinder conscious above all else of the image his deeds might project when exhibited to the public in the kind of dashing report that, thanks to Jessie, had issued from his first two expeditions? We cannot know.

The next day, December 17, dawned milder, with the wind slackened to a breeze. Encouraged by the weather change, the men set off once more to push their way west. Taking advantage of rocky slopes bared by the tempest, they struck out directly over Mesa Mountain. For a while, the going was good, as the team followed the crest of a broad, featureless ridge in a steady plod from northeast to southwest.

This hinterland of the vast San Juan Range remains a bleak and lonely mountainscape today. Hikers and climbers seldom visit the bald domes and stony shoulders at the heads of West Benino and Embargo Creeks, for there are no peaks here to challenge even the timidest alpine ambition. Only sheepherders know this terrain well. It was their boots through the years that pounded out the La Garita Driveway, a narrow trail snaking near the 12,400-foot crest of the ridge along which, decade after decade, they moved their flocks. It was those solitary highlanders who built the low-walled rock shelters here and there, in which a man could take refuge from a sudden August lightning storm or a raw May blizzard.

Luxuriating in the absence of humans, a large elk herd ranges today among the sedges and willows at the head of Embargo Creek. But in 1848, the men found no elk or deer in their snow-smothered wilderness. Not since December 10, a week before, had the men been able to fill their bellies with wild game, when Alexis Godey had shot the last two elk the party had seen, down on the flats of the San Luis Valley.

Having topped Mesa Mountain, the men drove their stumbling mules three miles along the barren ridge above timberline. Though the wind had dropped, Charles Preuss still found that the "cold on the summit was almost unbearable." Even now, on otherwise mild summer days, that high, dreary crest where the Driveway winds tends to summon stiff winds out of the west. Vague rounded summits stretch almost limitless in the blue haze to the west.

The mules were on their last legs. Benjamin Kern's diary, breathlessly unpunctuated as usual, recorded the demise of his own beast of burden: "[M]y old friend (riding mate) packed with meat gave out was unpacked & started loose ahead gave out half way up the hill—I reached her to encourage her—She stopt & trembled cries of go ahead we're freezing I gave her a slight push with my knees she fell over off the trail & died that night."

At 3 P.M., the men staggered north off the ridge and reached a grove of trees at 11,800 feet, near the head of what is known today as Wannamaker Creek. Once more, the camp bore Frémont's signature: a timberline stand of pines on the west edge of the headwaters basin, facing the dawning sunlight that, after fifteen hours of cold and darkness, might send hope surging back through the veins of the stupefied explorers. But here, beneath the wind-racked ridge, the men were forced to camp once more in deep snow. Ben Kern thought it 13 feet deep, his brother 15; in reality, the drifts that blanketed the Wannamaker grove ranged up to 25 or even 30 feet off the frozen ground.

Before dark, the men herded the animals—still almost one hundred in number—up to "a bald place on a neighboring hill in hopes of their finding a little feed." There, during the subsequent days, they would die of cold and starvation, down nearly to the last mule.

In the grove at the head of Wannamaker Creek, the party would spend the next five days, as an incessant storm thwarted all their efforts to forge farther west. "Camp Dismal," the dispirited men named their pine-shrouded prison. Yet rather than accept defeat, Frémont lingered on, even as the team's plight grew grimmer by the hour. Along with Old Bill Williams, the colonel was in the grips of the delusion that had hounded him to this fatal impasse: he was convinced that he had crossed the Continental Divide. The valley stretching north, he was sure, flowed into a yet-unnamed river (the Gunnison) that ultimately emptied into the Colorado. California lay beyond.

In actual fact, Wannamaker Creek flows north into the Saguache River, which then bends back toward the north and east, entering the very San Luis Valley Frémont had fought so hard to put behind him. In Camp Dismal, the team still lay nine miles east of the Continental Divide. The snow that had drifted all around them would ultimately find its way, melted and gushing next May and June, down the Rio Grande to the Gulf of Mexico.

In the grove of pines, the men hunkered down to outlast the storm. Thomas Martin would later recall the misery of the men's effort to make a livable camp:

> We were obliged to keep a large fire always burning. At night we would clear a place and spread on it one of our large rubber covers used to cover our bag[gage] 14 by 16 feet, a few blankets on top of this and our bed was made. We slept together by messes, our covering was as many blankets as we could pile on and over these another of the rubber covers. It was not unusual to wake up in the morning and find from 3 to 6 feet of snow on top of us.

The campfire of each "mess," or group of men eating together, gradually melted a pit in the snowdrift so deep that its denizens were out of sight of the other messes, ensconced in their own frigid pits. Wood smoke and spindrift effectively blinded the men. From the surrounding slopes avalanches cut loose at all hours, sometimes, in the words of Thomas Breckenridge, "so close that the sound was like the crash of artillery. It is impossible for one who has never been placed in a similar position to imagine the state of terror we were in during our stay in that camp." Yet in the long intervals between thundering reports of the snowslides, a "lofty and dreary solitude" reigned, according to Micajah McGehee: "not even the ravens uttered their hoarse cry, nor the wolves their hollow and dismal howl."

To try to make the time pass, on December 19 the men manufactured moccasins out of whatever rawhide lay at hand. Meanwhile the mules were perishing up on their storm-lashed bald hill. "At night their cries of hunger but added to the horror of our situation," wrote Breckenridge. "The mules stood huddled together on the mountain," added McGehee, "after vainly searching for grass, their ears frozen and their limbs cracked and bleeding from cold; they would drop down and die, one by one. . . ."

By this point, the men themselves were ravenous with hunger. Except for a small store of delicacies Frémont would save for Christmas Day, there remained for the thirty-three explorers only fifty pounds of sugar and fifty pounds of coffee, along with a quantity of macaroni. As the mules died, the men thawed and cooked their carcasses, then resorted to slaughtering the doomed animals while they were still clinging to life. "In butchering them," reported McGehee, "some of the men would return to camp with fingers perfectly hard frozen." Eventually the famished team broke open their supply of candles for food, which, according to Breckenridge, "were found afterwards to be a luxury indeed."

Finally the men had begun openly to acknowledge the possibility that they might not emerge alive from their ordeal. Some essayed a feeble gallows humor, like the Scot Andrew Cathcart, who had served in the British army only two years before: "Who'd 'a thought it? A Captain in the 11th Prince Albert's Hussars eating mulemeat and packing his baggage amongst the snows of the Rocky Mountains!" On the eighteenth, Benjamin Kern, bivouacking beside his brother Richard, "waked up and found 8 inches snow on my bed, peeped out and told Dick the expedition was destroyed and if we all got to some settlement with our lives we would be doing well." For five days, Benjamin Kern felt too weak to write in his diary. When he took up his pen again, on December 24, it was to memorialize "these days of horror desolation despair."

Around 1928, an old-time miner and settler in the San Juans, Albert Pfeiffer, Jr., rediscovered Camp Dismal. He brought his twelve-year-old nephew, Charles Elliott, to the site. Standing atop the saddle on his horse, Elliott could not reach the tallest of the stumps still standing from the pines that Frémont's wretched men had cut down for firewood between December 17 and 22, 1848.

Fifty-two years later, Elliott guided Patricia Richmond to the camp. By 1980, the tallest stumps had fallen, but Richmond measured them as they lay prone in a summer meadow, finding that they ranged from sixteen to thirty feet in length. Thus the heavy snows of Frémont's ordeal that long-ago December had drifted here nearly as deep as thirty feet. By 1997, several of the tallest trees still lay in the grass, rotting to sodden pulp, but still showing the peculiar bites of the 1848 party's hacking assault on the life-sustaining evergreens. Within the heart of the grove, a number of Frémont's chopped pines still stand, their stumps eight feet off the ground.

In 1942, a local game warden named George Ward, riding up Wannamaker Creek to check hunting licenses, had come across the bald hilltop where the party had pastured their doomed mules. Bleached bones littered the tundra. Ward and a companion gathered the bones and skulls into a sizable mound. Nine months later, Ward returned to find the bone pile vanished. He concluded that some sheepherder or hunter-turned-entrepreneur had found the mound and carted out the bones, to sell to a sugar factory. In the hard times of World War II, such factories bought prairie-dog bones wholesale, to pulverize and use to bleach their sugar.

Another old-timer, Frank White, told Richmond that in his childhood the bones of Frémont's mules that had expired on the hard march to Camp Dismal lay scattered all over the slopes of Mesa Mountain. Out of respect for the 1848 tragedy, White's parents had forbidden him to play with these forlorn remnants of the "animals that belonged to men who had died on the mountain."

By December 22, even the ever-stubborn Frémont had realized that the game was up. That he waited so long to order a retreat (we know from an aside in Micajah McGehee's reminiscence) sprang in large part from the fact that the colonel had still not abandoned his preoccupation with the 38th parallel. For even as he gave the command to start back toward the Rio Grande and the San Luis Valley, Frémont hoped to reinforce himself with new animals and supplies and set out once again, via a different route through the jumbled San Juans, along the vector of his mad obsession.

In his first letter to Jessie after the debacle, the Pathfinder analyzed his predicament as if it were the working of blind Fate, of sheer bad fortune beyond his control:

Westward the country was buried in snow. The storm continued. All movement was paralyzed. To advance with the expedition was impossible: to get back, impossible. Our fate stood revealed. We were overtaken by sudden and inevitable ruin.

Even in the maw of the disaster that was opening around him, Frémont felt it appropriate to lay most of the blame not on his own rash decisions, not even on Old Bill Williams's mistakes, but on the character of his loyal followers: "The courage of the men failed fast; in fact, I have never seen men so soon discouraged by misfortune as we were on this occasion; but, as you know, the party was not constituted like the former ones."

With all but a few mules dead, on December 22, Frémont ordered the men to begin ferrying their supplies—carrying everything they owned on their own backs—to a relay site a mile to the east, over the "divide," at the headwaters of the south-flowing west fork of Rincon Creek. It was the first step in the reordering of the expedition's priorities: to forget about railroad routes and try to save men's lives. But for ten of those men, it was already too late.

10

WOLF BONES

So debilitated was the party by December 22 that it took them the better part of four days to manhandle their baggage only two miles to the southeast, where they set up a new camp in a mere six feet of drifted snow. Camp Hope, as the men called it, lay at the same altitude as Camp Dismal, but was sheltered by a much larger stand of pines and spruces. Apparently the team lacked even a decent shovel, for to prepare their blanket-and-rubber-cover bivouac sites, they scraped away the surface snow with pot lids and dinner plates.

With only a handful of mules left alive, and these too weak to bear loads, the men portaged their considerable truck themselves, shouldering burdens of sixty to seventy pounds apiece. Even so, it required many relays to transport all the equipment those two miles toward salvation. On his last ferry back to Camp Dismal, Benjamin Kern surveyed the wreckage of the expedition's dreams: "a desolate looking place a smouldering fire at Scotts mess aided the effect. The remains of the Cols [Frémont's] dead mule. . . . A raven floating thro the cold air gave the music of its hoarse notes a perfect addition to camp dismal."

Yet the weather had ameliorated, so much so that Ben Kern's brother Richard gloated in his terse diary, on five successive days: "cold but not unpleasant. . . . passed very comfortable day. Weather pleasant. . . . day pleasant. . . . day pleasant. . . . Camp in beautiful

valley about 2 miles dist. day very warm and pleasant." In the circumstances, it is hard to comprehend how a man on the edge of survival could deem a day of backbreaking toil in the snow "pleasant,"
a valley fraught with the threat of death "beautiful." What spoke in
Richard Kern's bland adjectives was the enormous relief of having
turned toward home and safety. During the first days after December
22, the whole expedition seems to have been caught up in a mood
of giddy optimism.

Among the diaries and reminiscences of the survivors, only
Thomas Breckenridge's memoir—written forty-eight years later, by
which time he was the last living veteran of the ordeal—comments
explicitly on the logic that dictated Frémont's tardy retreat: "It was
soon evident that to remain in camp [Dismal] meant to us starvation and death, and it became our main topic of conversation how
to get relief."

On Christmas Day, in Camp Hope, the party indulged in the
closest approximation to a feast it could scrape together. Richard
Kern recorded, "Had Elk stew & pies, rice dough nuts coffee biscuits
& hot stuff." His brother Benjamin lovingly detailed the same
repast: "[W]e made a good supper of elk meat which we had saved
from elk camp (Dec—) Rice coffee & a little Alcohol." But so rich
did even this meager dinner prove that Ben paid the price: "Sick all
night attack of intermittent with severe vomiting."

Many years later, Breckenridge published a "bill of fare" of the
feast (possibly recorded at the time), in the mock-formal style invented earlier in the century by British naval expeditions frozen
into the Arctic ice:

—MENU—
MULE.

SOUP.
Mule Tail.

FISH.
Baked White Mule.
Boiled Gray Mule.

MEATS.
Mule Steak, Fried Mule, Mule Chops,
Broiled Mule, Stewed Mule, Boiled Mule,
Scrambled Mule, Shirred Mule,
French-fried Mule, Minced Mule,

DAMNED MULE.
Mule on Toast (without the Toast)
Short Ribs of Mule with Apple Sauce
(without the Apple Sauce)

RELISHES.
Black Mule, Brown Mule, Yellow Mule,
Bay Mule, Roan Mule,
Tallow Candles

BEVERAGES.
Snow, Snow-Water, Water

To pass the time before dinner that Christmas Day, Frémont read many pages of Blackstone's Law, several volumes of which he had borrowed from Thomas Hart Benton's library—curious books to have carted along on an exploring expedition in the Rockies. In his letter to Jessie a month later, he reconstructed the melancholy feelings that had smitten him in Camp Hope:

Like many a Christmas for years back, mine was spent on the summit of a wintry mountain, my heart filled with gloomy and anxious thoughts, with none of the merry faces and pleasant luxuries that belong to that happy time. You may be sure we contrasted much this with the last in Washington, and speculated much on your doings, and made many warm wishes for your happiness.

(At the moment, Jessie and her six-year-old daughter, Lily, were ensconced in a hotel in Panama City, stalled in the tropics in the middle of their sea voyage to California, while a survey team desultorily scouted a quite different railroad route from her husband's—a path across the isthmus near where the Panama Canal would be dredged sixty years later.)

Caught up himself in the optimism of his party's flight toward safety, Frémont now concocted a plan of action that in retrospect raises many doubts. The colonel decided to send a small party ahead, traveling as fast and light as possible, to reach the nearest settlement and organize a relief expedition. He called for volunteers; not surprisingly, many men stepped forward, for the sooner the sufferers could escape the hell of the La Garita snows, the better. Frémont chose four: Old Bill Williams, Thomas Breckenridge, Henry King, and Frederick Creutzfeldt. He did not put Williams, still ostensibly the expedition's guide, in charge; indeed, so disgruntled was the Pathfinder with Old Bill's performance that he might well have left him out of the rescue party altogether had the man not known the country far better than any other member of the expedition. Instead, Frémont designated King the leader. Not much is known about this man today. A captain in the army, he had served ably on Frémont's third expedition in California. He lived in Georgetown, then a community neighboring the nation's capital, and thus may have been a regular acquaintance of the colonel between expeditions. Perhaps still in his twenties, he had married only two weeks before leaving for the 38th parallel. And he seems to have been well liked: in the phrase of an expedition teammate, King "gained the friendship and esteem of every member."

Glazing his memory perhaps with a fulsome estimation of his own role in this emergency jaunt, Thomas Breckenridge decades later recalled the Pathfinder's very words as he sent the four men off on their mission:

> "Breckenridge," he said, "we have been in many tight places together, and I know you are one of the hardest and toughest men I have, and you are able to endure more than the average man; but what I shall ask of you will try both your nerve and endurance to the utmost. Relief we must have, and as soon as possible, and a small party can get along faster than a large one. . . . King, Kreutzfelt [sic] and Williams have volunteered—now will you go?" I said, "I will go. If any one can make the trip, I can."

Frémont and Old Bill Williams knew that the nearest settlement was Abiquiú, in northern New Mexico. Benjamin Kern reported that the leaders guessed this Hispanic hamlet lay 160 trail miles away; Charles Preuss put the distance at 100 miles as the crow flies. The four emissaries sat down with the colonel to map out day by day the stages by which they might achieve their errand of help. Yet the diaries and memoirs from the expedition vary wildly in reporting the remaining twenty-nine men's expectations. Micajah McGehee recorded that sixteen days were allowed for the quartet's retreat and return with reinforcements. Alexis Godey reckoned eleven days. The blithest anticipation was Preuss's: according to his diary, King planned to lead his trio on a forced march, day and night, taking advantage of moonlight, and to reach Abiquiú in three or four days. "The return trip on fresh animals could be made in no time. . . . The most difficult part seemed to be getting back to the river [Rio Grande], but he hoped to reach it the first evening." Summing up the situation equanimously on December 27, Preuss convinced himself, "[W]e could now expect relief in about a week, and until then, and even beyond that, we had enough provisions."

The euphoria of turning back had blinded even the most skeptical of the expedition members to their true predicament. During the last few weeks' struggle toward the Continental Divide, even with mules carrying their gear, the party had usually advanced only two or three miles a day. To be sure, traveling light, King's quartet could move faster than the heavy-laden expedition. But to think (as the congenitally pessimistic Preuss unaccountably did) that those men could cover more than thirty miles a day as the crow flies, or some fifty as the trail wends, was fatally misguided. Even McGehee's more sober allowance of sixteen days coming and going would have required the rescuers to average twenty miles a day.

On the morning of December 26, King's party left. "We took one blanket apiece, a few pounds of frozen mule meat, about one pound of sugar, a little macaroni, and a few candles," Breckenridge remembered. "We had three Hawkins' rifles for defense against the Indians, about fifty bullets, and one pound of powder. We also had one shotgun."

Second-guessing a disastrous expedition's mistakes from the hindsight of a century and a half is altogether too facile an exercise.

But at this juncture, Frémont's decisions and omissions cry out for analysis. Why did the Pathfinder put such faith in a relief mission? For even if King's splinter party reached Abiquiú quickly, how might a rescue team, burdened with fresh mules and supplies of food, fight its way in only a few days back to the high, snowbound basins that it had taken Frémont's team so much time and such arduous travail to reach?

The strongest of all Frémont's men was indubitably Alexis Godey. Why had Frémont not appointed this man—whom three years earlier he had likened to one of Napoleon's marshals—to lead the rescue team? In the event, Godey accompanied King's men partway down to the San Luis Valley, then returned to join Frémont's entourage—an action that saved the party from even worse tribulations.

Would a better chance of survival not have lain, after December 25, in the whole party's stripping to a minimum of gear and pushing hard, en masse, toward the San Luis Valley? Yet even after all but a few mules had died, the men still painfully hauled their saddles, bridles, and halters from one camp to the next, along with all kinds of other unnecessary stuff—surveying instruments, trade goods for the Indians, specimen-preserving presses, a telescope, trunks and barrels, and Frémont's volumes of Blackstone, among other items. The gear had a certain value, to be sure, but life itself must have loomed as more precious. (Yet returning from the South Pole in 1912, Robert Falcon Scott had died of cold, starvation, and exhaustion, without having jettisoned some thirty pounds of rocks—geological specimens—from his sledge.) Finally, there is no ignoring that, no matter how grim the party's outlook was by Christmas, Frémont fully intended to resupply and head back into the San Juans, bashing his winter way to California through sheer willpower. To make a second push, he would need all that otherwise superfluous gear.

Why didn't the explorers make snowshoes? Every mountain man knew how to fashion such footgear out of a little rawhide and some willow boughs: Bill Williams could have taught the craft in half an hour. Yet the option comes up only once in the men's memoirs and diaries, when on December 27 Preuss bafflingly mutters, "[W]e could not find material for snowshoes."

Perhaps most crucially, why did the men fail to butcher the dead mules and lug with them as much meat as they could carry? For food meant life, and in the meat of a hundred mules there would have been enough food to sustain the men for weeks. A kind of apathy seems to have seized the party once King's quartet had set out. Preuss says only, "To take meat with us seemed to be too troublesome because we already had plenty to drag." Frémont believed that by Christmas, between what was left of his macaroni, sugar, coffee, and bacon, he had less than two weeks' provisions. Yet as King departed, the colonel could not imagine that in two weeks all his men would not be resting safe, sound, and well fed.

It was not Frémont's plan simply to sit in Camp Hope and wait for rescue. Since hauling the massive piles of gear on his comrades' backs had proved so grueling, he set them to work on December 26 constructing sledges out of the available timber. By the next day, the team was ready to slide their gear down the steep grade of forest and talus that led to Rincon Creek. In Patricia Richmond's pithy evocation, "Bundles of equipment were shot down the steep slope or ridden like giant inner tubes." And by the end of that day, the grand experiment had proved itself a complete failure, as the runaway sledges bounced off rocks, spilling their baggage, hung up in trees, and simply fell apart. Ben Kern's diary glumly recorded this careening travesty: "[O]ne fell down very often & slid with the baggage 20 or 50 ft at a time. . . . Very weak & miserable with difficulty reached our camp."

In the 1920s, Albert Pfeiffer, Jr., the local miner and settler, stumbled across the remains of Camp Hope (which would come to be renamed Christmas Camp). A few years later, the Forest Service put up a sign marking the site of Frémont's yuletide vigil. Faded but still legible, the sign still hangs from a sturdy pine on the edge of the level grove. Back in the woods some thirty to fifty yards, a number of stumps, only a few feet off the ground, stand placid in their decay, scarred into the softened splinters of the characteristic 1848 hacking effort that felled the trees for firewood. Christmas Camp is the only site from Frémont's ordeal sign-posted today, and yet it is seldom visited, for it is not easy to find, clumped on a nondescript timberline shoulder between the west and main forks of Rincon Creek.

In 1930, a sheepherder and a forest ranger found a pair of hand-crafted sledge runners below the camp. These were removed to the Rio Grande County Museum in Monte Vista, where, preserved in a glass case, they center a forlorn collection of relics from the tragic expedition, recovered over the years in the high La Garitas: a butcher knife, porcelain moccasin beads, a piece of an old leather boot, a mule jawbone and skull coated with green-gray lichens.

Although the sledges proved unworkable, by the end of the day on December 28 the men had wrestled all their unwieldy gear down into the V-shaped canyon where Rincon and Embargo Creeks join to hurtle southward. Somewhere in that basin, the team set up camp. They had reached their lowest elevation in weeks, perhaps below 11,000 feet; they were sheltered by the valley and surrounded by a limitless supply of firewood. Despite the sledging fiasco, the men were full of optimism, for their looming task seemed a straightforward matter of pushing on down Embargo Creek, as King's rescue party had two days before, until it emptied into what they called the Rio del Norte (the Rio Grande).

Then Alexis Godey returned from his scout with King, and he brought with him bad news. Below the men's camp, the canyon of Embargo Creek became far too precipitous, seamed with cliffs and talus slopes, for the party to haul their baggage down it. Their only choice was to carry all the heavy gear back up the valley, then cross another ridge to the east, as high as Camp Hope. Devastated by the news, the men named their hapless bivouac Camp Disappointment.

Of all the camps from the 1848 ordeal in the La Garitas, Camp Disappointment is the only one that has never been relocated, though Patricia Richmond has searched for it for years. Benjamin Kern's diary mentions that for the party's campfire on December 28 "our fuel is quaking asp easily cut & soon consumed." Today a good trail winds its way down Embargo Creek, cleverly skirting the precipices that blocked Frémont's retreat; but one need only glance to the wayside to perceive the impossible gauntlet of deadfall, scree, and raw ravine that Godey had fought his way back up that snowy December day.

There are a number of aspen groves in Embargo Creek, the lowest of which has been all but leveled by beavers to construct a maze of ponds. Since an aspen tree, unlike pine or spruce, seldom lives a hundred years, there is no hope of finding the standing stumps from Camp Disappointment. Richmond's only clue as to where the disheartened men received their setback came from an old-time rancher named Carl Keck, who told her that in 1941 he and his father had "passed a rock ledge littered with brass rings and buckles. Two logs resembling the runners of a sledge lay among the trees. . . ." Yet no further search on Richmond's part has found any trace of these fugitive artifacts.

So on December 29, the men began the Sisyphean job of hauling their baggage back up to timberline. "[A] long toilsome march for a weak man," wrote Ben Kern, and the next day, "got ¼ mile from next camp & gave out left the load & crawled on my hands & knees back again very much exhausted." It took the twenty-nine men three full days to ferry their enormous piles of gear over to the next drainage to the east; yet still, Frémont was unwilling to abandon even a book or a specimen press.

As if there were not already abundant evidence that the party was in a fight for their lives, a new sign of disintegrating morale emerged on December 31. Unable to keep up with their teammates, the three Kern brothers and their three mess partners set up their own camp at the head of Embargo Creek, one mile and a low divide short of the rest of the party. They tried to make a festive occasion of New Year's Eve, eating "boild mule meat for pies," singing "several songs in our crude way." But the forced joy could not dispel what Ben Kern noted as "quite a feeling of novel loneliness."

Occupied only one night by six men, the New Year's Eve Camp is vestigial in the extreme today. It rests in a tiny grove clinging to a steep slope just west of the headwaters of the stream. In the summer of 1997, a group of delinquent teenagers led by an officer from a youth camp based in Monte Vista, authorized by the Forest Service, was tearing up the ground with picks and shovels, prying loose boulders and chainsawing downed logs, as they built a new trail right through the grove. Ignorant of any notion of Frémont's expedition, they labored within a few feet of several stumps bearing the 1848 hatchet work. Nearby, some more sensitive passerby had built a small cairn of rocks, inside which he had cached two eloquent relics from the ordeal: a smashed metal bucket, inside of which was stashed a dried-out black leather boot sole, the pegging holes intact.

The next day—January 1, 1849—the Kerns managed to struggle east to the main party's camp on Groundhog Creek. It was this drainage by which Frémont intended to escape the snowy prison of the mountains. But here the Kerns effectively gave up. They would spend the next eleven days in the Groundhog Creek Camp, waiting apathetically for someone to rescue them, even as their teammates ferried gear up and down the valley below. With them for several days lingered Raphael Proue, a Frenchman getting up in years who had nonetheless served under Frémont on all four of the Pathfinder's expeditions.

Richard Kern's already laconic diary was reduced on Groundhog Creek to the essence of apathy:

SAT JAN 6th in same camp
SUNDAY JAN 7 Same camp
MONDAY JAN 8th Same camp.

Ben Kern's more loquacious jottings offer some detail. To wait out their fate, the men built a "shanty" out of evergreens they felled. Richard read out loud to the others and played his flute. The men's hunger was so intense that Ben noted, "[S]aw several mice looked at them with a hungry eye long for a mouse trap." On January 7, Ben recorded only the date, then laid his diary aside for good.

Today, in the grove at Groundhog Creek Camp, there are abundant signs of the Kerns' feckless vigil. Many low stumps still stand, sheared with a series of diagonal cuts that seem to be the signature of the chopping style of one of the Kern brothers. Remarkably enough, the rectangular base of the shanty lies intact in the grass at the edge of the grove, logs all but decomposed but still proclaiming a feeble hold on human life.

In summer, it takes only twenty-five minutes to walk across the grassy alp that separates Groundhog Camp from West Benino Camp, into which the expedition had staggered through the snowstorm on December 15. In 1848, it had required sixteen days of severe privation and relentless toil to complete the trek that closed the party's anguished loop between those two camps—a trek, moreover, that had effectively sealed some of the men's fates.

Meanwhile, Frémont, Godey, and the other strongest veterans

forged their way down Groundhog and La Garita Creeks, first reaching the Rio Grande on January 2. Still ferrying gear, the men climbed up and down the seven-mile-long valley, some returning to Groundhog Camp to try to rally the Kerns. The relatively warm spell between Christmas and New Year's dissolved in a new snap of bitter cold, against which the weakened travelers had few defenses. By January 10, the food had given out, and the men started eating rawhide. Micajah McGehee memorably recalled this grim fare: "[W]e began eating the rawhide tugropes and parfleches [leather pouches], cutting it in strips and boiling it to a sort of glue, or burning it on the coals until it was soft enough to bite."

Frémont was beside himself with worry about what might have befallen King's rescue party. By January 10, the four putative saviors had been gone sixteen days—the longest span allowed by the most pessimistic among the party. As the colonel later wrote to Jessie of these early January days: "Now came on the *tedium* of waiting for the return of the relief party. Day after day passed, and no news from them. Snow fell almost incessantly in the mountains. The spirits of the camp grew lower. Life was losing its charm to those who had not reasons beyond themselves to live."

Among the objects of that sneering aspersion was Frémont's old companion, Raphael Proue. On January 9, somewhere on Groundhog Creek, Proue's legs froze so badly he could not walk. A companion wrapped him in his own blankets and went for help, but by the time he returned, Proue was dead. By now, the men were locked into the kind of solipsistic callousness that a survival ordeal commonly brings on. Micajah McGehee recalled seeing Proue's frozen corpse beside the trail: "[W]e passed and repassed his lifeless body, not daring to stop in this intense cold to perform the useless rites of burial." Frémont seemed to blame his old comrade for giving up: "Proue laid down in the trail and froze to death," he wrote Jessie. "In a sunshiny day, and having with him the means to make a fire, he threw his blanket down on the trail, laid down upon it, and laid there till he froze to death!"

Meanwhile, what indeed had happened to King's rescue party? The only firsthand source for its tribulations is the memoir Thomas

Breckenridge penned forty-eight years after the fact. Yet that recital gives a vivid account of agony and despair.

Expecting to reach the Rio Grande the first day, King's party had instead taken three, averaging a mere five miles per day down precipitous Embargo Creek. Cold and starvation dogged their dragging steps: by the time they reached the Rio Grande, they were "as hungry as wolves. Two tallow candles, the last of our supplies, had served as breakfast hours before. The situation was growing desperate."

On the fourth day, the team hiked down the frozen bed of the river. Their feet were now frostbitten, swollen so badly that they took off their leather boots and bundled their feet in strips of blanket. Rather than discarding the boots, they carried them along as emergency rations. "That very night," Breckenridge recalled, "one of them was nicely browned over the fire."

During the next week, the quartet advanced at the pitifully slow pace of two to three miles a day. "My memory is clouded concerning a portion of the time, so near was I to death," Breckenridge confessed, "but to the best of my recollection we lived eight days on our boots, belts, and knife scabbards." The only supplement to such fare came when Breckenridge managed to shoot a hawk, and when the team found a dead, rotting otter on the ice—"a delicious morsel, though it was, by long odds, the gamiest I ever attempted to swallow."

By now the party had reached the western edge of the great, bleak San Luis Valley, near today's town of Del Norte. The walking was far easier than in the mountains. But at this point, Old Bill Williams paused, shaded his eyes with a flat hand, and stared toward the eastern distance. That night in camp, he told his companions he had seen a thin plume of smoke—" [A]nd, boys, that smoke don't come from the camp-fire of a white man—it is the smoke of an Indian camp, and if these are Indians, they are Utes.'

> We were glad to hear him say they were Utes; we knew that Bill had lived among this tribe and could speak their language, and I had heard that he had a squaw among them. We would engage them to go back with us to the camp in the mountains and rescue our comrades.

Bill sat with his head between his hands for a long time as if in deep thought. Then he looked up and said: "I have an explanation to make. When I was a young man I was adopted by the Utes and lived among them. I was sent to Taos for supplies for my friends and was betrayed into a drunken spree. It was during this time that I blindly led the soldiers against my comrades. It was the meanest act of my life. For my treachery every Ute Indian rightly seeks my scalp."

Disheartened by this revelation, Old Bill's companions agreed to avoid the Ute camp by leaving the course of the river and striking out on a beeline "short-cut" across the stark San Luis Basin. It was a consequential and probably unwise decision—for on the open plain, the men were exposed to the merciless wind and could find virtually no firewood. For a century and a half, historians have wondered whether Williams made up the story as an excuse deliberately to delay the rescue mission—for reasons that will later become clear.

According to Breckenridge, during the hellish jaunt across the basin, the men became snow-blind. At night, without a campfire, they bivouacked sitting up in a snow hole, a blanket beneath them and the remaining pieces of blanket drawn over their heads to shield them from the wind. "Sleep was out of the question except for a few minutes at a time."

The men saw no game to shoot. "Our stock of burnt boots was now gone. We began to chew the leather of our knife scabbards as we staggered on. When these were gone we began on our belts."

On January 12 or 13, as the team came within a quarter-mile of finishing their beeline and rejoining the Rio Grande, King stopped in his tracks and said, "I can go no further, I am sorry, but I am tired out, and will sit here until I am rested. You three leave me and push on to the river and make your camp. When I am a little rested, I will follow."

No amount of exhortation could persuade King—nominally the leader of the rescue mission, but by now its weakest member—to continue. Limping ahead on their frozen feet, the other three took two hours to cross that quarter-mile of ground to the river bottom. At 4 P.M., with the day fading to dusk, they built a bonfire of cottonwood branches and warmed themselves for the first time in a week.

Creutzfeldt offered to go back in the night and try to drag King to camp, but Williams insisted the man was already dead, for he had seen a raven circling over the carrion their companion would soon become. Yet Creutzfeldt set off on his errand of mercy anyway. When he returned several hours later to report that King had indeed died, he was in a kind of dementia: "I could see that the shock was affecting his mind," remembered Breckenridge. "He could talk of nothing else.

> That night I dreamed of my mother's kitchen at Christmas-time: of the roast meats and turkeys, the pumpkin pies, and the cakes and fruit. Then I would awake to the terrible feeling of emptiness, the indescribably painful craving for food.

Breckenridge's narrative implies that the men broke camp the next morning and headed on down the river. But from the second-hand testimony of three other members of the expedition, a far more gruesome aftermath of King's death in the snow emerges. Wrote Charles Preuss matter-of-factly in his diary, around January 17, when the main party had reunited with their "rescuers," "King had died of exhaustion four days before, and the others had eaten part of his body." Thomas Martin later corroborated the claim: "They brought his body into where they camped and it is supposed that they lived on it, although they never would acknowledge it." So did another expedition member, Charles Taplin, telling a St. Louis reporter only three months after the disaster, "King had died, and his remains, which the party carried with them, had been more than half eaten up by his companions."

The question of whether the survivors of Frémont's ordeal were reduced to cannibalism, like the Donner party only two years before, has been fiercely debated ever since 1849, but the preponderance of evidence supports the claim. (Frederick Ruxton's remarkable quasi-memoir, *Life in the Far West*, implies that cannibalism was almost a routine practice among mountain men.) Old Bill Williams's biographer, Alpheus Favour, went to some lengths to deny the imputation, arguing that if Frémont's main party, trailing the relief team, came upon the remains of King's body, they might have mistaken the ravages of ravens and wolves for cannibalism; and also that the charge, which surfaced during the nasty 1856 presidential campaign, was a calumny of Frémont's political opponents. But Favour wrote before the discovery of Preuss's diary. Most likely Preuss and others in the party learned about the flesh eating from the rueful admissions of its perpetrators. Many years later, Jessie Frémont insisted that Kit Carson had later told her, "In starving times no man who knew him ever walked in front of Bill Williams." (Jessie, of course, was at pains to buttress her husband's contention that the whole catastrophe of the fourth expedition ought to be blamed on Old Bill.)

Stumbling on down the Rio Grande, the three survivors had to pause once more when Creutzfeldt collapsed, "and lying down refused to go further." His companions built a fire on the spot and dragged and rolled the stricken man near it. In the morning, Breckenridge, stronger than the sixty-one-year-old Williams, set off alone in the lead; soon, however, he was reduced to crawling.

At that moment, all three survivors of the rescue party were on the verge of death. Then, abruptly, Breckenridge saw five deer standing only a few yards away. He raised his rifle and aimed. "This was the supreme moment," he dramatized later. "Life or death rested on that shot." He fired, then crawled to the carcass of the three-pronged buck he had felled. "I cut the deer open, and tearing out its liver devoured it as ravenously as I have seen hungry wolves devour the flesh of a buffalo."

Rejuvenated by the raw venison, Breckenridge carried meat back to his comrades. He found Williams waiting over Creutzfeldt's deathbed. Yet the first taste of deer meat so galvanized the failing man that, according to Breckenridge, "He sprang to his feet and hugged and kissed me, calling me his savior and preserver." The men set up camp near the slain deer.

That night we were three of the happiest men on earth. We sat up and cooked and ate venison until midnight, then turned into our remnants of blankets. We cooked and ate deer meat all the next day. Strange as it may seem, none of us were inconvenienced in the least from over-eating.

* * *

Meanwhile, as the rest of Frémont's party struggled down Groundhog and La Garita Creeks, all semblance of expeditionary discipline vanished. By twos and threes, no longer organized even by the messes in which they had camped and cooked for weeks, the men stumbled toward the Rio Grande. When Elijah Andrews collapsed, his friend Micajah McGehee, rather than abandon him, managed to get him into a nearby cave, then rolled piñon logs down the hillside from above for firewood. Later Andrew Cathcart and Richard Kern, at last roused from their apathy at Groundhog Camp, joined the bivouac. The four men spent two days in the cave, waiting out a snowstorm. Over the fire, they prepared the very last of their rations—a cup of sugar and a cup of macaroni apiece—but the shaky Andrews tipped the whole concoction into the fire. "Thus went the last mouthful we had to eat on earth, and we half starved," recalled McGehee. This resourceful survivor, however, found a roll of rawhide strings which he cut into pieces, as well as some old wolf bones in a den in the nearby talus. "[T]hese we pounded to pieces between rocks and boiled them with the strings and, upon this mess, we four lived for two days."

At last, though far too late, Frémont had agreed to cache all the expedition gear that the party had wrestled down from Camp Dismal. He chose the base of a prominent cliff he called Point of Rocks, near the mouth of La Garita Creek, for this depot, as the site ought to be easily spotted from a distance by a party returning to gather it up. With his fondness for gadgets and instruments, it must have been painful for Frémont to leave behind his telescope and compasses, thermometer and barometer, chronometer and sextant, his specimen presses, as well as his father-in-law's Blackstone and a gilt-edged Bible.

By January 11, Frémont resolved to march ahead on a second rescue mission. It had been eighteen days since the departure of King's quartet; by now, the colonel was convinced they had either lost their way completely or been ambushed by Indians. And already he had rediscovered King's first campfires, sited discouragingly close together in mute testimony to the party's pokey progress. (From the campfires, Preuss calculated that their predecessors had gained only ten or eleven miles in four to five days.)

With his four strongest colleagues, Frémont set off on the eleventh. They included, of course, Alexis Godey, but also Charles Preuss, who on this, his third Frémont expedition, had seasoned from the effete bumbler of 1842 into a competent explorer. In charge of the twenty-five stragglers he left behind, the Pathfinder appointed Lorenzo Vinsonhaler, a forty-one-year-old sergeant who had served under him in California.

Richard Kern, by then embittered against his former commander, published in 1856 what he claimed to be the text of Frémont's note giving orders to Vinsonhaler as he departed:

> I am going to start for Abaca [Abiquiú]; I want all the men to bring the baggage down the lodge [Point of Rocks]. If no relief come then, let them take down their guns and blankets, and follow the river down to Rabbit [Conejos] Creek; and if no relief at Rabbit Creek, then come to Abaca; and come quick, or you will not find me there, as I shall have left for California.

If this text is accurate, the selfish inhumanity of its concluding phrase takes one's breath away. The ever-loyal Godey vehemently denied that the note mentioned any plan to head on for California, and by 1856, Richard Kern had motivation aplenty to besmirch the Pathfinder's integrity. But Micajah McGehee independently vouched for the California clause, reporting, "He left an order that we scarce knew how to interpret, to the effect that we must finish packing the baggage to the river and hasten on down as speedily as possible to the Mouth of Rabbit River where we would meet relief, and that if we wished to see him we must be in a hurry as he was going on to California."

Frémont's team of five moved more efficiently along the Rio Grande than King's party had. Even so, the ordeal had taken its toll, and these men were as famished as their comrades left behind. On January 15, by sheer chance, the party ran into a solitary Ute who spoke some Spanish. In his letter to Jessie, Frémont detailed this encounter in his usual cavalier fashion:

> He proved to be . . . son of a Grand River chief we had formerly known, and behaved to us in a friendly manner. We encamped

near them at night. By a present of a rifle, my two blankets, and other promised rewards when we should get in, I prevailed upon this Indian to go with us as a guide . . . and take with him four of his horses, principally to carry our little baggage. These were wretchedly poor, and could get along only in a very slow walk.

Frémont thus implies that the meeting with the Ute was a mere happy convenience; in truth, it may have saved the lives of all the members of the expedition who eventually escaped the ordeal. For that night the Indian brought the starving men to his camp and fed them well ("Miserable as the place looked," wrote Preuss, "we prepared here a magnificent breakfast of corn mush and venison"). From then on, Frémont's men rode horseback rather than walked, and turned over to their guide—whose Ute name has not come down to us, though Anglos may have known him as Chief San Juan—the considerable task of navigating the way to the nearest New Mexico settlement.

As was his wont, Frémont was inclined to credit his own decisions rather than the Ute's heaven-sent aid for the deliverance of his party. To Jessie, he smugly reflected, "I look upon the anxiety which induced me to set out from the camp as an inspiration. Had I remained there waiting the party which had been sent in, every man of us would probably have perished."

Thomas Martin put the business in proper perspective: "Frémont and party would have in all probability perished had they not had the good fortune to take an old indian prisoner [?] . . . [who] afterwards guided them all to the settlements. Frémont and whole party were snow blind when they ran across the old indian."

Toward sunset of their first day on horseback, the colonel's revived team saw a thin column of smoke rising from a grove near the river. They rode up, only to discover the three survivors of King's relief mission. It had been twenty-two days since these men had set out for help, and they were not even halfway to Abiquiú. Frémont did not recognize Creutzfeldt until Breckenridge reminded him who his companion was. The three emaciated, starving men were, the colonel wrote, "the most miserable objects I have ever seen."

11

THE STRONG

AND THE WEAK

FRÉMONT'S discovery of the starving trio—Williams, Brecken-ridge, and Creutzfeldt—saved their lives. In his letter to Jessie, the colonel insisted, "By aid of the horses, we carried these men with us to the Red River settlement. . . ." Yet Breckenridge's own account is quite at odds with this assertion: "Frémont remained just long enough to cook some venison, then pushed on, ordering us to follow as fast as we could . . . and leaving ten or fifteen pounds of jerked venison."

If Breckenridge's memory is accurate (and there is no reason to doubt it), the three men continued toward New Mexico not on horseback, but limping along on their frostbitten feet, which soon gave out: "We were compelled to get down on our hands and knees. For nearly the entire distance we crawled on ice or through snow." Their feet, freezing and thawing daily, had become masses of open sores: "Truly, that last forty miles was a trail of blood." It took the trio "ten days of the most excruciating pain" to reach the nearest New Mexico settlement.

Meanwhile, riding on south, Frémont's party of five covered the same distance in four days. They arrived not at Abiquiú, but at the "Red River settlement," an Hispanic colony that had sprung up on the site of today's Questa, New Mexico. There Preuss waited to greet his comrades as they straggled in, while Godey and Frémont rode on down the Rio Grande to find mules and volunteers for a relief party.

Seven years later, Godey, who the rest of his life would never utter a negative word about his commander, remembered Frémont's courage during the escape from the La Garitas:

> [He] never, during all the trying perils that beset us, evinced for a single moment that his eminent energy and determination had deserted him, bearing up against the most forbidding prospects, wearing a bold and hopeful front among his men, and infusing into their drouping spirits a portion of his own indomitable fortitude. . . . That man, a mere stripling in stature, prosecuted his weary way on foot to the settlements when stout mountaineers had given up in despair. . . . If anything had been wanting to knit me close to Frémont, . . . the few brief days passed with him on that fearful journey, within which were compressed a life time of experience, would have perfected it.

Frémont reached Taos the next evening, where he at once set out to find Kit Carson. Entering the shop of an old acquaintance, he discovered three veterans of his California campaign engaged in idle talk: Lucien Maxwell, Dick Owens, and Carson. As the colonel wrote in the manuscript notes for the illustrated report on the fourth expedition that he would never produce: "Owens fails to recognize me & Maxwell does instantly—Why don't you know the Captain? Hospitable reception. Carson takes me to his house."

Shocked by the appearance of his old comrade, Kit and his wife, Josefa, nursed Frémont slowly back to health. Every morning, she brought him a cup of hot chocolate, which he drank in bed. After six years of marriage, Josefa was pregnant with the couple's first child. (Born prematurely on May 1, the son survived only a little more than a year.)

As he waited for news of the rest of his party, Frémont wrote to Jessie, already framing his self-exculpatory exegesis of the catastrophe even as it continued to unfold. And, as if oblivious to the tragedy, but mindful above all of how posterity might judge his fourth expedition, he explained, "At the beginning of February (about Saturday) I shall set out for California, taking the southern route. . . . I shall break up my party here and take with me only a few men." In-credibly, Frémont seems still to have cherished his delusions about the railroad route, for he added, "The survey has been uninterrupted up to this point, and I shall carry it on consecutively."

Godey, however, without even pausing to spend a night in bed in Taos, had headed back north, in charge of a rescue party he, Fré-mont, and Carson had hastily assembled. He had thirty mules, a few horses, ample food, four Mexican volunteers, and eight or ten U.S. soldiers assigned by the commander of the local military district. Unlike the Pathfinder, despite his own exhausted state, Godey would spare no effort to save the men he had marched with through the worst ordeal of their lives.

Back in the San Luis Valley, it was not until January 16, the same day that Frémont and his Ute guide had discovered the campsite of the three original "rescuers," that the last of the surviving men fi-nally emerged from La Garita Creek and started to hobble south along the Rio Grande. It had been thirty-eight days since they had passed through Hell Gate on the Carnero, beginning their climb into the La Garitas full of high expectations already tempered with doubts.

Carrying a handful of sugar each, along with candles and rawhide strips as food, a blanket strapped to each man's back, a rifle in hand, the played-out men walked down the ice-covered river. "Tottering from weakness and some with frozen and bleeding feet," remem-bered Micajah McGehee, "we made slow progress."

The ordeal had already driven some of the men to the edge of madness. As McGehee foreshadowed the subsequent events, "Now commenced a train of horrors which it is painful to force the mind to dwell on. . . ." Manuel, a mere teenager, a California Indian whom Frémont had befriended on his third expedition, his feet gone to frostbite, stopped and begged the leader of this sorry band, Lorenzo Vinsonhaler, to shoot him. When Vinsonhaler declined, Manuel abruptly turned around and headed back toward the cache at Point of Rocks. He was given up for dead by his teammates, but remarkably enough, he would survive.

On January 17, in McGehee's terse phrase, Henry Wise "lay

down on the ice and died." We know almost nothing about this unfortunate, except that he was a tax collector Frémont had recruited
in St. Louis: his first expedition proved to be his last. On the
evening of the seventeenth, a man named Carver—so lost to history that we cannot even retrieve his first name—"crazed by hunger,
raved terribly all night," McGehee reported. "He told [his compan-
ions], if any would follow him back, he had a plan by which they
might live. The next day he wandered off and we never saw him
again."

Two old friends, Frenchmen Vincent Tabeau and Antoine
Morin, the latter a veteran of Frémont's third expedition, were the
next to die, on January 22. At first, they had seemed among the
stronger survivors, setting off down the Rio Grande in advance of
Vinsonhaler's main band. But Tabeau fell into "a violent fit, which
lasted upon him for some time," according to McGehee. "Poor fellow, the next day he traveled as long as his strength would allow,
and then, telling us we would have to leave him, that he could go
no farther, blind with snow, he lay down on the river bank to die."
Refusing to leave his friend, Morin sat with him and perished at
Tabeau's side.

Two other young Indians Frémont had befriended in California,
known only as Gregorio and Juan or Joaquin, now concluded that
the men they had shared a mess with for weeks might be plotting to
kill and eat them. They refused to travel farther with their erstwhile
comrades.

Trudging south, the abler men kept their eyes out for game to kill,
but no animals appeared. Recalled McGehee,

Occasionally we could hear the distant, dismal howl of a wolf
weary with waiting for its work, but none came near, and, at distant intervals, a raven would go screaming by, beyond our reach,
but never stopping within sight. We found a handful or two of
rosebuds along the river which we divided and ate, and Dr. [Ben-
jamin] Kern found a few small bugs upon the water where the ice
was broken and ate them. We had already devoured our moccasin
soles, and a small sack made of smoked lodge skin. We dug in the
ground beneath the snow with our knives for roots, but it was a
useless labor.

Under the stress of such extreme conditions, a deadly schism began to develop within the team, as it sorted itself into the stronger
and the weaker. Instead of traveling together, the stronger men
voiced the intention of pushing ahead, abandoning their slower
comrades to their inevitable fate. The catalyst was the division of
spoils after Thomas Martin shot a deer on January 19. Richard Kern,
one of the weakest stragglers, complained in his diary that Vinsonhaler intended to take the deer with the stronger men and "[leave]
the rest of us to perish." As it was, "Our share of meat was so unjustly small that it did us no good." In his retrospective account,
Thomas Martin baldly admitted the schism: "We then waited 4 days
until the rest of the company should come up. When they arrived
we divided the deer with them. . . ." Then, at midnight, while the
weaker men were all asleep, Martin, Vinsonhaler, and four other
men "crept out of camp and started again."

The three Kern brothers, who tended, as well-educated Philadel-
phians (Edward the topographer on the third expedition, Richard
the expedition artist, Benjamin a doctor), to antagonize their lower-
born teammates by expecting special treatment, and who had loafed
in Groundhog Camp, shirking the hard job of hauling baggage
down to Point of Rocks, blamed Vinsonhaler for allowing the
schism to develop. Edward Kern's later remarks were especially bitter: he thought Vinsonhaler "a weak & cowardly person to whose
imbecility and cowardice may be laid the subsequent deaths of most
of the men who were lost." In fact, on January 21, Vinsonhaler had
abdicated his impossible role as leader. As Richard Kern wrote in his
diary that night, "Mr. Vinsonhaler resigned all command of the
party, declared it broken up and said each one must take care of
himself. A piece of rascality almost without parallel."

The deaths continued: Henry Rohrer and Elijah Andrews on January 22, Benjamin Beadle and George Hubbard a few days later.
There can be little doubt that the survivors cannibalized some of the
corpses. McGehee later recounted a campfire proposition made by
one of his comrades (left unnamed in his reminiscence), explicitly
raising the option of devouring the dead. McGehee talked the others
into waiting another three days. In 1878, Thomas Martin wrote, "I
know positively that the men we left behind lived on those of their
companions who gave out, as I had it from some of the same men."

By this time, even the relatively strong Micajah McGehee admitted that "to walk thirty steps once a day after some dry cottonwood sticks to keep up our fire fatigued us greatly." One by one, the men prepared for death. "Remained in camp—too weak to move," wrote Richard Kern on January 23. "We looked for muscles & snails & earth worms—found none." His brother Edward later recalled "gradually sinking into a sleep. . . . I felt happy and contented sitting nearly all day by the fire in a kind of stupor listless and careless of when my time would come—for I was expecting it and in anticipation of it had written and closed all my business."

On January 25, Micajah McGehee and his four companions sat in camp, too tired to move, "in the deepest gloom." Suddenly the men thought they heard a call. " 'Hush!' said one, and we all listened intently."

Taken in sum, the pageant of Frémont's fourth expedition unfolds as a tale of unremitting folly. The common men were brave enough, and some of them rose to occasional acts of compassion and self-sacrifice. In Old Bill Williams, the expedition had at best an ineffectual guide; at worst, a true villain. And it is hard not to read Frémont's pigheaded obstinacy and fateful decisions as verging on the villainous.

But the expedition had one genuine hero. That man was Alexis Godey. Knowing that every hour counted, he had left the Red River settlement at the head of his rescue team on January 22. In less than four days, he had ridden back to the San Luis Valley and located the vanguard of the helpless survivors. As Edward Kern wrote to his sister two weeks later, "To the perseverance of Godey must be accredited the salvation of those of us that remain and he was the only man capable of performing such an exploit."

The men in McGehee's camp were so snow-blind, at first they took their savior to be Frémont himself, who looked nothing like Godey; they saluted him and addressed him as "Colonel." At once, Godey gave the men, delirious with joy, several loaves of bread, "with commendable forethought giving us but a small piece at first," as McGehee put it. "It required considerable persuasion to prevent us from killing the old horse which the Spaniard had, in order to eat it; but Godey informed us there were two colts in the camp below, which, if we would wait, we might have."

As Breckenridge recalled, "Next morning Godey left me in the care of 5 or 6 men to get wood and cook for us, and keep us from eating too much, as we were totally unable to help ourselves." Then Godey set out to search for the rest of the survivors—no easy task, for they were scattered up and down the Rio Grande, some camped at a distance from the river, each small contingent utterly unaware of the whereabouts of the others.

During the next few days, Godey found Hubbard dead, and nearby, John Scott at death's door, "sitting in a listless manner by a fire he had just kindled, his head resting upon his hands, almost totally snowblind." Godey fed the man and gave him a horse and a Mexican escort to take him to McGehee's camp. Pushing on, Godey discovered the bodies of Tabeau, Morin, and Beadle, but he found and rescued one survivor after another. A month later, Benjamin Kern replayed his own salvation in a letter to a friend. As Kern sat with several others in a snowstorm around a small fire of willow twigs, Charles Taplin abruptly cried, "By God, there is a halloo!"

Tis but a wolf again we said—rising to his feet he said Christ there's a man on horseback over the river, we gave a shout you may be sure, almost in an instant Alexis Godey was with us. Well boys I am damned glad to find you alive. He then pulled some bread from his pocket Oh he has bread we cried and some of us trembled with joy at the sight of it. Yes boys and there is a mare you may kill.

Even after being restored with food and blankets and given horses to ride, some of the refugees barely endured the slow trek south. Thomas Breckenridge, till now one of the stronger survivors, could not ride a horse unless someone held him on it. McGehee, too, had to be hoisted onto his horse ("for we could not lift even our skeleton frames").

So full of pluck was Godey that, after finding what he assumed was the last of the survivors, he rode on north to Point of Rocks to see if he could retrieve the party's cache of equipment. This proved impossible, but there he discovered the Indian boy, Manuel—given up as dead by all the others—and so saved one more life.

On February 9, the bedraggled column reached the Red River

settlement. "[G]ot there about sunset, and slept in a house," Richard Kern told his diary with understated jubilation.

Ten of the thirty-three men on Frémont's fourth expedition perished in the La Garitas and the San Luis Valley. Without Godey's extraordinary mission of succor, another fifteen would have died.

On February 12, the survivors reached Taos, where they were reunited with their commander. That same day, Frémont chose the men he wished to accompany him and set off for California, as if impatient to obliterate the memory of his great failure and redeem it by completing some sort of "survey." In the seven pages of notes he eventually jotted down as his plan for a book, the whole ordeal is telescoped into less than a page. There follow three pages of blithe reminiscence of the utterly routine trip he subsequently made along established trails to reach California.

In a letter to Thomas Hart Benton, written on February 24, from Socorro, New Mexico, Frémont gives himself the credit for the rescue: "In four days afterwards I reached the settlements, in time to save many, but too late to rescue all the men." Godey's heroic return to the San Luis Valley is depersonalized into a single vague sentence in the passive voice: "Relief was immediately sent back, but did not meet them in time to save all."

If one were to seek evidence of the narcissism that his recent biographer Andrew Rolle sees at the core of the Pathfinder's character, his behavior at the end of the disastrous expedition in pursuit of the 38th parallel offers it in spades. From his letters and notes detailing the catastrophe, not one germ of genuine remorse leaks out. Instead, Frémont takes refuge in his habitual conceit that his men depended vitally on his leadership. Writing to Jessie from Taos on January 29, he voices a token of concern: "I am anxiously waiting to hear from my party, in much uncertainty as to their fate." But then he adds, with fatuous complacency, "My presence kept them together and quiet, my absence may have had a bad effect."

In March, Old Bill Williams, Benjamin Kern, and eight New Mexicans returned to Point of Rocks to retrieve the cache. The mission cost the two survivors from the La Garitas their lives. All the histo-

ries that cover this postscript to the fourth expedition insist that at or near the supply cache, the party was attacked by Utes, embittered against white men by recent army raids on their villages. Kern and Williams were killed, while the others fled for their lives. Williams's biographer, Alpheus Favour, claims that the Utes admitted the slayings to an Indian agent who investigated the matter, and that "when it was discovered who it was they had killed, [Williams] was given a chief's burial by the Indians."

After her years of sleuthing along the paths of the La Garita disaster, Patricia Richmond has come to a different conclusion. Her definitive book, *Trail to Disaster*, stops short of unequivocally advancing her alternative theory; but by 1997 she was ready to voice it. A scholar friend of Richmond's, doing research at the Library of Congress and the Smithsonian Institution, had come across an army document reporting that Benjamin Kern and Bill Williams had been killed not at Point of Rocks, but separately, far from the cache: Kern near Culebra Peak, just north of what would become the Colorado–New Mexico border; Williams on the Mora River, southeast of Taos.

"I think the party had already recovered the baggage," says Richmond. "A lot of the gear later showed up in Abiquiú. I think Ben Kern was killed by the others in the party, because he wouldn't go along with their plan to appropriate the equipment for themselves. If Old Bill was killed on the Mora, it may have been by Utes, or by members of the recovery party, as he was trying to link up with the Santa Fe Trail and trade the stuff."

Richmond also believes that Williams deliberately led the party into a mountain cul-de-sac, hoping they would be forced to cache their equipment (valued at some $8,000 to $10,000), planning beforehand to recover it in the spring for his own personal profit. This scenario seems hard to square with the fact that Old Bill twice came very near to dying himself on the expedition, and with the fact that when he set out to recover the cache in March, he enlisted so many confederates in that mission.

In any event, Williams's death was convenient for Frémont, for the mountain man never had a chance to defend himself against the Pathfinder's charge that the disaster was entirely the guide's fault. The notes for his book, complete with bracketed annotations as to

where the engravings might appear, indicate that for a while Frémont planned a report in the style of the two that had made him famous. But then, perhaps, he thought better of it, realizing that
silence was preferable to any account of an expedition that had
failed in its objective, at the cost of the lives of ten men, some of
whom had then been cannibalized by their desperate teammates. Or
perhaps his habitual writer's block simply stalled the project.

A century and a half after the fact, it is hard to escape the conclusion that blame for the debacle of the fourth expedition can be
almost entirely laid to the Pathfinder. All the crucial decisions that
led, one by one, to the catastrophe—from pushing into the La Garitas long after the dream of the railroad route lay in ashes, to failing
to turn back when both mules and men could have been saved, to
hauling the useless gear from camp to camp, thereby exhausting the
men—were Frémont's choices, not Williams's. Finally the fact that
Frémont felt no obligation to accompany Godey on the rescue mission argues a leadership of the most cowardly and heartless sort.

Yet it is remarkable how well, in subsequent years, Frémont managed, in the modern phrase, to "control the spin" on the disaster.
This misguided and tragic expedition, whose participants' sufferings
rivaled those of the Donner Party, remains little known today.
Because Frémont's was a privately funded jaunt, no government
agency ever felt the need to investigate the expedition of 1848–49.
Had he commanded this fiasco as an army officer, Frémont would
probably once again have been court-martialed and convicted. As a
private citizen leading a band of volunteers, he could traipse on to
California unscathed. During the 1856 presidential campaign, rumors about the catastrophe resurfaced, but men like Godey rose to
his eloquent defense. The deaths in the La Garitas did little or
nothing to damage the Pathfinder's chances in a close election
against James Buchanan.

Left behind in Taos, the Kern brothers were the most vocal of
Frémont's detractors. As Edward wrote, shortly after his deliverance,
Frémont was

> jealous of anyone who may know as much or more of any subject
> than himself (for he delights to associate among those who *should*
> be his inferiors—which may in some measure account for the rep-

utation he has gained of being, for a man of his tallents, so excessively modest[)] . . . [T]he greatest dread he has at present is that a *true* and *correct* account of the proceedings above and here be made public.

This bitter but perceptive analysis, however, found the ear only of Kern's sister; it was not published until 1960.

During the 1856 campaign, Richard Kern published his 1848–49 diary, with retrospective derogations of Frémont added in, in the *Washington Daily Union*. But it was buried beneath the widely reprinted encomium of Alexis Godey, who passed down the portrait of a courageous and exemplary leader whom, for the rest of the nineteenth century and well into the twentieth, the public wished to believe in:

Frémont, more than any man I ever knew, possessed the respect and affection of his men; he ever lived on terms of familiarity with them. Yet never did commander possess more complete control. He ever partook of the same fare; underwent like hardships; rode when they rode; walked when they walked, and unhesitatingly exposed himself to every danger and privation.

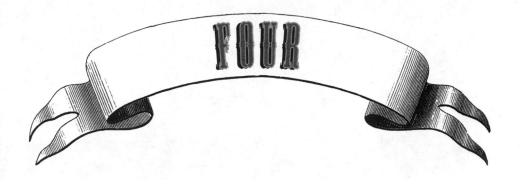

THE LONG WALK

12

ROUNDUP

A s Kit Carson rode south from his home in Taos toward the ruins of Fort Stanton, in south-central New Mexico, he was overtaken by a messenger. It was October 1862, with the country eighteen months into the Civil War that was threatening to tear even the West apart. Carson was serving as a colonel in command of the New Mexico Volunteers. He had been sent on his errand into the homeland of the Mescalero Apaches by his commander, Major James H. Carleton, in charge of the Union forces in New Mexico. The Confederate army had been recently driven from the territory, and Carleton was turning his zealous attention to the Indians.

Carson knew that his job was to pacify the Mescaleros, who had made numerous raids on the far-flung settlements of New Mexico. And he knew Carleton well, having first gained the general's approbation as Carson guided him in another Indian campaign eight years before.

But now, as he opened the letter from the major that forwarded his official instructions, and shyly asked one of his men to read it out loud to him, he was chilled and disgusted by the directive:

All Indian men of that tribe are to be killed whenever and wherever you can find them: the women and children will not be harmed, but you will take them prisoners and feed them at Fort

Stanton until you receive other instructions about them. If the Indians send in a flag and desire to treat for peace, say to the bearer . . . [that] you have been sent to punish them for their treachery and their crimes: That you have no power to make peace; that you are there to kill them wherever you can find them. . . .

Carleton closed this extraordinary missive with an equally extraordinary self-appraisal: "I trust that this severity in the long run will be the most humane course that could be pursued toward these Indians."

A weary fifty-two years old, Kit Carson was a far different person from the greenhorn who, at nineteen, had gleefully killed Apaches in Arizona under the command of Ewing Young. He knew twenty times as much about Indians as Major Carleton did. And though, as an on-and-off member of the U.S. Army, he believed in following orders as faithfully as the next soldier—had in fact followed Frémont's orders in California even when he disagreed with them—he could not bring himself to carry out the letter of Carleton's genocidal imperative.

Other men could. Before Carson reached Fort Stanton, a regiment under Captain James Graydon met up with a band of Mescalero men, women, and children heading north. These Apaches, under the command of two chiefs, the seasoned Manuelito and his protégé, José Largo, were on their way to Santa Fe to sue for peace. On seeing the soldiers, Manuelito raised his hand in the universal peace sign and slowly rode forward. Without warning, Graydon ordered his men to fire. Both chiefs, nine warriors, and one woman were killed, and twenty other Apaches were wounded.

Thus began the most extensive—and, arguably, the most wrong-headed—roundup of Indians ever prosecuted in the United States, which would culminate in the Long Walk of the Navajos and in five years of starvation and demoralization at the Bosque Redondo—in conception an Indian reservation; in truth, nothing more than a prison camp.

As the best Indian fighter in the West, a reluctant Kit Carson would be pressured by Carleton into spearheading the roundup. In his lifetime, the campaign against Apaches and Navajos capped Carson's glory, making him even more famous and uniformly honored than he already was. Today, thanks to the revisionism of history, Carson's role in that campaign has all too often been seen as the most shameful deed in a long, occasionally brilliant, more often checkered career in the West.

The crowning irony, perhaps, is that the average Navajo today has never heard of James H. Carleton, but he reviles the very name of Kit Carson.

Thirteen years had passed since Carson had nursed Frémont back to health and sent him on to California. During that period, Kit had made his most concerted effort yet to settle down—only to find some new adventure or campaign periodically luring him away from Taos. Assuaging the sorrow of losing her firstborn, Josefa gave birth to another son in 1852, a daughter three years later, and two more sons in 1858 and 1862; eventually seven of the couple's children would live to adulthood. On a trip to St. Louis in 1852, Carson at last performed the task he had long set his heart on, of bringing Adaline, his daughter by his Arapaho wife, to Taos. Fourteen at the time, she would spend only a short part of her sad life in New Mexico, marrying Louis Simmons within a year; heading for the California goldfields, only to be abandoned by her husband; and dying at twenty-two, apparently destitute.

At Rayado, near the Cimarron River, forty miles east of Taos, Carson went in with his old friend Lucien Maxwell on the most serious farming venture he would ever attempt. In the heart of magnificent grasslands and piney hills, the isolated ranch was too vulnerable to Indian attack for Carson to feel secure in bringing his family there: Josefa and the children continued to live in Taos. For all his wanderlust, it pained Carson deeply to be separated from his children and his wife. One army friend left a memorable vignette of Kit's ways with his children:

> [H]e used to lie down on an Indian blanket, in front of his quarters, with his pockets full of candy and lumps of sugar. His children would then jump on top of him, and take the sugar and candy from his pockets and eat it. This made Colonel Carson very happy, and he derived great pleasure from these little episodes.

According to the friend, Kit's nickname for Josefa was "Chepita," "and he was most kind to her." Another acquaintance observed, "Only with children and the child-like Mexicans did he seem able to lay shyness aside."

Yet during the early 1850s, Carson twice succumbed to the urge to strike out on a long journey. In 1852, with several cronies, he trapped the Arkansas and the North and South Platte Rivers once more, even though the bottom had fallen out of the beaver market. The following year, with Maxwell and another partner, he pulled off the remarkable feat of driving a herd of 6,500 sheep to California, via Laramie and the Oregon Trail, to sell to the gold seekers who had thronged the new state. The men managed to ward off the wolves and mountain lions that might have wreaked havoc among their flocks, and bought off Indian raiders with the occasional gift of a sheep. Having purchased the animals in New Mexico for $2.50 a head, they sold them in California for $5.50 apiece. The three men netted a windfall of nearly $20,000, and Carson was for a short time richer than he had ever been.

Everywhere he went, celebrity seekers dogged his heels; in California, the papers announced his advent. Carson hated the attention and went to great lengths to avoid it. "Men sitting next to him," wrote Carson's first biographer, DeWitt C. Peters, in 1859, "would speak of him and Kit would quietly eat his meal and walk off, signaling his friends not to give him away." More than one journalist, on first meeting Carson, was dumbfounded at his unprepossessing appearance. "He . . . looked like an Illinois farmer," wrote one; and another found "a little weazen-faced, light-haired, active frontiersman, who wore his hair long, and swore in a horrible jargon of Spanish and English, and who didn't 'fear no Injun livin'.' "

In California, Kit visited with many old friends from Frémont's third expedition, saw Adaline for the last time, and marveled at the changes wrought on the place by the Gold Rush. The Pathfinder himself was back east at the time, however. Though each would hold the other in the highest esteem for the rest of his life, the two men, once so inextricably bound together, would meet only once again—in Washington, when Carson had a mere three months to live.

When Kit returned to Taos with his small fortune in sheep speculation, he learned that he had been appointed Indian agent to the

Utes. His domain was that of the Mohuache Utes, a subtribe ranging mostly across northern New Mexico; but during the next eight
years he would minister also to the Jicarilla Apaches and the
Puebloans living along the Rio Grande.

As agent, he was required to strike the delicate balance between
providing for the welfare of the Indians under his charge and hunting down and punishing those who had committed "depredations."
It was on one such mission, in 1854, that Carson first met Major
Carleton, when Kit served as his guide for an army pursuit of a band
of Jicarillas. The soldiers trailed the Apaches up into Colorado Territory, along the east edge of the San Luis Valley (retracing the very
route Frémont had followed six years before toward his ordeal in the
La Garitas). Though Apaches were masters at hiding their tracks,
Carson followed them east along the Huerfano River and back
south into the mountains near Raton. Still without having glimpsed
a single Indian, Carson told Carleton on June 4 that they should
meet up with the fugitives by two o'clock. The major was so skeptical of this prediction that he promised his scout that if it came true,
he would buy Carson the finest hat available in New York City.

Precisely at two, the battle was joined, and the Jicarillas were
routed. A few weeks later, back in Taos, Carson received a package
in the mail: it contained a splendid hat, with gilt lettering on the inside band:

AT 2 O'CLOCK
KIT CARSON
FROM
MAJOR CARLETON

Carleton went on to describe Carson in print as "the best tracker
among white men in the world."

Many a mountain man who had formed his views of Indians during his trapping years never altered them thereafter. But Carson,
though taciturn by habit, and the furthest cry from an intellectual,
was a thoughtful and perceptive student of human nature. His sympathy toward Indians had begun to gestate in California. Now he
used his years as an agent to deepen immeasurably his perspective
on the problem of the natives of the Southwest.

More than almost any other veteran Indian fighter, Carson apprehended a central conundrum: that the decline of wild game attendant on the white man's flooding into the country ineluctably drove the Indians toward a raiding life. On one punitive mission against the Apaches, he was disturbed to find the tracks of barefoot children in the mud and snow. As Carson's recent biographers Thelma S. Guild and Harvey L. Carter write, "Those prints . . . were eloquent signs to Carson that the battle was not simply against a band of reckless adventurers, but against a people—old and young, mothers and children."

In the annual reports that his post required him to dictate and forward to Washington, Carson articulated the Indian policy that had gradually formulated in his mind. For their own good, the natives needed to be settled on reservations, preferably far from white settlements with their corrupting influences (as early as the first rendezvous in the 1830s, Kit had seen what alcohol could do to Indian culture). Like even the most liberal theorists of his day, Carson believed the best way to "civilize" the Indian was to teach him agriculture. It would take the anthropological relativism of the mid twentieth century to recognize what a profound injury forcibly converting nomads and hunters into sedentary farmers inflicted.

In these views, Carson was fairly conventional among Indian agents. Where he surpassed most of his peers was in his recognition of raiding as a desperate necessity, not simply a nasty penchant of "savages," and in insisting that it was the agent's job to come to the Indians, not vice versa. As he complained against the reservation practice of the day, in his dictated 1856 memoir,

> I cannot see how the Superintendent can expect Indians to depart satisfied that he has called to see him from a distance of two or three hundred miles, compelled to go several days without anything to eat, unless they have carried it with them. They are given a meal by the Superintendent, then the presents are given. Some get a blanket; those that get none are given a knife or hatchet or some vermillion, a piece of red or blue cloth, some sugar, and perhaps a few more trinkets. They could more than earn the quantity they receive in one day's hunt, if left in their country.

Even more powerfully, Carson concluded, "They should not be allowed to come into the settlements, for every visit an Indian makes to a town, it is of more or less injury to him."

By now, Carson longed for nothing more than to stay at home with Josefa and his children, but as agent, again and again, he rode out to the Ute camps to give his charges bushels of wheat, blankets, and other supplies. In his 1857 report, he confessed, "It would promote the advance of civilization among the Indians if . . . I could live with them." Many of the Indian agents of the day were corrupt, skimming off a good percentage of the annuities forwarded them by the government or selling supplies to white settlers. Carson was scrupulous to see that every penny went toward Indian welfare. Best of all, when he visited Utes or Apaches, he spoke to them in their languages.

Despite these sometimes far-flung missions, Kit was earnestly trying to embrace the domestic life. He had sold off his interest in the Rayado ranch in order to stay in Taos. To an eastern journalist who interviewed him, he insisted that, having passed the age of fifty, "he designed thenceforward to avoid horseback riding and travel only in carriages." He even joined the Masonic order in Santa Fe. (The image of Kit Carson as a Master Mason, trading esoteric banter with his colleagues over dinner at the fraternal lodge, is as bizarre a picture as his life affords.)

The question of how Carson came to dictate the memoir that stands today as virtually his only autobiographical document is a murky one. Given his distaste for celebrity, as well as his congenital taciturnity, it is certain that Kit did not initiate the project himself. Since the manuscript of the memoir was lost for almost half a century, to be rediscovered in a trunk in Paris in 1905, we cannot even be sure of the identity of the amanuensis who recorded Carson's reminiscences. The modern editor of the memoir, Harvey L. Carter, has studied the problem more assiduously than any other scholar. He concludes that the man writing down Carson's stolid but honest sentences was John Mostin, one of four scribes he employed during his years as Indian agent to handle his correspondence. In turn, an entrepreneur from Missouri named Jesse B. Turley took the manuscript and tried to peddle it as the raw material for a professional biography. Turley approached, among others, Washington Irving, who had converted a comparable manuscript by the mountain man Benjamin Bonneville into a lively and popular book; but the prolific Irving indicated he had no interest in cranking out a life of Carson. Eventually the memoir formed the basis of Carson's first biography (if we discount the dime novels that celebrated his derring-do), DeWitt C. Peters's grandiloquently titled *The Life and Adventures of Kit Carson, the Nestor of the Rocky Mountains, from Facts Narrated by Himself,* published in 1859. When a friend read parts of the book to Kit, he said only, "Peters laid it on a leetle too thick."

All this, of course, leaves unanswered the question of whose idea the memoir was in the first place, and how he persuaded Carson to cooperate. After 1856, unfortunately, we have no account in Kit's authentic voice (save such dry correspondence as he churned out as army officer and Indian agent) to narrate the last twelve years of this remarkable man's career.

A month after the Civil War broke out, Carson resigned as Indian agent and accepted his commission with the New Mexico Volunteers. He seems to have had no hesitation in joining the Union side in the fray, even though most of his far-flung family, including a number of brothers, were Confederate sympathizers; perhaps the years with Frémont had inculcated abolitionist and Republican views.

For most of a year, New Mexico was hotly contended. Legend has it that early in the campaign, as Confederate partisans assembled in the Taos plaza to hoist their banner, Carson was one of several men who nailed the Stars and Stripes to a cottonwood pole, erected it in the plaza, and kept it under guard day and night. The Confederate army was composed mostly of Texans who had marched north along the Rio Grande. For a good part of the first year, they held both New Mexico and Arizona Territories.

Lacking true military training, far more skilled at the guerrilla tactics of Indian fighting than in the brutal pitched battles of the Civil War, in charge of a motley band of volunteers even less well trained than he, Carson participated in only one battle, though it was the important and bloody carnage at Valverde. The fight was won by the Confederates, though the toll was high on both sides: 68 dead in the Union ranks, 40 among their opponents. Carson's troops succeeded in forestalling a Confederate capture of a 24-pound cannon, with which they fired a shell at the enemy, "with fatal effect," Carson reported. But in the panic of battle, many of the volunteers were useless, and about a hundred of them broke and ran.

A month later, after the decisive battle at Glorieta, the Union army retook the New Mexico Territory, sending the graycoats scurrying back to Texas. Carleton, heading east at the head of his California Column to help rout the Texans, was too late to fight at Glorieta, but when the colonel in charge of that victory was ordered to Washington, Carleton stepped into the breach. On September 18, 1862, he assumed command of the Union army in the Department of New Mexico. With no more Confederates to fight, he turned his eye on the Apaches and Navajos.

Forty-eight years old that autumn, Major James Henry Carleton had his virtues. In the words of C. L. Sonnichsen, historian of the Mescalero Apaches, he was "an extremely competent and aggressive officer who was always driving himself and his men, a stickler for discipline, a man without weakness or mercy. . . . He had a heart which could be touched, and a conscience which never slept. He was a Christian and a gentleman; he had friends and loved his family."

Earlier historians were kinder toward Carleton than more recent ones have been. To Edwin L. Sabin, Carson's 1935 biographer, Carleton was "a fighter, a gentleman and a Christian, at once the soldier and the citizen. A very dynamo of energy, relentless as a chastiser, kindly as an adviser"—all in all, "a mentor admirably endowed for further shaping the character of Carson."

But in the view of Edwin R. Sweeney, whose 1991 biography of Cochise is the definitive work on the great Chiricahua Apache chief, Carleton "had become obsessed with a psychopathic hatred of Apaches." As Sonnichsen adds, "His trouble was that he could not admit an error, change his mind, or take a backward step." In the best surviving photo of the major, his eyes are fixed in a fanatic stare, beneath dark cornices of frowning eyebrows, above a bushy beard and mustache that seem to hide a clenched jaw.

The logic of Carleton's campaign was far from inescapable. As far back as 1855, the Mescaleros had been soundly defeated by army troops in their homeland. That year they were confined on a reservation (whose boundaries remain more or less unchanged today); Fort

Stanton was built at the junction of the Bonito and Ruidoso Rivers to oversee it. The fort had been burned down by the retreating Union army in 1861, lest it fall into Confederate hands. Over the years from 1855 to 1861, periodic raids had been conducted by Mescaleros, as by the Jicarillas and all other Apache bands. With the American army suddenly divided into blue- and graycoats killing each other after April 1861, Indians all over the Southwest were emboldened. As troops retreated, burning their forts behind them, some of their shamans and chiefs dared to believe that the scourge of the white men was about to be lifted, that supernatural powers had intervened to cause them to flee the West they had so eagerly invaded.

A gloomy concomitant to Carleton's roundup, however, was the fact that the major had ridden into New Mexico with fully 2,350 volunteers under his command. With the Confederates routed, these men were itchy for further action: soldiers who have mustered to fight an enemy have a hard time abiding idleness and peace. One captain whose troops prowled through the Guadalupe Mountains in search of Apaches but found only deserted camps reported all his men were disappointed, "but none so much as myself, in not getting a fight out of the redskins." As much as for any other reason, Carleton launched his campaign against Apaches and Navajos to give his soldiers something to do.

By November, three separate companies had pushed deep into the Mescalero heartland. The demoralized Apaches offered little resistance. Knowing Carson's reputation for fairness and humanity, rather than fight the army they sought out Kit at Fort Stanton and put themselves under his protection. Carson could not bring himself to execute men who had come to him to surrender, nor to imprison the women and children. He sent five leading Apaches to Santa Fe under an armed guard. There, before Carleton, one of them, a chief named Cadete, made a mournful speech of submission that lost none of its eloquence when translated into English:

> "You are stronger than we. We have fought you so long as we had rifles and powder; but your weapons are better than ours. Give us our weapons and turn us loose, and we will fight you again; but we are worn out; we have no more heart; we have no provisions, no means to live; your troops are everywhere; our springs and water-

holes are either occupied or overlooked by your young men. You have driven us from our last and best stronghold, and we have no more heart. Do with us as may seem good to you, but do not forget we are men and braves."

Incredibly, Carleton seemed unmoved by these words. He had already made up his mind about the ultimate disposition of the Apaches. He told Cadete that no treaty of peace would be signed until all the Mescaleros had walked and ridden to a place far to the east of their homeland, on the Pecos River.

Despite the deepening of his sympathies for the natives over the past decade, Carson's stance was still a far cry from that of certain prominent easterners—Quakers, pacifists, and ministers, for the most part—who from time to time inserted themselves into the Indian wars of the West, only to earn from the white settlers of the territories that most withering of epithets, "Indian lover." On the trail, Carson kept up his guard as staunchly as he had during his trapping days. As he brought Adaline back west with him from St. Louis in 1852, he foiled a plot that would have cost the lives of a party led by almost any other white man. Camped on the plains of eastern Colorado, Carson's small entourage grew uneasy as about twenty Cheyenne men came riding up in twos and threes. Carson invited them to sit and smoke. The Cheyennes feigned peace, then in their own tongue began discussing the best way to kill the whole party: they would knife its leader, they said, while he was smoking and off his guard.

Kit understood every word. He summoned up an angry indignation, replying in Cheyenne: "So you wish to take my scalp! Why? I have done you no injury!" Then he ordered the Indians to leave his camp. "Any that refuse to leave will be shot. If any of you return, I will fire on you."

The Cheyennes retreated, only to plan an ambush down the trail. But Carson foiled this stratagem, too, by bluffing the Indians with the threat that troops were on their way from Bent's Fort.

By 1862, though he had come to admire such peoples as the Utes and Puebloans, Carson retained a distrust of the Apaches. The Jicarilla under his charge, he dictated in one report, "were truly the most degraded and troublesome Indians we have in our department. . . . [W]e daily witness them in a state of intoxication in our plaza."

For Carleton's roundup and removal, however, Carson had no stomach: the whole idea was anathema to him, and he knew Carleton's grand plan would prove a failure. Moreover, at the age of fifty-two, Kit was simply worn-out. Two years before, on a hunting trip in the San Juan Mountains, he had been thrown by a horse. Numerous times in his life, like any other veteran rider, Kit had been thrown; but this time he got tangled in the lead rope and was dragged brutally across the stony ground. He suffered internal injuries that, in his own estimation, never really healed; from them, in Edwin L. Sabin's words, "developed the malady which within eight years took his life."

In February 1863, Carson dictated his letter of resignation from the army. "There is no probability that we shall again be called upon to defend our Territory against hostile invasion," he pleaded with Carleton, explaining his withdrawal. Carson was right: never again would New Mexico be invaded.

But Carleton refused to accept Kit's resignation. There was only one man, he insisted, capable of carrying out the second phase of his grand scheme. Kit Carson must lead his forces against an enemy even more warlike and far more numerous than the Mescaleros: the Navajos, who had never in their long, proud span in the Southwest submitted to reservation life.

13

THE SIEGE OF TSÉLAA'

THE site Carleton had chosen for his "reservation" lay on an empty plain 140 miles southeast of Santa Fe, where a lonely bend of the Pecos River meandered beneath a stand of cottonwoods. Apaches had sometimes camped here. The place's Spanish name, Bosque Redondo, the Round Grove, alluded to that stand of tall trees. By late 1862, under Carleton's orders, soldiers had begun to erect Fort Sumner nearby.

Before settling on the location, Carleton had sent an inspection team. They had found little to like about the bleak site, warning, in their report, that "[b]uilding material will have to be brought from a great distance. The water of the Pecos contains much unhealthy mineral matter." But Carleton had made up his mind. Even after the Bosque proved a disaster, Carleton kept issuing rosy reports of well-being among the prisoners; his critics sardonically called the camp Fair Carletonia.

Coldhearted and stubborn though he was, Carleton was nothing if not shrewd. Two unacknowledged motives were central to his transplanting the Navajos and Apaches en masse to the Pecos. Bosque Redondo lay in a region so desolate that Carleton doubted white settlers would ever come into conflict with Indians situated there. And he hoped these desert nomads would serve as a buffer against the marauding bands of Kiowas and Comanches even farther east.

With a resigned fatalism, the Mescaleros—men, women, and children—trudged 130 miles to the new fort. By March 1863, some 400 Apaches had settled around the burgeoning stockade. Fewer than a hundred others had fled westward, joining their sometime allies the Gila Apaches in an ultimately futile struggle against other army forces intent on wiping them out. By midsummer at the Bosque, the prisoners had begun their apprenticeship as farmers, plowing fields, planting corn, and erecting a crowded and squalid city of tents in which to dwell.

On July 7, the campaign against the Navajos began, as Carson, full of misgivings, rode west toward Fort Defiance, yet another army outpost that had been abandoned by retreating Union forces in 1861. Just inside what would become the Arizona border, a few miles north of today's town of Window Rock, the fort—soon renamed Fort Canby, in honor of Carleton's predecessor as head of Union forces in New Mexico—lay in the southeast corner of the vast Navajo homeland. It would become the headquarters for Carson's campaign against the Diné, as the people called themselves.

Carson's orders were virtually identical to those he had received in the Apache roundup: the adult men were to be shot on sight, the women and children taken captive, and no peace treaty brokered until all the Navajos had marched to Bosque Redondo. And once again, for the most part, Carson softened his persecution so radically that, in any officer less vital to such a difficult mission than Kit seemed to Carleton, it would have amounted to insubordination.

The extended campaign by which Carson would round up most of the Navajo people took a course unlike that of any other Indian war in our country's history. Relatively few men were killed: only one white soldier lost his life. For six months, Carson regarded his effort as perhaps the greatest failure of his life, even while it took its devastating toll beyond the eyes of the soldiers who vainly sought an enemy to fight.

At the beginning of the campaign, Carson hired ten Utes and four Mexicans as guides; all were familiar with the Navajo country, and the Utes were delighted at the chance to pursue and slay their traditional enemies under the imprimatur of a grateful government. What killings were accomplished in the summer of 1863—three Navajo men here, eight there—could be laid chiefly to the credit of the canny Utes, who had no compunctions about scalping their victims. As was their long tradition, the Utes also expected to keep the horses and enslave the women and children they captured. Cognizant of the importance of these practices to Ute culture, Carson supported this idea; but Carleton, as both a Christian and a supreme autocrat, forbade it. When the Utes learned that not only their captives but the horses they had seized must be turned over to the government, they quit in disgust.

From July through November, Carson made three exhausting scouts deep into the Navajo heartland, pushing as far west as the three Hopi mesas of northern Arizona. At his peak strength, he commanded 736 soldiers. Everywhere they rode, they saw abundant signs of the Navajo—wheat and corn fields, flocks of stray sheep, empty hogans, even masses of footprints left in the dirt by recently departed Indians. But no matter how hard Carson pushed the pursuit—one comrade remembered his leader repeatedly "reeling in his saddle from fatigue and loss of sleep"—he found it all but impossible to engage the enemy. The Navajo were simply too skilled at fleeing and hiding. For the man Carleton considered "the best tracker among white men in the world," this endless and frustrating chase proved humiliating.

Carleton had anticipated this difficulty. "[I]f a hunter goes after a deer, he tries all sorts of wiles to get within gunshot of it. An Indian is a more watchful and more wary animal than a deer," the major wrote, condescendingly articulating what Carson knew far better than he. The Navajo must thus be "hunted with skill; he cannot be blundered upon; nor will he allow his pursuers to come upon him when he knows it." No matter how arduous the campaign proved, Carleton ceaselessly drove Carson to further efforts. In the major's black-and-white moral universe, the end justified the means, for the Navajos were by nature an "aggressive, perfidious, butchering" people.

Meanwhile, as he failed to fight or even catch sight of more than a handful of the Diné, Carson fed his troops and horses on the wheat and corn the Indians were forced to abandon, and seized the sheep and horses on which the Navajo way of life depended. In brilliant nighttime raids, the Navajo succeeded in stealing back some of the animals, but theirs was a desperate and ultimately a losing counterattack. By autumn of 1863, Carson had begun the practice not only of seizing flocks and grain, but of burning to the ground every field and hogan his troops rode past. It was this "scorched-earth policy" (in the phrase of the historian Clifford E. Trafzer, whose *The Kit Carson Campaign* strenuously indicts not only Carleton but Carson himself) that turned the tide. For no matter how successful the Diné were at escaping the army, they were beginning to starve.

Late in the fall, the first mass surrenders took place, which Carleton accepted as an alternative to his policy of genocide. In November, a group of 188 Navajos, including the important chief Delgadito, turned themselves in at Fort Wingate. As he sent them east toward Bosque Redondo, Carleton crowed his delight. In the major's vision, the reservation on the Pecos was a grand exercise in humanitarianism: there both Navajos and Apaches, "away from their haunts and hills, and hiding places of their country," could begin to become civilized, as their guardians would "be kind to them; there teach their children how to read and write; teach them the arts of peace; teach them the truths of Christianity."

During the first summer and fall at the Bosque, the Mescaleros had succeeded in planting and harvesting a corn crop. Many of them seemed, in the eyes of their wardens, to be embarking on their new life with zeal and enthusiasm. But just how ill conceived the Bosque would prove became evident as the first Navajos arrived. Having observed linguistic similarities between the two tribes, Carleton assumed the Mescaleros and the Navajos would live in peace together. Both were in fact Athapaskan peoples, who had migrated to the Southwest centuries before (perhaps as early as 1400 A.D.) from a former homeland in the Canadian subarctic. Long ago, however, the tribes had diverged from one another. By the 1860s, Apaches and Navajos had often raided and warred with each other.

Now, in the Round Grove, fights and murders broke out, even though the wardens segregated the living quarters of one tribe from the other. As the inspection team had predicted, the alkaline water of the Pecos caused severe intestinal and stomach problems. With the cottonwoods felled to build shelters, the Indians soon had to walk twelve miles to find firewood.

Far to the west, discouraged by what he still thought only a minimal result from his three strenuous scouting missions into the
Navajo heartland, homesick and deeply weary, Carson pleaded for a
winter's leave in Taos. Carleton did not even hesitate in refusing.
Instead, he ordered Kit to prepare an invasion of Canyon de Chelly.

Carson had paused at the western mouth of this twin-branched
sandstone gorge in northeastern Arizona in August, as he pondered
whether to send troops into its labyrinth. Recognizing the difficulty
of the terrain, he hesitated to penetrate the canyon. Then he moved
on, arguing in a dispatch to Carleton that "there are very few Indians in the Cañon, and these are the very poorest." For once, Carson
was wrong and Carleton was right—if only out of sheer dumb luck.
For neither man comprehended the paramount importance of this
place to the Navajo. Carson's sweep through Canyon de Chelly in
the winter of 1863–64 would prove to be the decisive action in the
whole campaign.

Although they had dwelt in the Southwest for less than five centuries, by the 1860s the Diné believed that they had always inhabited this desert homeland. They reckoned its boundaries by drawing
a parallelogram at whose corners stood the four sacred mountains:
Sierra Blanca and Hesperus Peak in Colorado, Mount Taylor in
New Mexico, and the San Francisco Peaks in Arizona. In the 1860s,
at least 12,000 Navajos, owning 200,000 sheep and 60,000 horses,
lived in this tract of some 45,000 square miles.

After Coronado's *entrada* into the Southwest in 1540, the Navajos (as well as the Apaches) increasingly came into conflict with
first Spaniards, then Mexicans. Yet even as they fought grimly to
drive these invaders from their territory, the Diné—among the most
adaptable of Indian peoples—learned from them. Above all, they
learned to breed and ride horses and to herd sheep.

After the Mexican War, in 1846, American soldiers and settlers
began to clash with Navajo sheepherders and warriors. By the
1850s, pushing heedlessly into the Diné heartland, Anglos and Hispanics alike were afire with the passion to ranch its grasslands and
dig up its hills in search of precious minerals. So fierce was the
Navajo resistance that by 1851, the governor of New Mexico Terri-

tory had already adopted a policy of extermination or total surrender. Yet in 1861, Colonel E. R. S. Canby, Carleton's capable predecessor in New Mexico, had signed a peace treaty with what he thought were fifty-four Navajo chiefs.

Two factors doomed that treaty. The first was the exigency Carson had recognized among the Utes—that starvation due to the depletion of wild game inevitably drove a people to raiding. The second was more subtle. Again and again, American leaders failed to recognize that the Navajo, like most western Indian tribes, had never been a unified nation. A given "chief" had authority, at most, only over a small band of followers mostly made up of his extended family. A treaty signed in formal solemnity with various chiefs had no binding effect on the majority of Navajos ranging elsewhere. In particular, in the early 1860s, the farther west a Navajo band roamed, the less likely it was to subscribe to Canby's illusory peace. Thus again and again officers such as Carleton complained, and newspapers screamed, about "broken treaties" and "treacherous renegades."

Beyond these considerations, Anglos—even such perspicacious observers as Kit Carson—remained virtually ignorant of the supreme importance of special sacred places within the Dinétah (as the people called their homeland). In Navajo religion, the world was made livable through the long journey of Monster Slayer and Born for Water, also known as the Hero Twins. In the course of their odyssey, they had killed most of the enemies of the Diné; the lava badlands all across the Navajo homeland, for instance, were the dried blood of slaughtered enemies. But the Twins had been unable to defeat Hunger, Poverty, Old Age, and Dirt, which remained ineluctable aspects of the human condition.

In the Navajo cosmos, specific places have deeply moral characteristics, depending on their role in the Hero Twins' journey, ranging from benevolent to ugly, evil, and terrifying. No place in their homeland was more sacred and blissful than Canyon de Chelly. Yes, the twin gorges had been inhabited by the Anasazi long before the Navajo, who left behind striking cliff dwellings such as Mummy, Antelope, and White Houses, which the Diné scrupulously avoided, out of fear of the spirits of the dead. And yes, Spanish soldiers had marched into the canyon in 1805, trapped the people in a high cave, and perpetrated a terrible massacre by firing bullets that ricocheted off the cave's ceiling. (In 1970, an archaeologist visiting Massacre Cave found hundreds of bullet scars on the cave's walls, as well as human bones, many of them those of children.)

But Canyon de Chelly was, among other things, the home of Spider Woman, a complexly benevolent supernatural being who dwelt on top of the pinnacle called Spider Rock. Spider Woman was used as a kind of bogeyman to frighten children into obedience, but she had also taught the Diné how to weave. Near the head of Canyon de Chelly, the Hero Twins had chased and slain a monster called Traveling Rock. The Anasazi ruin at White House was believed to be the locus of the Ye'ii Bicheii, supernatural beings in charge of rain and fertility; beneath it, once a year (where today's Navajos have set up jewelry stands), the Diné performed their Nightway ceremony, which lasted through nine consecutive nights.

By 1863, the Navajo believed that Canyon de Chelly was their ultimate stronghold, a place where they could hold out even if the rest of their world was torn asunder. Already, by midsummer many of the Diné had retreated here to await the inevitable attack.

At the western mouth, the twin gorges of Canyon del Muerto (to the north) and Canyon de Chelly proper join, dwindling between low sandstone walls. Twenty miles upstream, however, the arching cliffs rise to 900 feet above the valley floor.

In January 1864, Carson divided his army and swept the thirty-five-mile lengths of the gorges. He himself led a party from the west along the rims of both branches of the canyon, while Captain Albert Pfeiffer descended del Muerto from its headwaters to the east. In the process of reconnoitering the canyon, they discovered its geological complexities. As Carson biographers Guild and Carter point out, "More mystery surrounded the Cañon de Chelly than any other spot he had explored, with the possible exception of the Great Salt Lake."

Pfeiffer's four-day scout succeeded in killing 1 woman and 2 men, and in capturing 19 women and children, who were near starvation. A delegation sent off by Carson trailed and slew 11 Navajos even as they tried to surrender. Two other Navajo men were found frozen to death. In keeping with Carson's "scorched-earth policy," his soldiers cut down most of the 2,000 to 3,000 peach trees that were the Diné's pride and glory.

Within the vast stronghold of the canyon, the place of ultimate refuge was a great plug of sandstone with vertical walls, thrusting west like a small archipelago from the mesa that divides del Muerto from de Chelly proper. The only point by which the plug is attached to the canyon rim is a sharp gunsight notch on the east, 300 feet above the valley floor.

Anglos today call this stone peninsula Navajo Fortress Rock. The Diné knew it as Tsélaa', the most sovereign of hideouts; indeed, Tsélaa' had given rise to the legend of Canyon de Chelly itself as the people's last-ditch stronghold.

Fortress Rock goes all but unmentioned in the sketchy reports of Carson and his officers, but the Navajo oral tradition concerning it is precise and vivid. In the summer of 1863, six months before Carson would sweep through Canyon de Chelly, as they anticipated the roundup, the Diné began preparing their encampment atop the thrusting fin of rock. The climb to the gunsight notch, then farther upward by a series of ledges, chimneys, and cliffs, was an acrobatic undertaking; from many places on the route, a simple slip meant falling to one's death. But centuries before the Navajo, those consummate rock climbers the Anasazi had scaled the rock, leaving neatly gouged sequences of hand- and toeholds to mark their passage.

Now the Navajo improved the route to allow the passage of women, children, and supplies. They built a kind of wooden bridge across the notch. Near the top, two blank cliffs barred the way; to tame them, the people hauled a pair of eighty-foot ponderosa pines all the way from the Lukachukai Mountains, fifteen or twenty miles away, somehow wrestled these timbers up the route, propped them in place, and cut alternating steps in the wood to turn them into ladders.

For weeks, the Navajo relayed tons of food—corn, beans, dried meat, piñon nuts, and dried peaches—to the top. On the twenty-five-acre summit, they erected crude dwellings, found natural potholes in the sandstone that would serve for water storage, and even dug latrine trenches near the west end. By October, some 300 people had settled in on top of Tsélaa' to await the inevitable attack.

In early January 1864, atop Tsélaa', 700 feet above the canyon floor, the 300 refugees saw Pfeiffer's 75-odd soldiers come riding through snowdrifts from the east. In the early 1970s, Teddy Draper, Sr., remembered his great-grandmother's story:

> All mothers, children, older people and younger people were in-structed to stay quiet until the soldiers passed us. . . . From where I was they looked very small, but they were well armed and had good horses. They camped below us at the junction. Our men didn't try to attack them. The next day they moved down the canyon and disappeared.

The people rejoiced at their escape. But four days later, Carson's men, scouting the canyon rim to the south, spotted the fugitives and opened fire. Tsélaa' was too far away for the bullets to reach, but af-ter heading back to Fort Canby with an entourage of captives, Car-son detailed a company to lay siege to Fortress Rock.

No good account of this action survives in army annals, but once again the Navajo oral tradition is eloquent. At first, feeling invul-nerable, the Navajo threw rocks and hurled insults in Spanish down upon the army. Sentries posted behind breastworks 400 feet up the approach route guarded it against attack, and indeed, no soldiers ever dared enter the chimney at the base of the route.

One day, however, the troopers discovered, like the Spaniards in 1805, that they could fire cartridges over the heads of the sentries and count on ricochets from the looming walls behind to wreak a terrible toll. Twenty Navajo warriors were wounded and carried to the summit; most of them died. Even before the bluecoats had come, some Diné had lost their lives, falling off icy logs and ledges as they ferried supplies up the perilous route.

Now the soldiers settled in to besiege the Fortress. Unbeknownst to them, the Navajo had reached a crisis, for no snow or rain had fallen in weeks, and their pothole reservoirs had all but dried up. Some urged complete surrender, but several leaders worked out a desperate alternative.

Below the sheer north face of Tsélaa', Tsaile Creek runs smack against the cliff for a few score yards. On top, the women wove ropes out of yucca fibers. Then the best Navajo climbers worked out a de-scent route on the north face. One night in February, they headed down in utter silence, roping a chimney here, zigzagging back and forth on narrow ledges there, until they had set up a human chain spanning the 700-foot cliff. The full moon rose, threatening the enterprise, but the north-facing cliff stayed dark.

From a ledge only about twenty feet above a pair of sleeping army sentries, a Navajo lowered one pot after another by rope, dipping and filling each in the stream. The pots were relayed to the summit through the night. Not a single stone clattered loose, not a pot was dropped, not a man fell.

After that February night, their supply replenished with weeks' worth of water for three hundred thirsty souls, the Navajo stayed atop Tsélaa'. At last, the soldiers gave up and left the canyon. The people came down from the Fortress, rebuilt their homes, and lived on unmolested through the next four years, while their relatives were starving at Bosque Redondo.

Today, only the most fugitive traces of this siege remain. A mile up-canyon from Tsélaa', at the junction with Many Cherry Canyon, an old inscription is the best on-site record of Pfeiffer's sortie. Carved in the rock, in square, old-fashioned letters, are the name "Jose Pena" and the words, in Spanish, "passed here the 13th day of January, 1864." Pena had been a Hispanic volunteer in Carson's army. On the obscure south side of the Fortress, where the February siegers had camped, someone neatly etched a pair of insignia in period capitals: "U.S." and "U.S.A."

Halfway up the perilous climbing route by which the Diné scaled Tsélaa', a cave that might have held twenty refugees is still guarded by low stone walls built across its mouth. And perched on the edge of the cliff, a number of breastworks still lie—piles of flat sandstone rocks, behind which Navajo warriors had crouched to fire their rifles and arrows.

At the gunsight notch, all that is left of the Navajo bridge is a single thirty-foot timber, wedged tight across a void that drops a hundred feet. Above that, however, the great ponderosa logs hauled from the Lukachukais to serve as ladders breaching the summit cliff still rest in place.

Despite the survival of the 300 refugees atop Tsélaa', Carson's ride through Canyon de Chelly broke the Navajo resistance, for it proved that not even in their ultimate stronghold could the natives count on escaping the Bilagáana, as they called the white man.

When Carson returned to Fort Canby, he was surprised to find a crowd of defeated Navajos streaming in to surrender. Many of the warriors expected to be killed, but starvation had driven them to seek mercy for their families. Wisely, instead of shooting the Diné leaders, he sent them back out to tell the remaining refugees that food and blankets awaited them at a place called Bosque Redondo, not death.

14

HWÉÉLDI

So began the Long Walk. Yet even before most of the captive Indians could set out on the four-hundred-mile march from Fort Canby, the full catastrophe of the campaign started to unfold. By February 21, 1864, there were 1,500 Navajos at the rebuilt fort, and not nearly enough food, clothing, or blankets to keep them healthy. In vain had Carson requested supplies, for Carleton could not forward them fast enough to meet the demand. By March 10, the number of refugees slowly freezing and starving at the fort had doubled, to 3,000.

Carson himself had ridden east with 240 Navajos, setting out on January 20. Carleton allowed him six weeks' leave in Taos, where Josefa was pregnant with the couple's third daughter. Before Rebecca could be born, however, Kit was required to return to Fort Canby. In the words of a junior officer, despite his rest in Taos, Carson seemed "unwell and very much fatigued." Guild and Carter, Carson's biographers, attribute his ailment to an aneurysm, the long-term result of the 1860 accident when he was thrown from his horse in the San Juans, "aggravated by the hardships he had undergone during the past year." Back at the fort, Kit wasted no time pleading again for help for the captives. "I think one pound of beef or of flour, wheat or corn," he wrote Carleton, "as entirely too small an allowance for an able-bodied man."

What relief Carleton was able to muster came too late. By the end of spring, 126 Navajos had died of cold or dysentery at Fort Canby. One survivor recalled the misery of the stockade:

> Because the Navajo did not know how to fix the strange foods in the proper ways, and perhaps because of the change in diet and climate, many deaths occurred. There were medicine men, but they did not have herbs to cure the nutrition sickness. Different types of diseases also caused a lot of deaths. There was much suffering among the people.

In particular, the Navajos ate bacon, with which they were unfamiliar, raw; flour mixed with water in an uncooked paste; and coffee beans without roasting or boiling them.

Part of the problem arose because Carleton severely underestimated the numbers of Navajo people. He believed there were not more than 5,000 Diné in all of New Mexico and Arizona; today's estimates of the 1860 population range from 12,000 to 16,000. Carson knew better: even after thousands of Navajos had come in to Forts Canby and Wingate, he guessed that fully half the tribe was still at large.

Many Navajos, having survived Fort Canby, died on the Long Walk. Government records of the exodus tend to be vague on this score—and myopic to an extreme as to the effect of the forced march on its victims. One officer, leading a party of almost 950 men, women, and children, arrived at Bosque Redondo to admit that 110 had died en route; yet in his report he could still claim that the "Navajos were greatly delighted and expressed great satisfaction with what they saw." Another contingent, of more than 2,000 refugees, lost 197 to death on the Long Walk.

Many of the officers in charge of moving large groups of Navajos east to Fort Sumner never wrote reports of their missions. One who did, Captain Joseph Berney, was aware of his captives' desperate hunger, for time and again he saw Navajos take their daily ration of meat, go straight to the fire, and eat it all at once, the moment the portion was singed. To keep up the Indians' morale, the various headmen gave nightly speeches to their followers. Berney learned through his interpreter that the text was always the same: that "they had been fools for fighting against the white man, but now they would fight no more." Hoping to counter this despair with a rosy promise, Berney had his interpreter tell the Navajos that "they would do as directed by their white father, plant corn and become rich, and good people." The officer who had lost 197 of his charges nonetheless blandly commended "a spirit of activity and industry" among the Navajos, "which promises well for their rapid and complete civilization."

The Navajo oral tradition paints an utterly different picture. Though the government provided some wagons for the exodus, only children and the very elderly rode in them; most of the captives walked the whole four hundred miles. A recurrent theme of horror, passed on to the grandchildren of Navajos who made the Long Walk, held that stragglers in the procession, including pregnant women, children, and the aged, were simply shot and left unburied beside the trail. As Howard Gorman later remembered the accounts of his ancestors, "[T]he Navajos, if they got tired and couldn't continue to walk farther, were just shot down. . . . [W]hen those things happened, the people would hear gun shots in the rear. But they couldn't do anything about it." According to Gorman, after one young woman gave birth on the trail, her guards forced her to abandon the baby, telling her, "Your daughter is not going to survive, anyway; sooner or later she is going to die." No army report admits to such atrocities, but it is not likely that, had they occurred, officers would have recorded them.

Eli Gorman got his story from his father. Near Mount Taylor, two white settlers ran a big chain across a river bridge, blocking the procession. As the Navajos halted, one of the men called out, "What's the use of taking the worthless Navajos on the trip with you? Just kill them! Horse thieves! Foxes! Crows!" The commanding officer agreed with the settlers' opinion, but got them to unchain the bridge by saying, "Calm down; we have peace. . . . The Diné will kill no more White Men."

One young Navajo man, others remembered, went crazy on the Long Walk and threw himself into a bonfire. "[E]veryone just watched him burn up," Fred Bitsillie said in the 1980s, repeating his grandfather's story. "Nothing was done to stop him."

Alarmed by the deaths of their people at Fort Canby, many

Navajos assumed that Bosque Redondo was planned as an extermination camp. In the 1970s, Curly Tso, a seventy-eight-year-old stockman, remembered the rumors rampant at Fort Canby that his grandfather had told him about:

> The government in Washington had ordered that all Navajos be rounded up and . . . taken to [Bosque Redondo] where they would be put to death eventually—killing them by means of subjecting them to different diseases, starvation and exposure, as well as using every other possible way to kill all of them. The government's reason seemed to be that the white people, coming this way, needed more land, and Navajos were scattered out too far and lived on some of the best lands.

The centrality of the Long Walk to Navajo history cannot be overemphasized. As Clifford Trafzer writes, the exodus, with its aftermath of four years' imprisonment at Bosque Redondo, is "the most significant time in their past, . . . the period from which Navajo time is measured." If we had only the Anglo accounts by which to judge that ordeal, its true horror would have come down camouflaged beneath the bland and self-satisfied reports of the Indians' keepers. Fortunately, several oral historians have collected the traditions of the descendants of the Navajos at Bosque Redondo, most notably in two powerful volumes: *Navajo Stories of the Long Walk Period* and *Oral History Stories of the Long Walk*, both published by Navajo presses.

By the end of 1863, before most of the Diné had arrived, the construction of Fort Sumner had been completed. Seven adobe buildings of five rooms each were reserved as officers' quarters; another six housed up to 600 enlisted men. There were also a hospital, a kitchen, a guardhouse, four spacious storehouses, and stables. Carleton intended one-story adobe buildings for the prisoners, imposing on these Athapaskan nomads the architecture of their Puebloan enemies. "I fancy," he wrote smugly, "there would be no Indian village in the world to compare with it in beauty." The Navajos, of course, longed for traditional hogans set at a distance from one another, as in their homeland.

By the summer of 1864, Kit Carson was in charge at Fort Sumner. He granted the Diné the right to build hogans out of branches and brush but, yielding to Carleton's sense of order, insisted that these huts be laid out in square grids, with "streets" between them, as in some midwestern town. For all his sympathy for native ways, Carson was momentarily stymied by the Navajo terror of lingering on in a hogan where death had occurred. Finally he worked out a system of hogans in open-ended rows: when someone died, his family could destroy their old shelter, move to the end of the row, and erect another one.

The Diné were in awe of Carson. At first, they had nicknamed him Red Clothes, in gently mocking allusion to the red long under-wear Kit wore throughout the roundup. Soon, however, he had be-come Rope Thrower, for he had effectively snared all the Diné in his lariat. From New Mexico to Washington, D.C., Carson was hailed by his countrymen as the hero who had tamed the most wan-ton and bloodthirsty of all Indian tribes.

Though he believed in the Bosque Redondo as a solution to the Navajo problem, by now Carson was deeply weary of the whole business. After only a few months at Fort Sumner, he tried for the third time to resign from the army. Instead, Carleton posted him off to the next Indian uprising, on the plains south of the Arkansas River, where Kiowas and Comanches were terrorizing settlers.

By the time the Navajos began to arrive at the Bosque in large numbers, the effort to convert Mescalero Apaches into peaceful farmers had proved itself a failure. By one count, only 86 out of the 400-plus Apaches ever did any planting or harvesting. Carleton blamed the agent put in charge of the Mescaleros, but an old adage of the day came closer to the truth: "There was never a shovel made to fit the hand of an Indian." As historian Lynn Bailey writes of the Mescaleros in *The Long Walk,* "For centuries their culture had been oriented to the chase and the raid. . . . Their nomadic life was in-delibly stamped upon them."

Even so, the corn crop in the fall of 1863 had been moderately bountiful, keeping the Apaches tolerably well fed. That was the last year, however, that the harvest met with success.

By the spring of 1864, the Bosque was laid out as a forty-square-mile reservation. The newly arriving Navajos, who numbered al-most 5,000 by March, were put to work digging irrigation ditches to divert the water from the Pecos, planting cottonwoods, and weeding and plowing the fields. The camp, however, lacked not only clothing, blankets, and adequate food; there was a severe shortage of tools. Often a Navajo would be forced to spend a whole day trying to uproot a single mesquite bush with his bare hands. The government-issued rations were routinely contaminated with rat droppings and ground-up plaster. Dysentery became epidemic, and hunger was a constant fact of life. As Mose Denejolie was later told by his grandparents, "The U.S. army fed corn to its horses. Then, when the horses discharged undigested corn in their manure, the Diné would dig and poke in the manure to pick out the corn. . . ."

To supplement their inadequate rations, the men hunted rabbits and gophers, and even trapped rats. "If a rat was killed," testified Denejolie, "the meat, with the bones and intestines, would be chopped into pieces, and twelve persons would share the meat, bones, and intestines of one rat." In winter, barely clothed, the people suffered grievously from the cold. "With some Navajos their crotches were barely hidden, and they were ashamed," reported Howard Gorman. "Torn cloth was given them to wrap around their waists." Within months, most of the people were infested with lice.

Soon the only firewood was roots of the thorny mesquite bush, which men and women hiked miles to find, carrying bundles home wrapped in braided yucca leaves. The wood burned poorly, but there was little alternative. When mesquite was hard to find, the Diné burned cockleburs—the seed cases of a spiny weed that grew all over the reservation.

Even the best hunters grew so weak, remembered Mose Denejolie, that "when a Navajo got hold of a rabbit's hind leg, the rabbit would just run off his hands; or, when a rabbit ran out of a hole and bumped into a man, the man would fall down, and the rabbit would run over him."

Even today, the Navajo refer to the camp of their incarceration not as Bosque Redondo, but as Hwééldi—a Diné attempt to pronounce the Spanish word *fuerte*, or fort. The name is a synonym for "despair." There exists a series of pictures of Navajo prisoners taken by one or more now-anonymous U.S. Signal Corps photographers at Hwééldi. In these remarkable portraits, the captives' misery is etched in their faces.

Some descendants of Navajos imprisoned from 1864 to 1868 recall the difficulty their grandparents had even summoning up the event. "What my grandmother told us about her experience was terrible and horrifying," testified Jane Hasteen in her late seventies. "She did not want to talk about it. She used to say it was not worth telling others because they suffered from everything." "Every time their thoughts go back to Hwééldi," Mary Pioche heard her grandmother say, "they remember their relatives, families, and friends who were killed by the enemies. They watched them die, and they suffered with them, so they break into tears and start crying."

Some survivors insisted that "Mexicans" (probably Hispanic guards) "would kill the children who were crying and throw them in the ditch." Carleton's notion that the Navajos might serve as a buffer against the marauding Comanche backfired. On the farther reaches of the reservation, Comanches indeed attacked Navajos, killing and scalping at will; unarmed, the Diné could only run.

Pretty girls, many survivors insisted, were given as mistresses to officers and guards. Rape was a regular occurrence. And "the Navajos participated in bad parties," according to Mary Sandoval's grandmother. "From these parties, many pretty women were captured and died of venereal diseases." By the end of 1864, not only dysentery, but syphilis and gonorrhea ran rampant among the captives.

As the prisoners, now approaching 8,000 in number, gathered the 1864 corn harvest, hopes were high. It was soon discovered, however, that tiny larvae had hatched from eggs laid in the ears as they grew. The whole crop had been infested by the dreaded "cut worm," or "army worm." Three years running, this parasite devastated the harvest on which the prisoners' very survival depended. In 1865, for instance, the total yield of corn, wheat, pumpkins, and beans across 6,000 acres amounted to less than 500,000 pounds. Nine million pounds had been anticipated.

Starvation began to vie with disease in taking its toll on the prisoners. "They ate anything to survive, even dead animals," said Joe Billy. "They tried to eat crows or coyote meat, but it tasted bitter. Skunk meat was good enough even though the musk stank."

To make matters worse, tensions between the Mescaleros and the Navajos rose, until fighting and murders were almost routine. By the beginning of 1865, the former people were outnumbered twenty to one by their sometime enemies. C. L. Sonnichsen, historian of the Mescalero, describes the Apaches' response:

> In secret councils the plan evolved. No white man knew anything about it, and no white man knows anything about it yet. Just before winter set in, in 1865, they were ready. On the third of November, during the night, every Apache who could travel arose and vanished. In the morning only the sick and crippled were left, and within a few days they vanished too.

Mortifying though this mass escape was to Fair Carletonia, its architect was forced to accept it, for anything that would reduce the numbers at Bosque Redondo might also reduce the suffering. The Apaches were never again rounded up.

To visit Fort Sumner today in the midst of the sort of midwinter cold snap that so often seizes the New Mexico plains, with a skin of ice coating the ground and sleet on the wind, is to taste the misery of Hwééldi. Approaching from the west on U.S. 60, one passes forlorn ranch houses scattered miles apart. The bleak monotony of the prairie is broken only by the occasional lone juniper or cottonwood.

Abruptly one crosses the shallow Pecos River, creeps through the somnolent town of Fort Sumner, and finds his way a few miles south to the site of Bosque Redondo. Today, nothing remains of the ambitious complex of adobe barracks and offices that made up the camp. A small modern edifice, housing a museum and library, constitutes Fort Sumner State Monument. A mere 12,000 passersby stop here each year, the majority of them members of an outfit called Boots and Saddles, war buffs dedicated to visiting nineteenth-century western forts. (The region's chief—one might even say only—tourist attraction is the grave of Billy the Kid.)

A pair of quotations mounted in the museum neatly captures the bipolar perspective of Navajos and Anglos on the Long Walk and the Bosque. An 1863 ballad of the New Mexico Volunteers has a jaunty swagger:

> Come dress my gallant souls, a standing in a row.

Kit Carson he is waiting to march against the foe . . .
To meet and crush the savage foe, bold Johnny Navajo,
Johnny Navajo! Johnny Navajo!

Facing this boast are the mournful words of Navajo headman Barboncito, anticipating release from the prison camp in 1868: "I hope to God you will not ask me to go to any other country except my own. It might turn out another Bosque Redondo."

Not far from the monument visitors' center stands a pile of stones. Beginning in 1971, Navajos who ventured here from today's reservation adopted the practice of carrying a single stone each from their homes to deposit on this spot.

Farther south, beside the river, a 42,000-pound boulder, trucked in in 1994 from Fort Defiance, serves as a kind of Plymouth Rock for the returning pilgrims. A plaque in the Navajo tongue records the words of tribal chairperson Peterson Zah on the occasion of the stone's dedication. "We are the Diné," Zah orated; "our endurance lies in our beliefs, prayers, chants, language and wisdom. . . . In Beauty we walk."

In recent years, supported by a hefty grant from the New Mexico legislature, a permanent memorial to the Navajo tragedy, designed by a Navajo architect, has been planned. If all goes according to schedule, the monument on the banks of the Pecos will be built early in the next decade. Remarkably, it will represent the first structure ever erected to commemorate the Native American experience in any of the Indian wars.

Meanwhile, a retired local schoolteacher named Bob Parsons has discovered an odd memorial already in place. To reforest the region with firewood, and to line the irrigation ditches and the grandiose boulevard that officers named La Glorieta (after the decisive battle of the Civil War in New Mexico), the Apaches and Navajos had been forced to plant 12,000 trees, most of them cottonwoods. The normal life span of a cottonwood rarely exceeds a century. Yet Parsons and others, consulting old maps and prowling across the grounds, identified some twenty-five cottonwoods, still living after 130 years, that had been planted by Navajo or Apache hands.

In the last few years, Parsons has succeeded in taking cuttings from several of these ancient cottonwoods and sending them to the American Forestry Association. From the cuttings, the AFA has propagated new trees. Eventually sapling offspring of the historic cottonwoods will be planted at the headquarters of the Mescalero and Navajo reservations—as well as here, beside the Bosque Redondo memorial, as it begins to rise on this river bottom of old sorrows.

After the Apache escape on November 3, 1865, the Navajos lingered on, reduced to squalor and despair. They kept up such important ceremonies as the girl's puberty rite, improvising as best they could. "As the Squaw Dance required horses, and horses were scarce," recalled Yasbedah Silversmith at the age of ninety, "the *Diné* would put long sticks between their legs and pretend they were riding real horses." A group of women met regularly with Manuelito, one of the leading Navajo headmen, to chant and pray.

Linguistic confusion reigned at the Bosque. Virtually none of the Navajos spoke any English; they had a little more Spanish, but very few of the officers at the fort were Hispanic or spoke the tongue.

Constantly the captives sought a philosophical explanation for their fate. To some, it was simply unfathomable. "There must have been a reason for being treated like that, but I do not know the reason," Mayla Benally recalled one of her elders saying. One of the saddest strains in the oral tradition reveals that many Navajos blamed themselves for their incarceration. As seventy-two-year-old Charley Sandoval, for instance, told his interviewers, "It was the Diné's own fault to be rounded up. The Diné, using bows and arrows, had been having war with other tribes." And Henry Zah, a former tribal councilman, lamented, "It was because of our own angriness."

Comments Alan Downer, an Anglo who serves today as historic preservation officer for the Navajo Nation, "The Navajo Way hangs on a belief that the Navajos are given a way of living by the Holy Beings, and that there are real and nasty consequences for not living in that way. Illness, bad luck, the creek drying up—the drought last summer—all can be blamed on not living the old way. That may be why some Navajos blame themselves for the Long Walk."

* * *

Though Carleton remained largely unaware of the fact, many Navajos escaped Kit Carson's roundup, hiding out during the four years that their kin were imprisoned at the Bosque. The old-timers have stories about that, too. Recalled Frank Goldtooth in the 1970s, "I want to say here that a lot of people managed to avoid the march to Hwééldi. They hid in rugged areas, cliff dwellings and other places where enemies were not likely to find them."

It is possible that fully half the Diné—as many as 6,000 or 7,000 Navajos—escaped the dragnet. To do so meant to live in a constant state of furtive vigilance, in craggy outbacks better suited for defense than for planting and herding. For four years, these fugitives scanned the horizon every day for signs of the dreaded bluecoat soldiers.

One of the best hideouts lay north of Navajo Mountain, on what would become the Arizona-Utah border, near the junction of the San Juan and Colorado Rivers. Even today, it is a challenge simply to travel across this landscape, tortured with humpbacked sandstone domes, slot canyons, deep alcoves, and soaring pinnacles. To this marginal paradise, a band of Navajos under Chief Hoskininni had fled, avoiding capture from 1864 to 1868. Carson trailed the band to a ford of the San Juan, waited for days for the flooding river to lower, then gave up in the face of the rugged badlands he beheld to the south.

At first, Hoskininni's band scratched a living out of grass seeds and piñon nuts. The chief led sorties to round up stray sheep the army had overlooked, and gradually nursed the band back to affluence. He sought out other fugitives in dire want and gave them freely of his band's sheep and skins and meat, earning the sobriquet the Generous One.

Indian traders John and Louisa Wetherill got to know Hoskininni in his old age, in the first decade of the twentieth century. The ancient chief was regarded by his people as the greatest of heroes. A measure of his power was that he owned thirty-two Ute women slaves, whom he put to work herding his sheep. Astonished at Louisa Wetherill's fluency in Navajo, the old chief convinced himself that despite her white skin, she must be a long-lost granddaughter of his. On his deathbed, he bequeathed her the thirty-two Ute slaves.

After 1865, mindful of the Apache example, by threes and fours and tens and twenties the Diné started to escape from Hwééldi. When their wardens built a fence around the reservation, Navajos simply tunneled under it. Some refugees were slain by soldiers as they fled west (Carleton's orders were to kill any Navajo off the reservation). But most regained their homeland and lived out the span of their less fortunate comrades' incarceration unmolested. One man wandered for five years in alien Nebraska, bewildered and afraid, finally returning to Bosque Redondo to find the prison camp disbanded. Eventually some 1,000 Navajos escaped from Hwééldi.

By 1866, not even Carleton's rose-tinted reports could conceal the fact that the Bosque was an utter failure. The Navajos could be kept working only at bayonet point. Often they wailed out loud the single word that epitomized their woe: "Tséyi' "—their name for Canyon de Chelly, the lost stronghold of their homeland.

Even the New Mexico citizens who hated all Indians saw Carleton's experiment as an expensive mistake. Carleton himself was fired in September, while Congress launched investigations and pondered another Navajo solution. There was strong feeling for moving the Diné even farther east, to the Indian Territory of Oklahoma, but Navajo headmen at the Bosque pleaded so passionately for return to their homeland that eventually they won the day.

For months before the solution was revealed, Diné shamans held Vision Way ceremonies to try to divine their jailers' will. According to Howard Gorman, just before the Navajos were released, an officer tied a billy goat to a post, then beat it so savagely its brains spilled out. He then drew the moral: "If you get in trouble with Washington or the U.S. Government again and do the things you should not do, that is what is going to happen to you people."

On June 1, 1868, the historic treaty was signed, terminating the prison camp and returning the Navajo to the land enclosed by the four sacred mountains. On June 18, they began their slow but joyous march west. They had 1,550 horses left of their original 60,000; 950 sheep of the 200,000 they had owned only five years before. Perhaps 2,000 or 3,000 Navajo had died on the Long Walk and at the Bosque, but the people had survived. Today the Navajo Nation is the most populous Indian tribe in the United States.

* * *

Kit Carson failed by only a week to live to see the treaty signed. Four years before, having shifted the field of his campaign to the plains south of the Arkansas River, he engaged a massive force of Kiowas and Comanches. Carson had 259 men, including Utes and Apaches enlisted to combat their hereditary enemies; he also had superior firepower. The Plains Indians, witnesses swore, numbered between 1,200 and 1,500. On November 15, 1864, in the battle of Adobe Walls, Carson routed the Kiowas and Comanches, losing only three men to their more than sixty. This last of Kit's Indian battles was, in the view of biographers Guild and Carter, "the most brilliant that Carson ever fought." Carleton wrote his appreciation: "This brilliant affair adds another green leaf to the laurel wreath which you have so nobly won in the service of your country." The lasting effect of the battle of Adobe Walls was to persuade the Comanches and Kiowas to sue for peace the next autumn.

For two years, Carson served as agent to the Utes, operating out of Fort Garland, Colorado. Most of that time, he was once again forced to be absent from Josefa and his six children, who stayed on in Taos. Carson's service among the Utes, aided by the efforts of his ally Chief Ouray, time and again defused tensions that could, under a less able agent, have broken out into full-scale war.

One measure of how far Carson had by now come in his views on Indians from his mountain-man days can be gleaned from his reaction to the Sand Creek Massacre, perpetrated against peaceful Cheyennes and Arapahos by Colonel J. M. Chivington in 1864. A visitor at Fort Garland, General James Rusling, left a verbatim account in the vernacular of what for Carson must have been a heroically lengthy outburst:

> "To think of that dog Chivington, and his hounds, up thar at Sand Creek! Whoever heerd of sich doings among Christians! The pore Injuns had our flag flyin' over 'em, that same old stars and stripes that we all love and honor. . . . Well, then, here come along that durned Chivington and his cusses. . . .
>
> "I tell ye what; I don't like a hostile Red Skin any better than you du. And when they are hostile, I've fit 'em—fout 'em—as hard as any man. But I never yit drew a bead on a squaw or pa-

poose and I loathe and hate the man who would. 'Tain't nateral for brave men to kill women and little children. . . ."

During these years, Carson's health declined drastically. A doctor who attended Kit during his last illness, appealing to the limited understanding of heart disease that obtained in the 1860s, diagnosed Carson's problem as an aneurysm of the aorta that had grown so large "the tumor pressing on the pneumo-gastric nerves and trachea, caused frequent spasms of the bronchial tubes which were exceedingly distressing." Whether the problem had indeed issued as a result of his having been thrown from the horse and dragged in 1860, Carson believed it had.

In constant pain, Kit tried to quit the army again in July 1867. This time his superiors accepted the resignation. Yet the Ute peace meant so much to him that he accompanied a delegation of chiefs to Washington the next February to sign a treaty.

There Frémont saw his old companion for the last time. Kit was so ill that Frémont, deeply alarmed, tried to get him to see a good doctor when he traveled up to New York City, and invited him to stay at a country house on the Hudson to which he and Jessie had hoped to retire. Alerted by her husband's letter, Jessie found Carson sharing a New York hotel room with several Utes. Jessie later recorded an anecdote from the visit in one of her sentimental sketches: the incident may have occurred just as she told it, although she was fully capable of fabricating or embellishing it. Kit told her, she wrote, that a few days earlier in the hotel room he had suddenly felt the bed seem to rise: " 'I felt my head swell and my breath leaving me.' " He woke up on the floor to find a Ute chief stooped over him, weeping. "He said, 'I thought you were dead. You called your Lord Jesus, then you shut your eyes and couldn't speak.' "

Recalling this near-death event, according to Jessie, Carson then raved on, torn between family and duty:

"I must take the chiefs to Boston. They depend on me. I told them I would. Then we go home, straight. My wife must see me. If I was to write about this, or died out here, it would kill her. I must get home, and I think I can do it."

Having resigned from the army seven months before, Carson once more found himself almost broke. Just before heading for Washington, he made the curious decision to sell his beloved Taos house and move to a burgeoning hamlet called Boggsville, on the Arkansas River, a few miles below the former site of Bent's Fort. This settlement no longer exists, but it lay near today's site of Las Animas, on one of the bleakest stretches of prairie on the eastern Colorado plains. It is hard to imagine that, even if healthy, Kit and Josefa would have been happy there.

On April 11, 1868, pregnant once again, Josefa met her husband at La Junta, on the last leg of his utterly debilitating journey. She had arranged a horse-drawn carriage to trundle her husband the few miles to Boggsville. Two days later, she gave birth to Josefita, her fourth daughter and the couple's seventh child who would live to adulthood. But the birth had not taken place without complications. Josefa lingered in bed with a high fever. Within two weeks, she was dead.

The loss was more than Kit could bear. His disease rapidly worsened, and though he put up a stoic front—joking to his doctor as he pointed to his heart, "If it was not for this, I might live to be a hundred years old"—the pain he endured required chloroform to quell.

Carson died on May 23, in his Boggsville home, watched over by his doctor and his best friend in the new settlement. With his last breath, he did not call on his Lord Jesus. Holding his friend's hand, he said, "Goodby, Doctor. *Adíos, compadre.*" He was fifty-eight years old.

Some months later, in accordance with his wishes as dictated in an 1866 letter, the remains of Josefa and Kit were disinterred from their Boggsville graves and carried by wagon back to Taos. Inside a wrought-iron fence, shaded by massive cottonwoods, their headstones stand side by side today. Josefa's reads:

> Josephine
> Wife of
> Kit Carson
> Born Mar 19 1828
> Died Apr 23 1868.

Kit's inscription is even simpler:

Kit Carson
Died May 23rd 1868
Aged 59 Years.

Fellow Masons from Taos who designed and set up the headstones got Kit's age wrong and felt they must Anglicize Josefa's
name. Nonetheless, the grave is a simple, moving monument, at the
heart of the locality this inseparable yet too often separated pair
loved best on earth. Here, in his final resting place, Kit Carson at
last settled down.

EPILOGUE

AFTER the disaster in the La Garitas in the winter of 1848–49, Frémont walked the earth for another forty-one years. Like his life up to that point, the remainder of the Pathfinder's career was strewn with giddy triumphs and abject failures. He came close to becoming the first Republican president; but by the end of his days, he was an impoverished, embittered near vagabond.

In June 1849, Frémont and Jessie were reunited in San Francisco. Seventeen months earlier, gold had been discovered near Sutter's Fort, and the wildcat rush that would transform California was in full sway. Frémont's foresighted purchase of a sizable estate at Las Mariposas in 1847 now bore unexpected benefits, as one of the richest of all veins was discovered on the property. Within months, the couple could count themselves millionaires without lifting a finger, as a team of hired laborers mined the gold and brought it to market.

Yet for decades thereafter, Frémont found himself mired in financial and legal morasses, as envious fortune hunters disputed his claim to Las Mariposas and creditors sought to recoup their loans. Frémont's penchant for living on borrowed money magnified almost to a mania. Some of his lawyers went unpaid for a decade (the son of one challenged the Pathfinder to a duel). The couple ignored their debts as they incurred lavish further expenses. Even after they had lost most of their money, the Frémonts continued to live far beyond their means: at one point, they simultaneously maintained spacious residences in San Francisco, New York, and on the Champs Élysées in Paris.

After California was made a state in 1850, Frémont was chosen by the legislature to be one of its first two senators in Washington. In the event, however, he would spend only twenty-one working days on the Senate floor in Washington, losing a reelection in 1852.

For the fifth and last time, Frémont now set out to advance his prospects by leading an expedition across the West. The search for a viable cross-country railroad route had become a paramount goal in Washington. In 1852, Congress had made a generous appropriation to launch five simultaneous surveys. Here was the Pathfinder's last chance to redeem Thomas Hart Benton's dream; yet such were the doubts about his competence, the lingering rumors drifting back from the 1849 catastrophe, that in the end Frémont was passed over for all five. Undaunted, he scraped together funds once more for a private reconnaissance.

This "pathetic little expedition," in the words of biographer Andrew Rolle, did little more than limp through the Rockies on the trail of Captain John Gunnison's government-sponsored survey. In the Great Basin, the weakened stragglers had to be guided to safety by a group of friendly Utes. Frémont's party reached California, but it had accomplished almost no real exploration. Once again, its leader planned to publish a report, which he never got around to writing.

Despite these setbacks, during the 1850s Frémont had become not only famous but widely admired in Europe, as the reports from his first two expeditions fed a burgeoning taste for tales of the wild American frontier. His strong antislavery stance had much to do with his lionizing on the Continent, and the same iron principle made him a logical choice for the newly formed Republican Party as candidate for president.

The 1856 election campaign was one of the nastiest in the nation's history. Democratic candidate James Buchanan emerged as a harmless moderate, a career politician fond of his nickname, Old Buck. But Frémont's adversaries raked all the muck they could find or invent. Broadsides and polemics sought to prove that Frémont was a secret papist; that he was of illegitimate birth (which was true); that he had been born in France or Canada, disqualifying his candidacy (which was not true); that he was a womanizer and adulterer (true again); and that his La Garita expedition had degenerated into cannibalism.

Yet in the end, what probably defeated Frémont was his inflexible stand on slavery. In this respect, he was oddly ahead of his time: only four years later, in Abraham Lincoln (who gave some ninety speeches in support of Frémont in 1856), could the country afford to elect the president who would abolish slavery.

The popular vote was 1,831,169 for Buchanan, 1,341,264 for Frémont. The electoral vote was closer: as Rolle points out, had the Pathfinder won only two more states—Pennsylvania and either Illinois or Indiana—he would have become president.

In the Civil War, now a general, Frémont headed two armies, the first as commander of the Department of the West, headquartered in Missouri; the second in Virginia. In both, thanks to his unwillingness to compromise, his financial mismanagement, and his arbitrary and quixotic dealings with subordinates, he turned difficult campaigns into disasters. One experienced veteran censured Frémont as "certainly the most stupendous failure of the war." An infuriated President Lincoln dismissed the general from his western command after Frémont, consulting no one, issued his own Missouri emancipation proclamation months before Lincoln had drafted his national one. In Virginia action, Frémont was brilliantly outmaneuvered by Stonewall Jackson; Lincoln dismissed him again, and he sat out the rest of the war in idle humiliation.

The last thirty-five years of Frémont's life make a dreary story. He squandered his fortune on bad investments and harebrained railroad schemes, but continued to live like a country baron. He served briefly as governor of the Arizona Territory, without much heart in the effort; Jessie hated both Prescott and Tucson, and Frémont himself was absent so often the citizens clamored for his recall.

As Rolle was able to demonstrate, Frémont's womanizing now became almost blatant. Frequently apart from his wife, he lived for some time in Philadelphia with a mistress named Margaret Corbett, and toured Europe with her. Later, in New York, Frémont's liaison with another mistress was so ill concealed that one of Jessie's best friends assumed the marriage was in pieces, writing a confidante in

disgust, "And he too faithless even to pretend to live with [Jessie]."
Perhaps out of desperation, Jessie turned a blind eye to all her husband's infidelities, writing him letter after letter full of abject devo-
tion.

By the 1870s, no longer able to float above the bedrock truth
of their poverty, the couple was reduced to living off the meager
earnings Jessie could make writing articles for such magazines as
Harper's, *Wide Awake*, and *Will and Way*. These pieces endlessly re-
cycled vignettes from "the General's" glory years and anecdotes of
life on the frontier.

Frémont himself sank into a kind of bitter anomie. On one journey west in the 1870s, as he rode a train in a parlor car, he was so
smitten by nostalgia on recrossing the Rockies that he composed a
poem. It opens:

> Long years ago I wandered here,
> In the midsummer of the year,
> Life's summer too.
> A score of horsemen here we rode,
> The mountain world its glories showed,
> All fair to view.

But decades later (indulging in a kind of pathetic fallacy), Frémont
saw a different West:

> The rocks rise black from storm packed snow,
> All checked the river's pleasant flow,
> Vanished the bloom.
> These dreary wastes of frozen plain
> Reflect my bosom's life again
> Now lonesome gloom.

> The buoyant hopes and busy life
> Have ended all in hateful strife
> And baffled aim.
> The world's rude contact killed the rose,
> No more its shining radiance shows,
> False roads to fame.

Ever prone to what modern psychology would deem narcissism and entitlement, Frémont could not recognize what a huge part his own rashness and impetuosity had played in the "hateful strife," tempting him along "false roads to fame." It was his detractors who deserved the blame.

In the 1880s, with Jessie's constant encouragement, editing, and embellishing, Frémont managed to write his *Memoirs*, bringing the account only up to 1847, the year he reckoned that fortune and men's eyes had turned against him. The bulky book, much of it cobbled together from the 1840s reports, was published in 1887, but sold poorly and brought the couple virtually no cash. The years of this effort were further troubled by the assiduous research of the young Harvard professor, Josiah Royce, who even as he interviewed the aging general sought to demonstrate that the "conquest of California" had been an unalloyed cultural tragedy and a military farce.

There is a kind of forlorn poetic justice in the fact that Frémont died, in a Manhattan boardinghouse on July 14, 1890, during one of his prolonged absences from Jessie. Lingering in California, she learned of his passing by telegram. The Pathfinder had perished, at the age of seventy-seven, of peritonitis as a result of a burst appendix.

Jessie lasted another twelve years, constantly polishing "the General's" legend like an old brass heirloom, cranking out sketches and reminiscences. After her own death in 1902, according to her wishes, her remains were buried next to those of her husband, in a hilltop cemetery at Piermont on the Hudson, within sight of the place where the couple had briefly owned, then been forced to sell, the country house Jessie loved, in which she had hoped to while away a quiet dotage at her husband's side.

In 1906, the State of New York commissioned a monument for the grave site, incorporating a bronze flag, a sword, and a medallion bust of Frémont's head. The granite stone is inscribed with the Pathfinder's titles and florid encomiums on his deeds. Unlike Kit Carson's monument in Taos, Frémont's is seldom visited today. It lies neglected, overrun with weeds, far from the sovereign West that in his youth had turned an aimless surveyor into the country's most celebrated explorer.

* * *

At the time of his death, though he had in many respects fallen out of the nation's favor as a hero, Frémont would still commonly have been ranked among its greatest figures. At its most fulsome during his lifetime, the esteem in which the Pathfinder bathed can be summed up by a professor in the 1850s who hailed his deeds as one of "the three greatest events in the world," all three vital to the emergence of the United States as the paramount avatar of human liberty: "Columbus marked a pathway to the new-found world. Washington guided and sustained the patriots who consecrated that world . . . and Frémont lifted the veil which, since time first began, had hidden from view the real El Dorado."

At a testimonial dinner for Frémont in Los Angeles on his birth-day in 1903, held in the Fremont Hotel, his partisans inscribed the dedicatory program with mottoes that sought to sum up his achieve-ment. One read, "He Wiped Out the American Desert"; another, "The Hero Who Gave California to the Nation and Started Civi-lization in the West."

As late as 1928, the acclaimed historian Allan Nevins subtitled his staunchly laudatory, then-definitive biography of Frémont, "The West's Greatest Adventurer." Eleven years later, however, in re-sponse to new scholarship that argued that the Pathfinder's achieve-ment lay not so much in exploring new ground—for relatively little of the routes of his five expeditions had not been previously traced by Anglos—as in mapping it, Nevins gave the second edition a chastened subtitle, "Pathmarker of the West."

In subsequent decades, Frémont's fame slowly dimmed. It was not so much revisionist attack that put the Pathfinder's deeds in the shade as the moldy neglect of half-remembered history. After Nevins's monumental biography, other admiring lives appeared, most notably Ferol Egan's 1977 *Frémont: Explorer for a Restless Na-tion,* which focused on California. But the tenor of modern appraisal of the explorer's achievement is perhaps summed up in the glumly perceptive, relentless psychoanalytic 1991 biography by Andrew Rolle, *John Charles Frémont: Character as Destiny.*

The fate in recent years of Kit Carson's reputation makes for a more perverse lesson in the vicissitudes of fame. In the anti-Viet-nam climate of the late 1960s and 1970s, Carson found himself ap-propriated as the villain of an earlier genocidal campaign at home, against the American Indian. Such works as Clifford Trafzer's 1982 *Kit Carson Campaign: The Last Great Navajo War,* though restoring a much-needed emphasis to the tragedy that the Long Walk and the Bosque Redondo became, went overboard in laying the blame not only on Carleton but on Carson. Trafzer all but ignored the many acts and omissions by which Carson ameliorated and humanized a roundup that might otherwise have turned truly genocidal.

In keeping with the spirit of such sanctimonious and ahistorical screeds as the Kevin Costner film *Dances with Wolves,* Carson-as-villain entered the popular conception of the West. The Discovery Channel's trendily revisionist 1995 series *How the West Was Lost* summed up Kit in its program notes thus: "The gun-toting good guy of Hollywood westerns, the real Kit Carson was a pint-size, illiterate Indian-killer whose scorched-earth campaign ensured that the Navajo could briefly run but never hide." The reaction against this cartoon villain, who was made to stand for all that was wrong with the wild and woolly West, took visceral, emotional forms. A young professor of anthropology at Colorado College noisily and success-fully demanded the removal of a period photograph of Carson that decorated the R.O.T.C. office. In 1992, a reporter for a Santa Fe newspaper overheard a tourist, pausing outside the Kit Carson mu-seum in Taos, say, "I will not go into the home of that racist, genoci-dal killer."

In 1973, militants in Taos demonstrated to try to change the name of Kit Carson State Park, which encloses the cemetery where he lies. Six years later, Kit Carson Cave, near Gallup, New Mexico, was vandalized; and in 1990, protestors spray-painted Kit's and Josefa's tombstones with the epithet NAZI.

As historian Marc Simmons has noted, the Navajo themselves, who for more than a century had retained a complexly ambivalent view of the Rope Thrower, fearing his vengeance but admiring his prowess and fairness, began to buy into the revisionist rhetoric. In the late 1970s, Carson biographer Thelma Guild heard a Navajo at a trading post on the reservation say, "No one here will talk about Kit Carson. He was a butcher." When a symposium to air conflict-ing views of Carson was organized in Taos in 1993, invited Navajo spokespersons refused to attend.

That symposium, whose papers have been published in a slender book called *Kit Carson: Indian Fighter or Indian Killer?*, marks the beginning of a pendulum swing back to rational balance. By the late 1990s, it seems, America had wearied of Vietnam-era revisionism and begun to hunger anew for good old-fashioned heroes. The phenomenal success of Stephen Ambrose's deft and enthusiastic retelling of the Lewis and Clark saga, *Undaunted Courage*, points to such a shift. (Twenty-five years earlier, at the peak of the Vietnam War, Dee Brown's *Bury My Heart at Wounded Knee*, with its doleful recital of one Indian war after another from the losers' point of view, was the symptomatic bestseller.)

Whether Frémont and Carson emerge once again, like Lewis and Clark, as paragons of exploratory genius is largely beside the point. Both men had their faults, but pure heroes or villains do not exist outside the pages of bad literature.

What remains is to take the measure of their achievement. In particular, Carson's trajectory, over three and a half decades, from thoughtless killer of Apaches and Blackfeet to defender and champion of the Utes, marks him out as one of the few frontiersmen whose change of heart toward the Indians, born not of missionary theory but of firsthand experience, can serve as an exemplar for the more enlightened policies that sporadically gained the day in the twentieth century. (One other such conscientious veteran was General George Crook, who harried the Chiricahua Apaches into surrender, then advocated for them in captivity.) It is worth remembering that most sapient nineteenth-century observers believed the Indians of the West were doomed to extinction. That so many Native Americans not only live today, but in the best of circumstances flourish and preserve much of their cultures, is due in no small part to humanitarian changes of heart like Carson's.

For better or for worse, whether one views the Americanizing of the West as a glorious pageant or an unmitigated tragedy, that sea change stands as Frémont and Carson's enduring legacy. By 1842, it was by no means inevitable that the United States would eventually spread to the Pacific. Lewis and Clark's epochal voyage had had as its rationale merely a reconnaissance of the Louisiana Purchase. The gloomy and cautious reports brought back by Zebulon Pike and Stephen Long might well have turned American backs on the West.

Perhaps manifest destiny would have crossed the continent had

Frémont and Carson never existed. It seems unlikely that the Mexican government, weakened by internal strife, could have indefinitely held on to its far northern territories. But with only a few odd twists of history, much of Texas, southern California, Arizona, and New Mexico might still be Mexican land, while Washington, Oregon, and Idaho could be part of Canada. The mountain men, after all, had come and gone without sparking a lasting interest among Americans in settling the vast and empty West.

Moreover, as they prowled across that huge wilderness in search of its secrets, only months ahead of an unprecedented tide of emigrants and gold seekers, Frémont and Carson effectively closed the era of the discovery of the West. There would remain a few landmark explorations, such as John Wesley Powell's bold first descent of the Colorado River in 1869. But in that same year, the golden spike was driven in Utah, and explorers could begin to ride from the Atlantic to the Pacific in the comfort of a parlor car.

The enduring achievement of Frémont and Carson, then, is the extent to which they gave shape and meaning to the United States in the middle of the nineteenth century—and thus to the modern world today, at the inception of the third millennium. In this sense, indeed, they led the way.

One may toy with the fancy of how those two explorers might respond to the country they did so much to define, could they be roused from their graves and allowed to gaze once more over the West their wanderings wrought. Frémont would be avid to find his own footprints on the desert sands, in the mountain snows; if there were an index to the monumental volume the West has become, his own name would be the first entry the Pathfinder would look up. But Carson would survey the landscape, scanning impatiently past the snaking paths of the interstate highways, the sprawling smog-hung cities, his eye cocked for some yet untraveled corner of the wilderness into which he might plunge for one last adventure.

NOTE ON SOURCES

PART ONE: SAVAGE SUBLIMITY
Frémont's government reports on his first two western expeditions are reprinted, with many useful footnotes, in *The Expeditions of John Charles Frémont*, Volume 1: *Travels from 1838 to 1844*, edited by Mary Lee Spence and Donald Jackson (Urbana, Illinois: 1970). The only other significant primary source for that expedition, Charles Preuss's secret diary, was translated from German to English by Erwin G. and Elisabeth K. Gudde and published as *Exploring with Frémont* (Norman, Oklahoma: 1958).

Shadowy glimpses of the now extinct Sheepeater Indians emerge in Osborne Russell's *Journal of a Trapper* (Lincoln, Nebraska: 1965) and in Washington Irving's *The Adventures of Captain Bonneville* (New York: 1861). William Alonzo Allen's fanciful and romantic *The Sheep Eaters* (New York: 1913) may glancingly reflect some of the true experience of that doomed people's past.

For Kit Carson's life, three works are indispensable. The first, originally published in 1935, is Edwin L. Sabin's zestful and monumental two-volume biography, *Kit Carson Days* (Lincoln, Nebraska: 1995), which gathers together an immense amount of raw material, although too often Sabin takes hearsay at face value. The definitive recent biography is Thelma S. Guild and Harvey L. Carter's *Kit Carson: A Pattern for Heroes* (Lincoln, Nebraska: 1984). This book is closely complemented by Carter's superbly edited version of Carson's own memoir, dictated in 1856: *"Dear Old Kit": The Historical*

Christopher Carson (Norman, Oklahoma: 1968), replete with valuable notes and ancillary essays.

For Carson's appearance in the dime novels of the day, see Darlis A. Miller, "Kit Carson and Dime Novels: The Making of a Legend," in *Kit Carson: Indian Fighter or Indian Killer?*, edited by R. C. Gordon-McCutchan (Boulder: 1996). The best book on the Santa Fe Trail is Marc Simmons's *The Old Trail to Santa Fe* (Albuquerque: 1996). The life and deeds of Ewing Young, Carson's first mentor in the beaver trade, are ably recounted in Harvey L. Carter's "Ewing Young," in *Mountain Men*, edited by Leroy L. Hafen (Lincoln, Nebraska: 1965), volume II. (Hafen's series of short biographical sketches of principal mountain men offers a rich account of the lives and tribulations of the beaver hunters. And the Museum of the Mountain Man, in Pinedale, Wyoming, displays a first-rate assemblage of artifacts, paintings, and documents from that most arduous of trades.) For a pithy compilation of primary sources on the rendezvous from 1825 to 1840, see Fred R. Gowans's *Rocky Mountain Rendezvous* (Layton, Utah: 1985).

The incomparable first-person account of mountain-man life through the eyes of the English adventurer George Frederick Ruxton, first published in *Blackwood's Edinburgh Magazine* in 1848, remains in print as *Life in the Far West* (Norman, Oklahoma: 1951). Several good essays in *Kit Carson: Indian Fighter or Indian Killer?* address the thorniest of biographical questions about the scout and mountain man. Joe Meek's unreliable but vivid as-told-to autobiography, *The River of the West,* by Frances Fuller Victor, was first published in 1870 (Columbus, Ohio: 1950).

For an excellent ethnography of the Blackfeet, consult John C. Ewers, *The Blackfeet: Raiders on the Northwestern Plains* (Norman, Oklahoma: 1958). The story of John Colter's amazing escape from the Blackfeet is well told by Burton Harris in *John Colter: His Years in the Rockies* (New York: 1952). Two modern works exhaustively document Bent's Fort on the Arkansas River: David Lavender's *Bent's Fort* (Lincoln, Nebraska: 1954), and Douglas C. Comer's *Ritual Ground* (Berkeley: 1996).

PART TWO: THE CONQUEST OF CALIFORNIA
Among the many Frémont biographies, three stand out. Allan

Nevins's well-written but idealized life, first published in 1928 as *Frémont, the West's Greatest Adventurer*, remains in print in its chastened revised edition as *Frémont: Pathmarker of the West* (Lincoln, Nebraska: 1992). Ferol Egan's *Frémont: Explorer for a Restless Nation* (New York: 1977), also an idealized account, is particularly useful for Frémont's doings in California. Andrew Rolle's gloomy and penetrating psychoanalytic life, *John Charles Frémont: Character as Destiny* (Norman, Oklahoma: 1991), contains many new revelations. The only biography of Frémont's wife, Jessie, is Pamela Herr's credulous but serviceable *Jessie Benton Frémont* (Norman, Oklahoma: 1987).

Frémont's own *Memoirs of My Life* (Chicago: 1887), written late in life, is often curiously at odds with his official reports. The definitive edition of documents relating to Frémont's third expedition, as well as a thorough dossier covering its aftermath and Frémont's court-martial, appears in Mary Lee Spence and Donald Jackson's *The Expeditions of John Charles Frémont*, Volume 2: *The Bear Flag Revolt and the Court-Martial* (Urbana, Illinois: 1973). The best map of Frémont's four important expeditions (his fifth being a sorry trek in the wake of other government explorers) appears in William H. Goetzmann and Glyndwr Williams's *The Atlas of North American Exploration* (New York: 1992).

Few documents bear directly on the massacre of more than 100 Indians near Lassen's Ranch by Frémont's men in 1846. Thomas Martin's dictated memoir, the only detailed first-person account, appeared as *With Frémont to California and the Southwest, 1845–1849*, edited by Ferol Egan (Ashland, Oregon: 1975). Slender ethnographies of the Maidu and Wintu, offering hints about the cultures of the massacre's possible victims, are found in Marie Potts, *The Northern Maidu* (Happy Camp, California: 1977) and Cora DuBois, *Wintu Ethnography* (Berkeley: 1935). The tragic classic account of Ishi and the extinction of the Yahi-Yana is Theodora Kroeber's unforgettable *Ishi in Two Worlds* (Berkeley: 1961).

For a comprehensive picture of the complex mosaic of Indian peoples in California, see *The Natural World of the California Indians*, by Robert F. Heizer and Albert B. Elsasser (Berkeley: 1980). An angry and devastating chronicle of the decimation of those peoples can be found in S. F. Cook's *The Conflict Between the California Indi-*

ans and White Civilization (Berkeley: 1943). Josiah Royce's equally angry and eloquent analysis of the "conquest," which appeared in 1886, can be found in California, from the Conquest in 1846 to the Second Vigilance Committee in San Francisco (New York: 1948).

There are no good modern ethnographies of the Klamath People. Carrol B. Howe's folksy Unconquered, Uncontrolled: The Klamath Indian Reservation (Bend, Oregon: 1992) has some useful information.

PART THREE: HORROR DESOLATION DESPAIR

Frémont's only known account of his disastrous fourth expedition appears as seven manuscript pages, chilling in their blasé indifference to the fate of his men, kept in the Bancroft Library of the University of California at Berkeley. Yet the day-by-day details of that ordeal can be reconstructed by a careful perusal of the diaries and memoirs of the survivors collected in two important books: Mary Lee Spence's The Expeditions of John Charles Frémont, Volume 3: Travels from 1848 to 1854 (Urbana, Illinois: 1984), and Leroy R. Hafen and Ann W. Hafen's Frémont's Fourth Expedition: A Documentary Account of the Disaster of 1848–1849 (Glendale, California: 1960). William Brandon's semi-novelistic The Men and the Mountain: Frémont's Fourth Expedition (New York: 1955) adds little of value. On the other hand, in her brilliant Trail to Disaster (Niwot, Colorado: 1990), Patricia Joy Richmond not only offers the definitive analysis of the catastrophe but reveals the sleuthing that led to her rediscovery of all but one of the party's camps in the La Garita Mountains.

The standard biography of Frémont's guide is Alpheus H. Favour's Old Bill Williams: Mountain Man (Norman, Oklahoma: 1962).

PART FOUR: THE LONG WALK

The best historical account of the Navajo removal is L. R. Bailey's The Long Walk (Tucson: 1988). Even more valuable is a pair of collections of oral histories by descendants of the forced exodus: Navajo Stories of the Long Walk Period (Tsaile, Arizona: 1973) and Oral History Stories of the Long Walk (Crownpoint, New Mexico: 1990). The classic Navajo ethnography is The Navaho, by Clyde

Kluckhohn and Dorothea Leighton (Cambridge, Massachusetts: 1974). Also valuable for the Navajo point of view are Robert S. McPherson's *Sacred Land, Sacred View* (Salt Lake City: 1992) and *Navajo Sacred Places*, by Klara B. Kelley and Harris Francis (Bloomington, Indiana: 1984). A small and quirky book, self-published by David F. Kipp, called *Tsélaa': The Incredible True Story of Navajo Fortress Rock* (Chinle, Arizona: 1983) affords many details of the besieged people's holdout atop the great plug of sandstone in Canyon del Muerto.

The best account of the Mescalero Apache experience at Bosque Redondo is C. L. Sonnichsen's *The Mescalero Apaches* (Norman, Oklahoma: 1973).

For Kit Carson's role in the roundup and Long Walk, see the Guild and Carter biography, *Kit Carson: A Pattern for Heroes*. An excellent summation of the Navajo view of Carson emerges in " 'Rope Thrower' and the Navajo," by R. C. Gordon-McCutchan, and in "Kit and the Indians," by Marc Simmons, both in *Kit Carson: Indian Fighter or Indian Killer?*

ACKNOWLEDGMENTS

Sitting down to compile this roster of gratitudes, I thought suddenly of Browning's lines, in "A Light Woman," "'Tis an awkward thing to play with souls,/And matter enough to save one's own." The relevance of that passage to the present task is not exactly clear even to me, but it has something to do with wondering whether the various helpers who took my hand on my three-year journey through archives and outbacks would be entirely pleased to see where I ended up. In any event, thanks must be freely offered with no hope of a receipt, as prayers are whispered to a *deus absconditus*.

A number of generous souls served hours and even days as my aides and guides in Carson and Frémont country. Patricia Joy Richmond laid a bountiful load of tips and hunches on my shoulders before clapping me on the back and sending me off alone into the high La Garita Mountains. Archaeologist Steve Lekson held forth in his usual dazzling manner about Bent's Fort. Bob Parsons showed me the cottonwood trees that Navajo and Apache prisoners had planted more than a century before at Bosque Redondo. Architect David Sloan shared his vision of the Bosque Redondo memorial he has been chosen to design. Alan Downer, cultural preservation officer for the Navajo Nation, gave me a rich insight into the legacy of that sorrowful imprisonment.

The folks attending the Kit Carson Rendezvous in Kit Carson, Colorado, let me see firsthand what a mountain man did with his time.

Brenda Frank and Gordon Bettles, from the Klamath Tribal Head-quarters, spoke of the impact of Frémont's assault on their people. Authorities at the Wind River Reservation allowed me to prowl into valleys where once only the now-vanished Sheepeater Indians lived. And Jim Johnston, archaeologist for Lassen National Forest, helped me guess just which natives Frémont's men massacred on Deer Creek.

In virtually every library, museum, and scholarly archive that I visited, I was treated with kindness and helpful advice. I am thus grateful to the many librarians, rangers, and curators—some of whose names I never learned, while others I have forgotten—at the Museum of the Mountain Man in Pinedale, Wyoming; the Bancroft Library at the University of California at Berkeley; Sutter's Fort State Historical Park in Sacramento; the California State Indian Museum in the same city; the Sonoma Barracks in Sonoma, California; Bent's Fort on the Arkansas River; Fort Bridger in southwestern Wyoming; the Kit Carson Museum in Taos; the Morada Archives, also in Taos; the Museum of New Mexico archives in Santa Fe; Fort Sumner State Monument in eastern New Mexico; the Klamath, Oregon, County Museum and the Klamath Falls Library; the Shasta County Library in Redding, California; the Rio Grande County Museum in Monte Vista, Colorado; the Denver Public Library; and Widener and Tozzer Libraries at Harvard.

With my longtime friend and climbing partner Jon Krakauer, I spent a blissful week in the Wind River Range, trying to figure out, among other gambols, where and how Frémont had made his way up the mountain later named after him. And with another old crony, Fred Blackburn, and Navajo guide Dave Wilson, I spent several uncharacteristic days on horseback revisiting the scene of the proud Diné resistance to Carson's roundup.

My wife, Sharon Roberts, gave me guidance and a close reading, as always. So, in my faltering initial stages, did Jon Krakauer. My ever-loyal agent, Max Gartenberg, went to bat for me at the right moments. At Simon & Schuster, Johanna Li and Gypsy da Silva were unstintingly useful in saving me from my worst habits and forgetful spells. And with this book, I come near the close of a decade of happy collaboration with my editor, Bob Bender, who seems to define how that most grueling and delicate of roles ought to be filled. May we share another decade of the same!

INDEX

Abert, J. J., 129, 131, 169
Abiquiú, N. Mex., 220–21, 232, 233,
    234, 242
Adobe Walls, battle of (1864), 282
Alaska, 166
Allen, William Alonzo, 42–43
Alps, Wind River Range compared
    with, 37–38, 39
Ambrose, Stephen, 294
American Fur Company, 95, 124
American Indians, 19, 55, 77–100
    beaver trapping of, 64
    evolution of KC's attitude to-
        ward, 20, 80, 137, 151–52,
        251–52, 257, 282–83, 294
    good vs. bad, 148–49
    Hispanic vs. American attitude
        toward, 154
    JCF's views on, 148–51
    Lajeunesse killed by, 31, 158–59
    massacres of, 19, 75, 79, 135–37,
        149–57, 159–62
    mission, 61, 135, 148, 149, 152,
        154
    mountain men's views on, 77–78,
        83–88, 92–94, 96–97, 191
    Nevins's views on, 168
    at rendezvous, 67, 68, 69, 71–74,

    82–83, 86, 96
    as wives, 69, 71–72, 74, 80, 83,
        96, 98–100, 190
Anasazi, 264, 265, 266
Andrews, Elijah, 238
Apaches, 52, 60, 61, 170–71, 252,
    253, 282
    Chiricahua, 154, 255, 294
    Gila, 260
    Jicarilla, 251, 256, 257–58
    massacre of, 150, 151
    Mescalero, see Mescalero
        Apaches
Applegate, Lindsay, 160
Arapahos, 88, 100, 150
    KC's marriage and, 69, 71–72, 74,
        80, 83, 98, 124
Aravaipa Creek, 150, 151
Argentina, JCF in, 115
Arizona, 133, 254, 280, 289, 295
    Apache massacred in, 150, 151
    KC in, 59, 60
Arkansas River, 58, 65–66, 72, 99,
    142, 195, 250, 282, 284
Army, U.S., 151, 161
    Corps of Topographical Engineers
        of, 24, 29, 30, 102, 117, 120,
        129, 141

Army, U.S. (cont.)
JCF's resignation from, 179, 183, 184
KC's resignation from, 258, 274, 283
Army of the West, 174–79
Ashley, William, 66, 67

Bailey, Lynn, 274
Bannocks, 74, 82–84
Barboncito, 278
barometers, 36, 39, 44, 45, 48
Beadle, Benjamin, 238, 240
Bear Flag Revolt, 166–71
beaver trade, 24, 58–59, 61–74, 97, 98, 191
ardors and risks of, 63–66
decline of, 68, 74, 95, 99, 191, 250
rendezvous and, 63, 66–74, 94–98
Benally, Mayla, 279
Bent, Charles, 99, 186
Bent, William, 72, 99, 101
Benton, Jessie, see Frémont, Jessie Benton
Benton, Thomas Hart, 117–22, 149, 165, 173
Jackson's quarrel with, 112, 121
JCF's correspondence with, 183, 194, 241
JCF's relationship with, 29, 30, 117, 120, 121–22, 131
Jessie's relationship with, 119, 121
Polk's relationship with, 178, 179
as railroad enthusiast, 183–84, 197, 209, 288
Western expansion advocated by, 29, 30, 112, 117, 119–20, 122, 126, 127, 133, 139, 164
Bent's Fort, 99–102, 257
fourth expedition at, 183, 184, 188–89, 196
KC as meat hunter for, 32, 72, 99, 101, 102, 123
reconstruction of, 19, 100–101, 144

Sutter's Fort compared with, 144
third expedition at, 139, 141, 142
trade at, 72, 100
Berney, Joseph, 271–72
Bettles, Gordon, 162
Billy, Joe, 276
Bitsillie, Fred, 272
Blackfeet, 19, 30, 84–94, 154
aboriginal affluence of, 91
as Algonkian people, 88–89
"Big Knives" vs., 88, 92–93
Crow vs., 92
in first contacts with whites, 88, 89–90
first expedition and, 24, 40
horses and, 89, 90
KC's fights with, 84–88, 294
Lewis and Clark expedition and, 91–92
Shoshone vs., 89, 90
smallpox and, 86, 87, 89, 94, 96
Blackfeet, The (Ewers), 94
Blackwood's Edinburgh Magazine, 76
boats, inflatable, 37, 130
Boggsville, Colo., 284
Bonneville, Benjamin, 31, 39–42, 254
Boone, Daniel, 53–54
Boon's Lick, Missouri, 54–58
Bosque Redondo, 18, 248, 259–60, 262, 268, 269, 271–81, 293
memorial at, 278–79
Boulder Lake, 26, 44
Brandon, William, 203–4
Breckenridge, Thomas E., 150, 196, 199, 203, 205, 212, 213, 240
"bill of fare" of, 217–18
rescue of, 240
in rescue party, 219, 220, 226–30, 233, 234
Breckenridge, William D., 153–54
Brewerton, George Douglas, 186–88
Bridger, Jim, 30–31, 62, 98, 130
first expedition warned by, 32, 36, 40, 124
as Indian fighter, 83, 84, 86, 87
Indian wives of, 71

at rendezvous, 83, 96, 97
surgery of, 73
Broadus, Andrew, 57
Brown, Dee, 294
Brown's Hole, 97, 98
Buchanan, James, 163, 165, 243,
288, 289
buffalo hunting, 32, 36, 64, 90–91
Bury My Heart at Wounded Knee
(Brown), 294

Cadete, Chief, 256–57
California, 28, 163–79, 232, 241,
250, 291, 292, 295
Bear Flag Revolt in, 166–71
Brewerton in, 186–87
British interests in, 133, 135,
145, 163–66, 171
ethnic complexity of, 152
gold of, 50, 96, 102, 185, 250, 287
Hispanic missions in, 61, 135,
148, 149, 152, 154, 166
horse stealing in, 97
Indians massacred in, 19, 135–37,
149–57
JCF as governor of, 178
JCF as senator from, 179, 288
JCF's midwinter crossing to,
131–34, 137
KC's early reconnaissance of, 59,
60–61, 132, 134, 153
legacy of Anglo–Hispanic racial
conflict in, 167–68
in Mexican War, 171–78
second expedition in, 134–37,
144
third expedition in, 143–57,
164–71
threat of Mexican civil war in,
145
U.S. efforts for peaceful annexation of, 139, 146, 163
*California, from the Conquest in 1846
to the Second Vigilance Committee in San Francisco* (Royce),
164–65
California, Republic of, 166–68

California, University of, 156–57,
194
California Battalion, 171–73,
176–78
California Column, 255, 256
Camp Disappointment, 223–24
Camp Dismal, 211–16, 231
Camp Hope (Christmas Camp),
216–23
Camp of the Mules, 24, 45, 47
Canada, Canadians, 66, 88, 94, 295
Canby, E. R. S., 161–62, 264
cannibalism, 18, 229–30, 238, 243,
289
Canyon de Chelly, 263–68, 281
Canyon del Muerto, 265, 266
Carleton, James H., 247–49, 251,
255–64, 270–71, 273–74,
280–82
Carnero Creek, 199–201, 203, 204
Carson, Adaline, 72, 98–99, 100,
193, 250, 257
death of, 102, 249
marriage of, 101–2, 249
Carson, Josefa Jaramillo, 130, 139,
140, 174–75, 235, 249–50,
282
appearance of, 124
death and burial of, 284–85, 293
KC's marriage to, 71, 98, 123–24,
170
pregnancies and childbirths of,
235, 249, 270, 284
in Taos Massacre, 185–86
Carson, Kit (Christopher Carson),
51–88, 93–103, 185–89,
247–85, 292–95
appearance of, 54, 56, 79, 186,
187, 250
background of, 24, 53–56
in beaver trade, 24, 58–59,
61–74, 97, 98, 99, 250
birth of, 54
bravery of, 70, 87
as buffalo hunter, 32
close calls and narrow escapes of,
80–81, 85–88, 160, 175

Carson, Kit (Christopher Carson)
  (*cont.*)
  death and burial of, 57, 124,
    284–85, 291, 293
  as dispatch rider, 173, 186–88
  duel of, 69–72, 80, 83
  early California reconnaissance
    by, 59, 60–61, 132, 134, 153
  evolution of attitude toward Indi-
    ans of, 20, 80, 137, 151–52,
    251–52, 257, 282–83, 294
  fame and heroism of, 17–18, 20,
    23, 50, 52, 60, 79, 109,
    186–87, 248–49, 250, 274
  on first expedition, 17, 18,
    23–26, 31–34, 38–40, 43–45,
    47, 49, 51, 55, 93, 102–3
  fourth expedition and, 185,
    188–89, 235, 236
  health problems of, 258, 270,
    283, 284
  homecomings of, 101, 193
  as horseman, 31, 258, 283
  illiteracy of, 33, 51, 52, 55, 102
  income of, 32, 55, 99, 123, 130,
    186, 250, 284
  as Indian agent, 250–54, 257–58,
    282, 294
  as Indian fighter, 52–53, 60–61,
    62, 75, 79–88, 93–94, 98,
    135–37, 149–52, 158–59,
    170–71, 247–49, 251, 252,
    282, 293, 294
  Indian languages of, 72, 75, 188,
    253, 257
  in Indian roundups, 18, 19, 152,
    247–49, 255–58, 260–69
  JCF as saving life of, 160
  JCF as viewed by, 107, 108, 160,
    250
  JCF's first meeting with, 17,
    23–24, 102–3
  JCF's last meeting with, 250, 283
  JCF's life saved by, 18, 160
  Kearny and, 174–76
  loyalty of, 18, 97, 99, 140, 178
  marriages of, 53, 71, 98, 100,

    123–24; *see also* Carson, Josefa
    Jaramillo; Waanibe; Making-
    Out-Road
  as Mason, 253, 285
  as meat hunter, 32, 72, 97, 99,
    101, 102, 123
  memoir of, *see Memoirs*
  Mexicans killed by, 169–71
  misjudgment of, 24–25, 39
  as mountain man, 24, 30–31, 54,
    58–74, 76–78, 80–88, 93–99,
    137, 186
  as myth, 52–53, 79
  near–death event of, 283
  Preuss's views on, 34, 40, 96–97
  ranches of, 139–40, 189, 249, 253
  at rendezvous, 66, 67, 69–74,
    94–97
  in resignations from army, 258,
    274, 283
  restlessness of, 24, 53, 58, 62,
    101, 130, 249, 250
  as runaway from home, 24, 56,
    71, 109
  as saddler's apprentice, 56
  Santa Fe monument of, 20
  search for essential nature of,
    51–53, 74–75
  sea voyages of, 172
  in second expedition, 128–30,
    132–37
  speech of, 74–78
  in third expedition, 139–40,
    142–43, 146–47, 149–51,
    158–60, 169–78, 187–88
  trade in Indians by, 96–97, 99
  will of, 32
  wounding of, 85
  Young as mentor of, 58–61, 80,
    137
Carson, Lindsey, 54
Carson, Mary Ann, 101
Carson, Moses, 54, 56
Carson, Rebecca Robinson, 54, 56
Carter, Harvey L., 75, 98, 252, 253,
    265, 270
castoreum, 64, 65

Castro, José, 145, 146, 147, 165–66, 169, 172
Cathcart, Andrew, 213, 231
Cave Creek, 204–6
Cecilia (Creole girl), 113–14, 115
Charleston, S.C., 112–16
Cherokees, JCF's views on, 116
Cheyennes, 88, 150, 257
    as wives, 71, 72, 99–100, 124
Chihuahua, 55, 58
Chivington, John M., 79, 150, 282–83
Chouteau's Landing, 32, 34
Christianity, 116
    see also missionaries; Roman Catholicism
Cimarron Valley, 139–40
Civil War, U.S., 51, 247, 254–55, 289
Clark, William, 28, 29, 30, 33, 91–92, 124, 127, 128, 294
Clyman, James, 148
Coast Survey, U.S., 33–34
Cochetopa Creek, 200, 201
College of Charleston, 113, 114
Colorado, 49, 59, 97, 133, 142, 257, 282
    fourth expedition in, 185, 189–90, 193–231
    Sand Creek Massacre in, 75, 79, 150, 151, 282–83
    see also La Garita Mountains; San Juan Range
Colorado River, 59, 61, 195, 280, 295
Colter, John, 30, 92–93
Colter's Hell, 30, 92
Columbia River, 122, 153
Columbus, Christopher, 184
Comanches, 81, 101, 259, 274, 276, 282
Confederate army, 247, 254–55, 256
Congress, U.S., 29, 138, 281, 288
    see also Senate, U.S.
Conquest of California, see third expedition
Continental Divide, 24, 46, 212
Cook, S. F., 153–56

Cooke, Philip, 192
Coolbroth Canyon, 204, 205
Corbett, Margaret, 289
Corps of Topographical Engineers, 24, 29, 30, 102, 117, 120, 129, 141
Costner, Kevin, 293
Crees, 88
Creutzfeldt, Frederick, 219–20, 229, 230, 233
Crook, George, 294
Crows, 40, 82, 86, 92

Dances with Wolves (film), 293
Daughters of the American Revolution, 160
Dau–nom (Bald Hills), subtribe of Wintu, 155
"Death of General Canby, The" (painting), 162
Deer Creek, 148, 149, 152, 155, 156, 157
de la Torre, Joaquín, 169, 170
Delawares, 74, 81, 84
    in third expedition, 139, 141, 158–61, 171
Delgadito, Chief, 262
Democrats, Democratic Party, 111, 288–89
Denejolie, Mose, 275
Denny Creek, 160–61
Derosier, Baptiste, 134
De Smet, Father Pierre–Jean, 90
De Voto, Bernard, 19, 108–9, 127, 146, 167, 172, 174
Diggers, see Paiutes
dime novels, 76
    KC in, 17, 52–53, 78, 79, 254
Diné, see Navajos
Dokdokwas, 159–62
Donner party, 133, 144, 229, 243
Downer, Alan, 279
Draper, Teddy, Sr., 267
Du Bois, Cora, 155
duels, 69–72, 80, 83, 287

Egan, Ferol, 108, 109, 170, 177, 292
election of 1844, 139

election of 1856, 111, 121, 170, 178, 179, 287, 288–89
 fourth expedition and, 200, 205, 230, 232, 243–44, 289
Elkhart Park, 26
Elliott, Charles, 213–14
Embargo Creek, 210, 223–24, 227
Eukskni, subtribe of Klamath, 159–160
Ewers, John C., 88, 90, 94

Far West Sketches (Jessie Frémont), 51
Favell Museum, 161–62
Favour, Alpheus H., 189, 191, 192, 229–30, 242
Fields, Ruben, 91–92
fifth expedition (1852), 288
first expedition (1842), 17, 23–49, 93, 102–3
 ascent of Fremont Peak in, 18, 19, 24–27, 38–40, 43–49, 69, 75
 Benton as champion of, 29
 daguerrotype camera and, 37
 food in, 34–35, 38
 funding of, 29
 Indian threat against, 32, 36, 40–41, 124
 JCF selected as leader of, 28–29
 in KC's memoir, 49, 51
 Lajeunesse's role in, 31, 117
 maps of, 31, 48, 127
 personnel for, 31
 predecessors compared with, 28, 30–31, 39–40, 124
 Preuss's diary of, 33–38, 40, 43–48, 75, 124
 purpose of, 24, 28, 29–30
 report on, 31–34, 36–38, 45, 47, 125–26
 supplies for, 32
Fitzpatrick, Thomas (Broken-Hand), 30–31, 62, 174, 185
 in second expedition, 128, 130, 132
Flatheads, 71, 90

Fontaine Qui Bouit (Pueblo), Colo., 189–90, 192, 193
Fort Bonneville, 100
Fort Canby (formerly Fort Defiance), 260, 267, 269–73, 278
Fort Davy Crockett, 97, 98
Fort Garland, 282–83
Fort Leavenworth, 179, 192
Fort Stanton, 247–48, 255–56
Fort Sumner, 259–60, 271, 273, 274, 277
Fort Sumner State Monument, 277
Fort Vancouver, 153
Fort Wingate, 262, 271
fourth expedition (1848–49), 34, 183–85, 188–244
 B. Kern's diary of, 195, 198, 203, 204, 208, 209, 211, 213, 216, 217, 220, 222–25
 California clause and, 232
 Camp Disappointment in, 223–24
 Camp Dismal in, 211–16, 231
 Camp Hope in, 216–23
 cannibalism and, 18, 229–30, 238, 243, 289
 December 15 and 16 camp in, 207–9
 decision to retreat in, 214–17
 election of 1856 and, 200, 205, 230, 232, 243–44, 289
 food in, 195, 196, 201, 203, 210–11, 213, 217–18, 220, 221–22, 224, 226, 227, 229–32, 237–40
 funding for, 184, 243
 gear cached in, 231, 236, 240, 241–42
 Godey as hero of, 236, 239–41, 243
 Indians and, 227–28, 231, 232–33, 236, 237
 losses in, 18, 208, 215, 226, 229, 236–38, 240–43
 New Year's Eve camp in, 224
 personnel of, 184–85
 railroad plans and, 18, 183–84,

185, 197–98, 199, 205, 209, 236, 243
rescue party sent ahead in, 219–23, 226–34
Richmond's reconstruction of, 204, 206–8, 214, 223–24, 242
R. Kern's diary of, 193, 194, 205, 207, 209, 216–17, 225, 238, 239, 241, 244
selection of guide for, 185, 188–93
Williams's role in, 97, 189–93, 196–201, 206, 208, 211–12, 215, 219–22, 227–30, 239, 241–43
"Frémon, Charles," see Frémont, Louis-René
Frémont: Explorer for a Restless Nation (Egan), 108, 292
Frémont, Elizabeth (Lily), 124–25, 218
Frémont, Jessie Benton, 33, 48, 113, 117–21, 125, 129, 185, 287–91
appearance of, 117–18, 119
death of, 291–92
education of, 118, 119, 126
JCF's correspondence with, 129, 143–44, 147–48, 149, 178, 194, 196, 199, 210, 214–15, 218, 226, 232–33, 235–36, 241, 290
JCF's first meeting with, 118–19
KC and, 186, 230, 283
marriage of, 29, 120–21
in Panama, 218–19
pregnancy and childbirth of, 124–25
Royce interview and, 165
willfulness of, 119, 120
writing by, 50–51, 55, 71, 80, 112, 118, 125–26, 138, 283, 290, 291
Frémont, John Charles, 17–20, 23–51, 107–80, 294–95
as abolitionist, 20, 113, 288, 289
appearance of, 113, 118, 131, 137
arrest of, 142, 178, 179
background of, 24, 31, 109–14
Bear Flag Revolt and, 166–71
birth of, 110
as botanist, 25, 30, 157
as Byronic hero, 108, 109
in Carolina survey, 115
in Cherokee survey, 116
court-martial trial of, 179, 183
death of, 291
Dokdokwas attacked by, 159–62
education of, 113, 114
in election of 1856, 111, 121, 170, 178, 179, 200, 205, 230, 232, 243–44
failures of, 108, 111–12
fall from grace of, 178–80
fame and heroism of, 17, 18, 20, 23, 31, 50, 120, 125, 127, 138, 165, 177, 183, 288, 292
fortune of, 50, 107, 179, 287
gadgets of, 36–37, 39, 44, 130, 231
good luck of, 114–17, 121, 129
as governor, 178, 289
grandiose pomposity of, 18, 109, 171, 177
health problems of, 26, 27, 38, 44, 47, 125, 138, 178, 291
illegitimacy of, 110–11, 288–89
KC as saving life of, 18, 160
KC dispatched to Washington by, 173
KC's first meeting with, 17, 23–24, 102–3
KC's last meeting with, 250, 283
KC's life saved by, 160
KC's views on, 107, 108, 160, 250
Kearny's correspondence with, 176–77
as leader, 20, 36, 108, 241, 243
mandate overstepped by, 30, 127–29, 131, 133, 141–42, 169, 173
marriage of, see Frémont, Jessie Benton
misjudgments of, 24–26, 40, 131–34, 163, 173, 195, 215, 219–22, 243

Frémont, John Charles (cont.)
  perseverance and stubbornness
    of, 107–8, 114, 131
  plumbing essential nature of,
    50–51
  post–fourth expedition life of,
    287–92
  Preuss's views on, 34, 35, 36–37,
    75, 130
  promotions of, 138, 169
  psychology of, 108, 120, 132,
    241, 291, 292
  reports of, 18, 31–34, 36–38, 45,
    47, 51, 80, 125–27, 134, 136,
    186, 187, 210, 288
  resignation of, 179, 183, 184
  Royce's interview with, 164–65
  secrecy of, 116–17, 120–21
  as senator, 179, 288
  stubbornness of, 198, 205, 214
  teaching jobs of, 114, 115
  as womanizer, 112–15, 118–19,
    178, 289–90
  writer's block of, 125, 138, 243
  see also specific expeditions
Frémont, Louis-René ("Charles Fré-
    mon"), 31, 110–12, 120
Fremont Peak, ascents of, 18, 19,
    24–27, 38–40, 43–49, 69, 75
Frémont's Fourth Expedition (Hafen
    and Hafen), 203–4
Fremont State Park, 146

Garrard, Lewis, 124
Gila River, 60, 61, 97
Gillespie, Archibald, 163–65,
    173–74, 179
Glorieta, battle of, 255
Godey, Alexis, 135–37, 176, 179
  in fourth expedition, 184–85,
    197–98, 200–201, 207, 211,
    220, 221, 223, 225–26, 232,
    234–36, 239–41, 243
  heroism of, 236, 239–41, 243
  loyalty of, 200, 243, 244
  in third expedition, 139, 143, 188
gold, in California, 50, 96, 102, 185,
    250, 287
Golden Gate, 172
Goldtooth, Frank, 280
Gorman, Eli, 272
Gorman, Howard, 272, 275, 281
Gray, Asa, 25
Gray, William, 74
Graydon, James, 248
Great Basin, 131, 143, 288
Great Britain, 66, 110, 111
  Blackfeet and, 90, 91, 94
  California and, 133, 135, 145,
    163–66, 171
  in Oregon, 29, 126, 128–29, 133
  U.S. relations with, 29, 126,
    128–29, 139
Great Plains, 28, 31
  arrival of Blackfeet on, 88–89
  "selling" of, 32, 127
Great Salt Lake, 62, 130, 138, 142,
    265
Green River rendezvous, 67–74,
    82–83, 86, 95, 97
Grinnell, George Bird, 88
Gros Ventres, 88
Groundhog Creek Camp, 225, 226,
    231, 238
Guild, Thelma S., 98, 252, 265, 270,
    293
Gunnison, John, 288
Gunnison River, 201, 212

Hafen, Leroy and Ann, 203–4
Handbook of American Indians North
    of Mexico (Hodge), 42
Hardscrabble, Colo., 193–95
Harper's New Monthly Magazine,
    187–88
Harrison, William Henry, 120
Hasteen, Jane, 276
Hawk's Peak, 146–47
Hayden Survey, 49
Head, Mark, 85–86
Herr, Pamela, 117–20
He-That-Looks-at-the-Calf, 92
Hodge, Frederick Webb, 42

Horse Creek, 68, 69, 72, 73, 95
horses, 87, 126, 160, 175, 194
    Indians and, 41, 81–82, 83, 89,
        91, 135–37
    in second expedition, 131–37
    theft of, 81–82, 83, 97, 135, 192
Hoskininni, Chief, 19, 280
howitzers, 128–29, 131, 133, 177
How the West Was Lost, 293
Hubbard, George, 238, 240
Hudson's Bay Company, 66, 89–90,
        94, 95
    second expedition and, 130–31
Huerfano River, 196, 251

Idaho, 62, 295
    Indians in, 41, 42
Indian agents, 160, 242, 250–54,
        257–58
Irving, Washington, 41, 253–54
Ishi, 156–57
Ishi in Two Worlds (Kroeber), 157
Island Lake, 27, 40–41, 45, 46–47

Jackson, Andrew, 112, 121
Jackson, Donald, 134, 164
Jackson, Thomas J. (Stonewall), 289
James, Edwin, 39
Janisse, Johnny, 44–45, 48
Jaramillo, Josefa, see Carson, Josefa
        Jaramillo
Jefferson, Thomas, 28, 29
Jefferson Fork, 93
John Charles Frémont: Character as
        Destiny (Rolle), 108, 292
Johnston, Jim, 154
José Largo, Chief, 248
Journal of an Exploring Tour Beyond
        the Rocky Mountains (Parker),
        71

Kansas River, 37, 128
Kearny, Stephen Watts, 174–79
Keck, Carl, 224
Kern, Benjamin, 205, 222–26, 237
    death of, 241–42
    diary of, 195, 198, 203, 204, 208,
        209, 211, 213, 216, 217, 220,
        222–25
    in Groundhog Camp, 225, 226,
        238
    rescue of, 240
Kern, Edward, 169, 171
    in fourth expedition, 185, 224,
        225, 226, 238, 239, 243–44
Kern, Richard, 193, 194, 207, 209,
        213, 216–17, 224, 238, 239,
        241
    election of 1856 and, 205, 232,
        244
    in Groundhog Camp, 225, 226,
        231, 238
Kernberg, Otto, 120
King, Henry, 219–23, 227–31
Kiowa Charley (dime novel), 79
Kiowas, 259, 274, 282
Kit Carson: Indian Fighter or Indian
        Killer? (Taos symposium pa-
        pers), 294
Kit Carson Campaign, The (Trafzer),
        262, 293
Kit Carson Cave, 293
Kit Carson Museum, 80, 293
Kit Carson State Park, 293
Klamath Falls, Ore., 161
Klamaths, 158–62
Kootenays, 90
Kroeber, A. L., 157
Kroeber, Theodora, 157

Lady of the Lake, The (Scott), 186
La Garita Creek, 206, 231, 236
La Garita Mountains, 19, 199, 201,
        203–31
Lajeunesse, Basil, 117, 128
    death of, 31, 158–59, 187
    in first expedition, 31, 32, 38, 45,
        47, 48, 117
    in third expedition, 31, 139,
        158–59, 187
Lambert, Clémont, 48
Larkin, Thomas, 145, 146, 147, 163
Las Mariposas, Calif., 185, 287
Lassen, Peter, 148

Lassen's Ranch, 148, 149, 151, 152, 154, 157
Lavender, David, 100
Lewis, Meriwether, 28, 29, 30, 33, 91–92, 124, 127, 128, 294
Life and Adventures of Kit Carson, the Nestor of the Rocky Mountains, from Facts Narrated by Himself, The (Peters), 254
Life in the Far West (Ruxton), 76–78, 229
Lincoln, Abraham, 289
Linn, Lewis, 126, 127, 131
Lisa, Manuel, 30–31
Long, Stephen, 28, 39, 55, 167, 195, 294
Longfellow, Henry Wadsworth, 126
Long Walk, 18, 152, 248, 270–73, 279, 281, 294
Long Walk, The (Bailey), 274
Los Angeles, Calif., 59, 61, 145, 170, 172, 292
    Gillespie in, 173–74
    KC in, 187
    reconquista of, 174–78
Louisiana Purchase, 28, 59, 91, 294

McGehee, Micajah, 190–93, 196, 197, 198, 201, 203, 207, 208, 212, 213, 214, 220, 226, 231, 232, 236–40
Maidus, 152–56
Making-Out-Road (Carson's Cheyenne wife), 71, 100, 124
manifest destiny, 19, 20, 138–39, 294–95
    Benton as proponent of, 29, 30, 112, 117, 119–20, 122, 126, 127, 133, 164
    Gillespie's message and, 163–65
    origin of phrase, 28
    Polk and, 139, 146
Mansfield, Cotton, 87
Manuelito, Chief, 248, 279
Martin, Thomas S., 149–50, 170, 200, 207, 212, 229, 233, 238
Massacre Cave, 264–65

Maxwell, Lucien, 32, 189, 191, 235, 249, 250
Médano Pass, 197, 198
Meek, Joe, 30–31, 62, 97–98, 189
    on Indian fighting, 80–81, 83, 87
    on white women at rendezvous, 73, 74
Memoirs (Carson), 55, 56, 58, 63, 71, 101, 123, 186, 193, 253–54
    duel in, 70
    expeditions in, 59, 60, 132, 136–37, 147, 171
    Indian fighting in, 60, 61, 81–88, 98
    JCF in, 107
    limitations of, 51–52, 74–75, 78
    rendezvous in, 67, 72–73
    straightforward telling in, 80, 81–82
Memoirs (Frémont), 50, 114, 115, 291
    fall from grace in, 179
    on first meeting with KC, 103
    Jessie in, 118
    plan for second volume of, 194, 241, 242–43
    third expedition in, 143, 146, 147, 149, 157, 159, 164, 165, 166
Men and the Mountain, The (Brandon), 203–4
Merced River, 149, 185
Merritt, Ezekiel, 166
Mesa Mountain, 206–11, 214
Mescalero Apaches:
    at Bosque Redondo, 260, 262, 274, 276–77, 281
    KC's roundup of, 18, 247–49, 255–58, 260
Mexican War, 133, 145, 164, 165–66, 171–78, 183, 263
    Andrés Pico's surrender in, 177
    San Pasqual battle in, 175–78
Mexico, Mexicans, 58, 99, 115, 139, 295
    Bear Flag Revolt and, 166–71

California wrested from, 18,
      163–78
   imperial problems of, 145
   independence of, 57, 166
   Indians as viewed by, 148
   second expedition and, 133,
      134–35, 144
   in Southwest, 57–62
   third expedition and, 145–47
Miller, Alfred Jacob, 69, 72, 74, 93
Miss English's Female Seminary,
      118, 119
missionaries, 61, 68, 190
   Hispanic, 61, 135, 148, 149, 152,
      154, 166
   at rendezvous, 71, 73, 74, 86,
      95–96
   wives of, 31, 73, 95
Mission San Francisco de Solano,
      166
Mississippi River, 117
Missouri, 54–58
   KC's returns to, 101, 193
Missouri, University of, 150
Missouri River, 24, 62, 66, 91, 102,
      117, 184
Modocs, 152, 160, 161–62
Modoc War, 161
Mohave Desert, 153
Montana, Indians in, 41, 42–43,
      91–92
Monterey, Calif., 148
   Gillespie's arrival in, 163
   JCF in, 145, 178–79
   Kearny in, 178–79
   Mexican administration in, 145,
      146, 165–66
   U.S. Navy in, 171
Morin, Antoine, 237, 240
Mormons, 138
Mostin, John, 253
mountaineering, 37–40
   see also Fremont Peak, ascents of
mountain men, 24, 30–31, 58–74
   in beaver trade, see beaver trade;
      rendezvous
   cannibalism of, 229–30

clothing of, 63, 192
   Colter as, 92–93
   food of, 63, 64, 191
   Indians as viewed by, 77–78,
      83–88, 92–94, 96–97, 191
   Indian wives of, 69, 71–72, 74,
      80, 83, 96, 98, 190
   packtrain of, 64
   speech of, 76–78
   trade in Indians by, 74, 96–97,
      99, 190
mules, 64, 98, 131–34
   in fourth expedition, 194, 195,
      196, 198, 201, 203, 205, 206,
      207, 210, 211, 213, 214, 216,
      217–18, 222
museums, 80, 156–57, 161–62, 223

Narrative (Thompson), 89–90
National Park Service, 69, 100
Native Americans, see American In-
      dians; specific peoples
Native Sons of the Golden West,
      167
Navajos, 249, 260–81, 293
   at Bosque Redondo, 262, 271–81,
      293
   Canyon de Chelly and, 263–68,
      281
   at Fort Canby, 269–73
   KC's roundup of, 18, 19, 152,
      258, 260–69, 293
   in Long Walk, 18, 152, 248,
      270–73, 279, 281, 293
   oral tradition of, 266, 272, 273
   treaties with, 264, 281
Navajo Stories of the Long Walk Pe-
      riod, 273
Navy, U.S., 171
Nebraska, 32
Nevada, 131, 133, 142
Nevins, Allan, 28, 31, 108–13, 116,
      125, 138, 292
   on California, 133, 145
   on expeditions, 128, 139, 164,
      203–4
   stereotypes used by, 167–68

Newell, Robert, 97–98
New Mexico, 133, 198, 232–36, 295
    Indians in, 52, 247–81
    KC in, 57–58, 59, 62, 71, 99,
        101, 123–24, 139–40, 170,
        185–86, 188–89, 235, 236,
        247–81, 284
    Kearny in, 173, 174
New Mexico Volunteers, 247–49,
    254–55, 277–78
New Year's Eve Camp, 224
Nez Percés, 71, 74, 83
Nicollet, Joseph, 28–29, 117, 120, 125
Northern Maidu, The (Potts) 155
North Platte River, 24, 32, 250
North West Company, 94

Ogden, Peter Skene, 59
Oral History Stories of the Long Walk,
    273
Oregon, 28, 31, 139, 295
    British in, 29, 126, 128–29, 133
    third expedition in, 31, 157–62,
        187–88
Oregon Trail, 55, 93, 117, 123, 127,
    250
    first expedition and, 24, 28
    JCF's search for alternative to, 145
    second expedition and, 128, 129
Osages, 190, 191
O'Sullivan, John L., 28
Ouray, Chief, 282
Owens, Dick, 97, 98, 179, 235
    KC's ranch with, 139–40
    in third expedition, 139–40, 143,
        149, 158, 159
Owl Woman (Bent's Cheyenne
    wife), 72, 99–100

Pacific Ocean, 59, 142, 164
paintings, 69, 72, 161–62
Paiutes, 135–37, 188
Panama, 218–19
Papagos (Tohono O'odham), 60
Parker, Rev. Samuel, 71, 73, 76, 77
Parsons, Bob, 278–79
Pecos River, 259, 262, 275, 277

Pena, Jose, 268
Pennsylvania, 53–54
Peters, DeWitt C., 250, 254
Pfeiffer, Albert, Jr., 213
Pfeiffer, Captain Albert, 265–68
Pico, Andrés, 175–76, 177
Pico, Pío, 145, 172, 175
Pike, Zebulon, 28, 39, 55, 124, 127,
    195, 294
Pikes Peak, 39
Pioche, Mary, 276
Platte River, 30, 37, 40, 66
    see also North Platte River; South
        Platte River
Poinsett, Joel, 115, 117, 120
Point of Rocks, 231, 232, 236, 238,
    240, 241–42
Polk, James K., 139, 146, 147, 165,
    169, 173, 174
    Benton's relationship with, 178,
        179
    KC's meeting with, 186
Popo Agie River, 39–40, 95
Potts, John, 92
Potts, Marie, 155
Powell, John Wesley, 295
Preuss, Charles, 139
    alpine snobbery of, 37–38
    beard of, 130–31
    in first expedition, 33–38, 40,
        43–48, 75, 124
    in fourth expedition, 185, 194,
        206, 208, 211, 220, 221, 222,
        229–35
    as greenhorn, 34
    on KC, 34, 40, 96–97
    in second expedition, 130–31,
        132, 134, 136
Preuss, Gertrud, 34
Proue, Raphael, 225, 226
Provost, Étienne, 66
Pryor, Anne, 109–12, 114
Pryor, John, 110
Puebloans, 185, 251, 257

railroads, 195, 288, 289, 295
    fourth expedition and, 18,

183–84, 185, 197–98, 199,
205, 209, 236, 243
Rayado Valley, 189
Reading, Pierson B., 154
Red Eagle, Chief, 43
Redford, Robert, 76
Red River, 141–42
Red River settlement (Questa, N.
Mex.), 234, 239, 240–41
rendezvous, 66–74, 94–98
of 1825, 66–67, 97
of 1834, 67–68
of 1835, 69–72
of 1836, 72, 73–74
of 1837, 69, 72–73, 74, 82–83,
94, 95
of 1838, 95–97
of 1840, 97–98
missionaries at, 71, 73, 74, 86,
95–96
*Report of an Exploration of the Coun-
try Lying Between the Missouri
River and the Rocky Mountains
on the Line of the Kansas and
Great Platte Rivers, A* (Frémont), 31–34, 36–38, 45, 47,
125–27
Jessie's role in, 125–26
publication of, 126
success of, 126–27, 138
Republicans, Republican Party, 111,
179, 287, 288–89
reservations, 42, 46, 252, 255–56
Klamath, 160, 161
Richmond, Patricia Joy, 201, 204,
206–8, 214, 223–24, 242
rifles, 63, 85, 90, 91, 175, 220
Rincon Creek, 215, 222, 223
Rio Grande, 62, 145, 206, 212, 214,
220, 226–31, 235, 236, 251
Rio Grande County Museum, 223
River of the West, The (Victor), 81
Robidoux, Antoine, 81, 196
Robidoux, Miguel, 60
Robidoux (Mosca) Pass, 197, 198
Rocky Mountains, 28, 39, 290
beaver lodges in, 65

see also Fremont Peak; La Garita
Mountains; San Juan Range;
Wind River Range
Rohrer, Henry, 238
Rolle, Andrew, 108–12, 114, 115,
116, 120, 132, 178, 179, 241,
288, 289, 292
Roman Catholicism, 111, 121, 123,
288
Royce, Josiah, 164–65, 167, 168, 291
Rusling, James, 282–83
Russell, Osborne, 42, 43, 73, 83, 84,
86
Russia, 166
Ruxton, George Frederick, 76–80,
137, 229

Sabin, Edwin L., 64, 71, 72, 81, 255,
258
Sacramento River, 59, 144–45, 148
Indians massacred on, 149–57
salmon run up, 154, 155
Sacramento Valley, 152, 153, 164,
165
Sagundai, 158, 160
St. Louis, Mo., 66, 74, 95, 101, 102,
131, 184, 249
Jessie in, 129, 137
St. Vrain, Céran, 99, 101
Salt River, 59, 60
Sand Creek Massacre, 75, 79, 150,
151, 282–83
San Diego, Calif., 172, 175, 176
Sandoval, Charley, 279
Sandoval, Mary, 276
San Francisco, Calif., 59, 167, 172,
184, 287
San Gabriel Mission, 61
San Gabriel Mountains, 135
Sangre de Cristo Range, 185, 189,
196–98
San Juan Range, 18, 34, 185,
198–201, 258
Carnero route in, 199–201, 203,
204
Cochetopa route in, 200, 201
see also La Garita Mountains

San Luis Valley, 59, 197–98, 209,
    212, 214, 221, 227, 236, 239,
    241, 251
San Luis Valley Historical Society,
    204
San Pasqual Valley, 175–76, 177
Santa Clara Valley, 145–46
Santa Fe, N. Mex., 20, 57
    KC in, 52, 185
    Mexicans in, 57, 61, 62
Santa Fe Trail, 52, 55, 57, 62, 99, 242
Santa Rita copper mines, 62
Scott, John, 240
Scott, Robert Falcon, 221
Scott, Sir Walter, 186
Scott, Winfield, 174
second expedition (1843–44), 61,
    96–97, 127–38
    accomplishment of, 128
    illegal activity in, 133
    Indian informants and, 131, 132
    losses of, 135
    Mexican detection of, 144
    midwinter crossing of Sierra
        Nevada in, 131–34, 137, 185
    Preuss's diary of, 130–31, 132,
        134, 136
    report on, 134, 136, 138
    weapons for, 128–29, 131, 133
Senate, U.S., 29, 121, 184
    JCF in, 179, 288
    Military Affairs Committee of,
        178
Seventh Cavalry, U.S., 151
sheep, bighorn, 27, 41
Sheep Eaters, The (Allen), 42–43
Sheepeaters (Root Diggers;
    Tukuarika; Tukedeka), 40–43
Sheridan, Philip H. (Little Phil), 82
Sherman, William Tecumseh, 186
Shoshone, 40–41, 89, 90
Shunar (Chouinard), 70–71, 72, 80,
    83
Sierra Nevada Range, 59
    December 1845 crossing of,
        143–44
    midwinter 1844 crossing of,

    131–34, 137, 185
Silversmith, Yasbedah, 279
Simmons, Louis, 101–2, 249
Simmons, Marc, 293
Simpson, Smith H., 71, 72
Sioux, 43, 75, 79, 89, 98
    first expedition and, 32, 36, 40,
        124
    at Wounded Knee, 151
slaves, slavery, 112–13
Sloat, John, 171
smallpox, 43
    Blackfeet and, 86, 87, 89, 94, 96
Smith, Jedediah, 30–31, 59, 66, 76,
        102, 108, 142, 143
Smith, Peg–Leg, 97, 102
Smith, Rev. Asa, 96
Snakes, 98
Society of California Pioneers, 167
Sonnichsen, C. L., 255, 277
Sonoma, Calif., 166–67, 169, 171
South Pass, 24, 26, 31, 38, 51, 93,
        129
South Platte River, 24, 32, 35, 250
Southwest:
    Mexican, 57–62, 295
    Spanish, 28, 55, 57, 263, 264–65,
        267
Souvenirs of My Time (Jessie Fré-
    mont), 51
Spain, 57, 166
    in Southwest, 28, 55, 57, 263,
        264–65, 267
Spalding, Elizabeth, 31
Spence, Mary Lee, 134, 164
Stegner, Wallace, 19
Stilts, George, 102
Stockton, Robert F., 171–76, 178
Sublette, William, 102
Sublette County Historical Society,
    69
Sutter, John, 96, 132, 134–35, 144,
    145, 148
    Bear Flag Revolt and, 168–69
Sutter's Fort, 132
    JCF's expeditions at, 134–35,
        144–45, 147, 169, 171, 185

reconstruction of, 19, 144
treatment of Indians at, 148
Vallejo at, 168–69
Sweeney, Edwin R., 255
Sweetwater River, 24, 30, 36, 40
Swonok, 159

Tabeau, Vincent, 237, 240
Taos, N. Mex., 57–60, 98, 241, 293
JCF in, 235–36, 241
KC in, 57, 58, 59, 62, 71, 99,
123–24, 170, 188–89, 235,
249, 250, 251, 253, 254, 270,
284
KC's grave in, 57, 124, 284–85,
291, 293
Kit Carson Museum in, 80, 293
1993 symposium in, 293–94
Taos Massacre (1847), 185–86
Taplin, Charles, 229, 240
Taylor, Zachary, 145, 165
Tennyson, Alfred, Lord, 15
Texas, Texans, 28, 295
in Civil War, 254–55
Mexican War in, 133, 165
third expedition (Conquest of Cali-
fornia) (1845–46), 18, 61,
128, 139–71, 193
Bear Flag Revolt and, 166–71
in California, 143–57, 164–71
desert crossing in, 142–43
funding of, 139
Gillespie's message and, 163–65
Hawk's Peak in, 146–47
Indian guide in, 142
Indians massacred in, 149–57,
159–62
losses in, 31, 158–61, 187–88
official orders in, 141–42
in Oregon Territory, 31, 157–62,
187–88
Sierra Nevada crossing in, 143–44
Thompson, David, 89–90
Titcomb Basin, 26–27, 46
Torrey, John, 25
trade:
at Bent's Fort, 72

of Blackfeet, 88–91, 94
in Indians, 74, 96–97, 99, 190
see also beaver trade
Trafzer, Clifford E., 262, 273, 293
Trail of Tears, 116
Trail to Disaster (Richmond), 201,
204, 206–8, 214, 223–24, 242
Trenholm, Virginia Cole, 72
Tsaile Creek, 267–68
Tsélaa' (Navajo Fortress Rock),
266–68
Tso, Curly, 273
Turley, Jesse B., 253–54
Tyler, John, 138, 139

"Ulysses" (Tennyson), 15
Undaunted Courage (Ambrose), 294
Union army, 247–49, 254–55, 256,
260
Upper Klamath Lake, 158–60
Utah, 133, 142, 280, 295
Utes, 190, 227–28, 242, 257, 280,
282
JCF rescued by, 232–33, 288
KC as agent to, 251, 253, 282,
294
in Navajo roundup, 260–61
peace of, 282, 283

Vallejo, Mariano, 166–69
Valverde, battle of, 254–55
Victor, Frances Fuller, 81, 98
Vinsonhaler, Lorenzo, 232, 236,
238

Waanibe (Carson's Arapaho wife),
69, 71–72, 74, 80
childbirths of, 72, 98
death of, 72, 98, 100, 124
Walker, Joseph Reddeford, 30–31,
147
Wannamaker Creek, 211, 214
Ward, George, 214
War Department, U.S., 127, 128,
129, 131, 138, 183
Washington, D.C., 118–22, 124,
138–39, 173

Washington, D.C. (cont.)
  JCF's court-martial trial in, 179,
    183
  KC in, 186, 250, 283
Washington Daily Union, 244
Washos, 132
Waterman, Talbot, 157
West, Americanizing of:
  as cultural tragedy, 19
  JCF's Report and, 127
  prior to first expedition, 28,
    30–31
  see also manifest destiny; specific
    people and expeditions
West Benino Camp, 225
West Benino Creek, 207–8, 210
Wetherill, John and Louisa, 280
Wet Mountains, 189, 195–96
White, Frank, 214
White, Mrs. James M., 52–53
Whitman, Narcissa, 31, 74
Wilkes, Charles, 144, 153
Willamette Valley, 145
Williams, William Sherley (Old
    Bill), 30–31, 99
  background of, 190–92
  death of, 241–43
  in fourth expedition, 97, 189–93,
    196–201, 206, 208, 211–12,
    215, 219–22, 227–30, 239,
    241–43
  JCF's disagreements with,
    198–201
  near death of, 208, 242
  in rescue party, 219–22, 227–30,
    234
  sinister ulterior motive of, 193,
    228, 242

Williamson River, 159, 161
Wind River, 95–96
Wind River Range, 18, 19, 24, 30,
    36–40, 68, 69
  Alps compared with, 37–38, 39
  Bonneville's ascent to summit in,
    39–40
  height of, 39, 44, 45, 48
  JCF's misjudging of, 24–26
  see also Fremont Peak
Wind River Reservation, 46
Wintu Ethnography (Du Bois), 155
Wintus, 152–56
Wise, Henry, 236–37
Wissler, Clark, 88
Wootton, "Uncle Dick," 189, 190, 196
Workman, David, 56, 71
Wounded Knee, S. Dak., 151
Wyeth, Nathaniel, 67–68
Wyoming, 18, 133
  first rendezvous in, 66–67
  Indians in, 41, 42
  see also Fremont Peak; Wind
    River Range

Yahi–Yanas, 156–57
Yahooskins, 161
Yanas, 152–57
Year of Decision, The (De Voto),
    108–9, 174
Yellowstone River, 30, 84, 92, 93
Young, Brigham, 138
Young, Ewing, 58–61, 80, 102, 108,
    137
  in California, 59, 60–61, 132,
    153

Zah, Peterson, 278, 279